Piotr Sztompka here presents a major work of social theory, which gives a comprehensive theoretical account of trust as a fundamental component of human actions. Professor Sztompka's detailed and systematic study takes account of the rich evolving research on trust, and provides conceptual and typological clarifications and explanations of the notion itself, its meaning, foundations, and functions. He offers an explanatory model of the emergence (or decay) of trust cultures, and relates the theoretical to the historical by examining the collapse of communism in 1989 and the emergence of a postcommunist social order. Piotr Sztompka illustrates and supports his claims with statistical data and his own impressive empirical study of trust, carried out in Poland at the end of the nineties. *Trust* is a conceptually creative and elegant work in which scholars and students of sociology, political science, and social philosophy will find much of interest.

Piotr Sztompka is Professor of Sociology at Jagiellonian University, Krakow, and has also been a visiting professor many times at Columbia University, New York, and UCLA. He is the author of twelve books, including *The Sociology of Social Change* (1993) and *Agency and Structure: Reorienting Sociological Theory* (1994).

Trust

Cambridge Cultural Social Studies

Series editors: JEFFREY C. ALEXANDER, *Department of Sociology, University of California, Los Angeles, and* STEVEN SEIDMAN, *Department of Sociology, University of Albany, State University of New York.*

Trust

A Sociological Theory

Piotr Sztompka

CAMBRIDGE
UNIVERSITY PRESS

PUBLISHED BY THE PRESS SYNDICATE OF THE UNIVERSITY OF CAMBRIDGE
The Pitt Building, Trumpington Street, Cambridge CB2 1RP, United Kingdom

CAMBRIDGE UNIVERSITY PRESS
The Edinburgh Building, Cambridge CB2 2RU, UK   http://www.cup.cam.ac.uk
40 West 20th Street, New York, NY 10011–4211, USA   http://www.cup.org
10 Stamford Road, Oakleigh, Melbourne 3166, Australia

First published 1999

Printed in the United Kingdom at the University Press, Cambridge

Typeset in Times 10/12$\frac{1}{2}$ pt [CE]

A catalogue record for this book is available from the British Library

ISBN 0 521 59144 9 hardback
ISBN 0 521 59850 8 paperback

Contents

Preface

For the last decade or so the problem of trust has come to the fore of sociological attention. Seemingly marginal and idiosyncratic concerns of some individual scholars at the beginning of the eighties – Niklas Luhmann in 1979, Bernard Barber in 1983 – have turned into rich intellectual enterprise with a large and constantly growing number of contributions. Sociological studies of trust have acquired considerable autonomy in comparison to the concerns of social psychology, economics, or political science. The field has diversified in theoretical and empirical directions. And it has been investigated from various theoretical and methodological perspectives: rational-choice, culturalist, functionalist, symbolic-interactionist, phenomenological, and others. Cutting across all those differences there is the emerging recognition of "the necessity for and the ubiquity of trust in human relations and the impossibility of building continuing social relations without some element of trust and common meaning" (Eisenstadt and Roniger 1984: 16–17). The sociologists have finally discovered "the clear and simple fact that, without trust, the everyday social life which we take for granted is simply not possible" (Good 1988: 32). Most would now agree that "the existence of trust is an essential component of all enduring social relationships" (Seligman 1997: 13).

As is usually the case in intellectual history, the career of the concept of trust has double sources. One has to do with immanent developments in the realm of ideas. In sociological thinking we have witnessed, to some extent, a depletion of the potential of organicist, systemic, or structural images of society, and a turn toward "soft variables," the domain of "intangibles and imponderables," or to define it more substantively – the mental and cultural dimensions of social reality. As Ulf Hannerz proclaims, "culture is everywhere" (Hannerz 1993: 95). The concern with trust fits squarely within this wider paradigmatic shift and the current focus on culture.

There are also numerous social reasons, which raise the relevance of cultural factors and particularly the salience of the problematics of trust. They relate to the peculiar features of human society at the end of the twentieth century, the dilemmas and challenges of our phase of modernity. "While some form of trust . . . among social actors is necessary for the continued operation of any social order (at any and all levels of differentiation), the issue of trust as a solution to a particular type of risk is a decidedly modern phenomenon, linked to the nature of the division of labor in modern, market economies" (Seligman 1997: 7–8). "Trust becomes a more urgent and central concern in today's contingent, uncertain and global conditions" (Misztal 1996: 9). If sociology's ambition is to become the reflexive awareness of society, then the current interest in trust seems to be wholly warranted. The focus on trust is a sign that sociology has not lost sensitivity to significant social issues and has not abandoned its calling to discover truths that are also socially relevant.

The present book is intended as a contribution to the cumulative, ongoing effort to disentangle the problematics of trust and apply the concept to the study of contemporary society. It attempts to take stock of the evolving investigations of trust, particularly those with theoretical implications, and to explicate, clarify, systematize, but also elaborate and synthesize, their findings. To use a famous metaphor: I try to "stand on the shoulders of giants" in order to see further and better (Merton 1965). My main ambition is theoretical: to provide conceptual and typological clarifications and explications of the notion of trust, and then to propose an explanatory model of the emergence (or decay) of trust cultures. In due course I shall also deal with the foundations and justifications of trust, functions and dysfunctions of trust, and the functional substitutes for trust.

In the reconstructive and synthesizing parts of the book I adopt the approach of "disciplined eclecticism": "the controlled and systematic use of complementary ideas drawn from differing orientations" (Merton 1976: 169). I refuse to be dogmatically one-sided and try to draw inspirations and insights from multiple sources in the attempt to integrate them into a coherent framework. In the elaborating parts I use, in a rather loose fashion, a combination of phenomenological and ethnographic methods. I try to figure out, phenomenologically, how trust could possibly operate, without contradicting our general sociological knowledge about human action, social structures, and social processes.[1]

But this imaginative reconstruction needs some raw materials to process. And here ethnography enters. Herbert Gans defines the approach in a general way: "Ethnography is now becoming an umbrella term to cover fieldwork, participant observation and informal interviewing. To me, it means being with and talking to people, especially those whose activities are not newsworthy, asking them thoughtful and empathic questions, and analyzing the resulting data" (Gans, in Wolfe 1991: xi). And he adds: "This method I consider the most scientific for understanding social life" (xii).[2] My ethnographic basis for concepts and models is found in the analysis of multiple and diverse illustrations: drawn from common sense observations, personal experience, historical accounts, sociological books, literature, newspapers, and journals. By playing with them imaginatively, using counterfactual arguments and thought experiments, testing tentative conclusions against those illustrations, I hope to arrive at coherent, unambiguous concepts, and comprehensive but parsimonious models.

Once this is achieved, I submit the results to confrontation with one selected historical case: the collapse of communism and emergence of a postcommunist social order, basing the analysis on the recent history of Poland. Here I enter the realm of empirical facts, supporting the claims by received historical accounts, existing sociological researches, but also the results of my own empirical study of trust, carried out in Poland at the end of the nineties. In this study[3] I carried out 403 in-depth interviews with a selected sample of respondents in five Polish cities.[4] In the search for heuristic and interpretative insights I have also conducted seven extended discussions in focus groups representing various occupational categories.

The vicissitudes and fluctuations of trust and distrust during the last fifty years of Polish history, as well as the condition of trust in the present turbulent period of postcommunist transformations have proven to be an excellent "strategic research site" (Merton 1973: 373), a kind of useful laboratory for applying and testing the viability of theoretical concepts and models.

I am a lonely writer, a strong believer in solitary, individual effort. Hence, regrettably, I cannot put here the typical long list of those who have read, commented, and improved the manuscript. Nobody did, except the co-editor of the series, Jeffrey C. Alexander, who does not need any perfunctory thanks on my part, as our friendship of almost thirty years allows me to take his generous help for granted. Therefore, the only people who are due my special gratitude are those many students of trust, whose work I quote profusely in the book. They may also be owed my apologies if I occasionally happen to misunderstand, misrepresent, stretch, or squeeze their ideas to fit my preconceived framework.

This book has been brewing for a long time. As is inevitable when one is working within the rich and evolving field of research, several times I have experienced that frustrating feeling of being beaten to the finish line by other authors publishing their accounts of trust.[5] Hence, the completed fragments of my work were rushed to publication, by means of articles, conference papers, or occasional lectures. The list of these is given below. But I have finally convinced myself that putting my thoughts together in book form and publishing yet another volume on trust will not necessarily be redundant. It is not for me to judge if I was right.

The final version of the manuscript was written in the friendly and cozy environment supplied generously by the Wissenschaftskolleg zu Berlin – Institute for Advanced Study, where I stayed as a Fellow in the spring of 1998. There are few places in the world that would provide a scholar with an equally stimulating habitat for academic work. I am indebted for the opportunity of having been there.

The early formulations of some basic ideas for this book have appeared in the following publications:

Sztompka, P. 1995, "Vertrauen: Die fehlende Ressource in der postkommunistischen Gesellschaft," in: *Kolner Zeitschrift fur Soziologie und Sozialpsychologie*, Sonderheft 35/1995 "Politische Institutionen in Wandel," ed. by B. Nedelmann, September 1995, pp. 254–276.

Sztompka, P. 1996a, *La fiducia nelle societa post-comuniste*, Messina: Rubbettino Editore.

Sztompka, P. 1996b, "Trust and emerging democracy: lessons from Poland," in: *International Sociology*, Vol. 11, No. 1, pp. 37–62.

Sztompka, P. 1996c, "Introduzione alla teoria della fiducia," in: F. Crespi and R. Segatori (eds.), *Multiculturalismo e democrazia*, Rome: Donzelli Editore, pp. 49–72.

Sztompka, P. 1998a, "Trust, distrust and two dilemmas of democracy," in: *European Journal of Social Theory*, No. 1, pp. 19–32.

Sztompka, P. 1998b, "Mistrusting civility: predicament of a post-communist society," in: J. C. Alexander (ed.), *Real Civil Societies*, London: Sage, pp. 191–210.

1

The turn toward soft variables in sociological theory

Double paradigmatic shift

Two sociologies

From its birth in the nineteenth century, sociology has been torn between two alternative emphases: the focus on social collectivities (societies) and the focus on socially embedded individuals (social actors). There have, in fact, always been "two sociologies" (Dawe 1978: 366), two distinct, parallel lines of sociological heritage. The "first sociology" was focusing on "social organisms," societal wholes, complex structures, social systems, with their own specific principles of operation, particular properties and regularities. The founding fathers of the "first sociology" were Comte, Spencer, and Marx. The "second sociology" focused on "human animals," societal members, human individuals, and particularly on their actions; what people do, how they behave individually and collectively in social contexts. The founding fathers of the second sociology were Weber, Pareto, and Mead. For a long time the first sociology has dominated the field. It was only in the second half of the twentieth century that the sociology of systems began to lose the contest to the sociology of action. At present we witness a consistent paradigmatic shift.

At the ontological level there is a turn away from "hard," organic, holistic, or systemic images of society, toward the "soft," field image of the social fabric, seen as a fluid and constantly moving pattern, a changing matrix of human actions and interactions.[1] At the epistemological level there is the corresponding turn from structural explanations invoking "hard" variables – like class position, status, economic situation, demographic trends, settlement patterns, technological developments, organizational forms – toward cultural explanations, focusing on "soft" intangibles like meanings, symbols, rules, values, norms, codes, frames, and forms of discourse.

Two sociologies of action

Within the "second sociology," with its focus on social actions, another paradigmatic shift seems to take place. There are also "two sociologies of action," two alternative images of what human actors do. And now we witness a turn from the "hard," utilitarian, instrumental, positivistic image of action (as exemplified by behaviorism, exchange theory, game theory, rational-choice theory), toward the "soft," humanistic, meaningful image of action (as exemplified by symbolic interactionism, phenomenology, hermeneutics, cultural studies).

At the ontological level, there is a shift from the image of action seen as purely rational, constantly calculating, consistently maximizing profit and minimizing cost ("homo economicus"), toward the richer picture including also emotional, traditional, normative, cultural components: value orientations, social bonds, attachments, loyalties, solidarities, identities. From here, two research directions open. One emphasizes psychological meanings – motivations, reasons, intentions, attitudes – and leads toward a socio-psychological theory of action. Its early forerunners are William I. Thomas and Florian Znaniecki in their theories of social actions (Thomas and Znaniecki 1918–20; Znaniecki 1967 [1934]). Another research direction, putting emphasis on cultural meaning – rules, values, norms, symbols – leads toward a culturalist sociology of action. The early forerunner of such an approach was George H. Mead with his theory of the act (Mead 1964). Another canonical author is Talcott Parsons with his emphasis on normative orientation of action (Parsons 1968 [1937]). A number of recent theorists elaborate the idea of cultural embeddedness of action, for example, Pierre Bourdieu's idea of the "habitus" (Bourdieu 1977), or Jeffrey Alexander's notion of "polarized discourses" (Alexander and Smith 1993). It is interesting to note that the less dogmatic representatives of the opposite, "hard" instrumental and rational image of action, also allow some "soft" cultural components into their analyses. This occurs – for example – in recent more liberal brands of rational-choice theory. Anthony Giddens reads Jon Elster's revisionist version of that approach as admitting that "rational choice theory needs to be complemented with an analysis of social norms; and that norms provide sources of motivation that are 'irreducible to rationality'" (Giddens 1990b: 223). In similar vein James Short Jr. writes about "social and cultural rationality" as embedded in social and cultural values and reflected in individual choice. He perceives human action as a mixture of self-interest and normative commitment derived from the engulfing cultural context (Short 1984: 719).

At the epistemological level this paradigmatic change is reflected by allowing various kinds of qualitative, interpretative, hermeneutical procedures, suitable for unraveling the cultural aspects of action. It is also marked by the reversal of perspective: from treating action as the dependent variable to be explained by rational appraisal of circumstances, toward treating action as an independent, creative variable, involved in constructing, shaping, and modifying all other social objects, including social wholes of all sorts: groups, communities, societies. Hence, the demand to explain those social objects by reference to actions which brought them about via the processes of structural emergence, or "morphogenesis" (Archer 1988).

The focus on culture

Duality of culture

The composite result of the double paradigmatic shift is the ascendance of culture to the top of sociological concerns. Describing the recent career of the concept, Ulf Hannerz calls it a true "success story" (Hannerz 1993: 95). But whereas social anthropologists or ethnologists have retained, at least in part, their traditional interest in culture *per se*, as a specific realm possessing its own anatomy and displaying its own tendencies of change, the sociologists have focused on the ways in which culture links with action. The new image of action has revealed that culture is intimately related to action in a double fashion. Paraphrasing Anthony Giddens' notion of the "duality of structure," it may be said that from the vantage point of action there exists a parallel "duality of culture." On the one hand culture provides a pool of resources for action that draws from it the values to set its goals, the norms to specify the means, the symbols to furnish it with meaning, the codes to express its cognitive content, the frames to order its components, the rituals to provide it with continuity and sequence and so forth. In brief, culture supplies action with axiological, normative, and cognitive orientation. In this way it becomes a strong determining force, releasing, facilitating, enabling, or, as the case might be, arresting, constraining, or preventing action. On the other hand, action is at the same time creatively shaping and reshaping culture, which is not a God-given constant, but rather must be seen as an accumulated product, or preserved sediment of earlier individual and collective actions. In brief, action is the ultimate determining factor in the emergence, or morphogenesis of culture.

Cultural intangibles and imponderables

Recognizing that in human collectivities actions do not occur separately and independently from each other, but rather interrelate in complex fields of actions (designated, depending on their various modes of cohering, as groups, communities, organizations, associations, institutions, states, markets, etc.), the sociologists also focused on some synthetic cultural qualities of such interactional fields, obviously bearing on their overall functioning. As such synthetic cultural features are highly intangible, hard to pin down empirically and operationalize, they are often addressed in metaphorical terms as social moods, social climate, social atmosphere, collective morale, social boredom, social optimism, social pessimism, social malaise, and so forth. The concept of "agency," in the special sense of the self-transforming potential of society and the prerequisite for social becoming (Sztompka 1991a, 1993a), as well as two concepts central for my argument in the present book, namely the trust culture and the syndrome of distrust, clearly belong to the same category.

Turning from the general synthetic qualities of the social field toward a more detailed picture of its anatomy, to the analysis of the fabric or tissue of which the social field is made, the culturalist perspective directs attention to a specific category of social bonds: the world of "soft" interpersonal relationships. After the long domination of the "hard" instrumental picture of social ties based on interests and calculation, fiscally mediated relationships, individualistic, egoistic rationality, we witness the rediscovery of the other face of society, the area of "soft" moral bonds. Viable society is perceived not only as the coalition of interests, but as a moral community. The term "moral" seems appropriate because it grasps all the main aspects of the phenomenon we described. Morality, as understood here, refers to the ways in which people relate to others, and it identifies the right, proper, obligatory relationships, invoking values rather than interests as the justification for prescribed conduct. As Francis Fukuyama characterizes it, moral community is based on ethical habits and reciprocal moral obligations internalized by the community's members (Fukuyama 1995: 7). "This idea of society has less to do with formal organization than with a sense of belonging, trust and responsibility, and duties towards others who share our values, interests and goals" (Misztal 1996: 206–207).

The moral community is a specific way of relating to others whom we define as "us."[2] Three moral obligations define the parameter of the "us" category. "Us" means those whom we trust, toward whom we are loyal, and for whose problems we care in the spirit of solidarity. In other words, according to this interpretation, there are three basic components of moral community. The first is trust, that is, the expectancy of others' virtuous conduct toward ourselves. The second is loyalty, that is, the obligation to refrain from breaching the trust that others have bestowed upon us and to fulfill duties taken upon ourselves by accepting somebody's trust.[3] The third is solidarity, that is, caring for other people's interests and the readiness to take action on behalf of others, even if it conflicts with our own interests. These three vectors delineate the specific "moral space" in which each individual is situated. Obviously, there are also more complex, multi-dimensional interpersonal relations of the "soft" type, incorporating those three components in various proportions. They are: friendship, love, patriotism, patron–client relationships (Eisenstadt and Roniger 1984: 3), ritual kinship, and others. The moral components may also appear as dimensions of quite formal, interested, and instrumental relationships: employment contract (e.g., team spirit, loyalty to the firm), business transactions (e.g., trust toward the partner). Moral community is reflected at the individual level in personal identity, that is, self-definition of one's place within the moral space and delineation of the limits of moral space in which one feels obliged to trust, to be loyal, and to show solidarity to others. In other words it is the indication of the "us" to which "I" feel that I belong.

The recognition of cultural embeddedness of each single action is one of the significant contributions of the culturalist focus. Another is the identification of general cultural traits characterizing a pluralistic and interconnected set of actions – a social field. Still another achievement is the analysis of the moral bonds linking individuals within a social field. I believe that all three contributions are crucially important for understanding the social life.

Intellectual origins of the culturalist turn

Seeking intellectual legitimacy for such a culturalistic orientation in classical sociological heritage, one can immediately point to two names. The first is Emile Durkheim, and his doctrine of "social facts" *sui generis*, or "collective representations" (Durkheim 1964a [1895]). As I read him, he had in mind precisely the cultural intangibles: shared by pluralities of individuals (therefore interindividual, predicated of the socio-individual field, rather than each individual separately), perceived by individuals as external to them (as the features of the field in which they are immersed), and constraining with respect to individual actions (providing actions with axiological, normative, and cognitive orientation). Law, morality, ideology, religion – the standard Durkheimian examples – clearly fit this description. And it was Durkheim who strongly emphasized the moral quality of bonds keeping people together, rejecting the purely instrumental, interest-centered image of social fabric. "Men cannot live together without acknowledging, and consequently making, mutual sacrifices, without tying themselves to one another with strong, durable bonds" (Durkheim 1964b [1883]: 228). No wonder that the contemporary culturalist school in sociology so often reaches back to Durkheim (Alexander 1988).

Another forerunner of the culturalist approach is Alexis de Tocqueville, and his idea of the "habits of the heart."

In order that society should exist and, a fortiori, that a society should prosper, it is necessary that the mind of all the citizens should be rallied and held together by certain predominant ideas; and this cannot be the case unless each of them sometimes draws his opinions from the common source and consents to accept certain matters of belief already formed.   (Tocqueville 1945, Vol. II: 8)

In spite of a somewhat misleading terminology of "the mind," which could suggest a psychological bias, he was as far from psychological individualism as possible. As I read him, he referred to collective mentalities, patterns for thinking and doing widespread in a society, and providing ready-made templates for individual actions. The habits of the heart did not originate in individual hearts (or minds), but rather were borrowed from the surrounding cultural milieu, internalized in personalities and displayed in actions. They clearly belonged to cultural intangibles, in the sense explicated above.

The concern for the condition of moral bonds and moral community has been expressed directly and indirectly by a number of other classical thinkers, especially those who, contrary to the prevailing mood, started to perceive dark sides of modernity. They have initiated long, critical debates that still continue. Five themes seem most persistent. First, the "lonely crowd theme," running from Tönnies (1957 [1887]) to Riesman (1950), indicating the atrophy of moral communities, isolation, atomization, and individualization of social life. Second, the "iron cage theme," running from Weber (1968 [1922]) to Bauman (1988), focusing on the formalization, depersonalization, and instrumentalization of interpersonal relations, bureaucratization of social organizations, and reification of individuals. Third, the "anomie theme," running from Durkheim (1951 [1897]) to Merton (1996 [1938]: 132–152) and emphasizing the chaotic and antinomic nature of axiological and legal regulations. Fourth, the "alienation theme" running from Marx (1975 [1844]) to Seeman (1959), pointing to the distancing of the individual from economic and political organization, which leads to the loss of identity, dignity, or sense of purpose in life. Fifth, the "revolt of the masses theme," initiated by Ortega Y Gasset (1957 [1930]) and Wirth (1938), delineating the negative sides of urbanization and the development of mass symbolic culture, as the de-moralizing milieu of day-to-day existence for the majority of people.

In modern sociology, apart from the continuation of those classical themes, there have appeared some new innovative lines of research, drawing attention to "soft" cultural intangibles and "soft" moral bonds. They have evolved around six theoretical concepts. First, as early as the 1960s there appeared numerous studies of "civic culture," initiated by the influential book by Almond and Verba (1965 [1963]). Addressing the domain of political life, they switched the research focus from the traditional concern with "hard" legal and institutional facts to underlying "soft" factors: values, beliefs, competences related to politics. They defined the concept as "attitudes towards the political system and its various parts, and attitudes towards the role of the self in the system" (Almond and Verba 1965: 13). Such attitudes were seen as including knowledge, feelings, and evaluations (cognitive, affective, and evaluative orientations toward politics).

Second, in the eighties, in the wake of pro-democratic movements and anti-communist revolutions in East-Central Europe, the classic notion of "civil society" was dug out from oblivion and significantly elaborated (Keane 1988; Cohen and Arato 1992; Alexander 1992, 1998; Seligman 1992; Kumar 1993). In one of its meanings, it clearly took on a cultural connotation. Robust civil society was seen as synonymous with axiological consensus and developed emotional community, bound by the tight network of interpersonal loyalties, commitments, solidarities. It designated mature public opinion and rich public life, the identification of citizens with public institutions, concern with the common good, and respect for laws. In modern sociology, such a neo-Durkheimian, culturalistic interpretation of civil society is put forward by Jeffrey Alexander: "Civil society is the arena of social solidarity that is defined in universalistic terms. It is the we-ness of a national community, the feeling of connectedness to one another that transcends particular commitments, loyalties, and interests and allows there to emerge a single thread of identity among otherwise disparate people" (Alexander 1992: 2).

Third, the analysis of the French educational system has brought Pierre Bourdieu to propose the powerful idea of "cultural capital." He was seeking for the secret of persisting social hierarchies, pronounced inequalities, elitist tendencies, surviving in spite of democratic and egalitarian forms of social organization. And again the key was found at the hidden cultural level. Cultural capital was defined as "institutionalized, i.e. widely shared, high status cultural signals (attitudes, preferences, formal knowledge, behaviors, goods and credentials) used for cultural and social exclusion, the former referring to exclusion from jobs and resources, and the latter, to exclusion from high status groups" (Bourdieu and Passeron 1979: 158). Such signals and resources for exclusion are transmitted by socialization and education and incorporated as dispositions, or "habitus."

Fourth, the study of the economic backwardness of Southern Italy has suggested to Robert Putnam the fruitful idea of "social capital," which has become immensely popular and widely applied in research (Putnam 1995a). He meant by that, "features of social life – networks, norms, and trust – that enable participants to act together more effectively to pursue shared objectives . . . Social capital, in short, refers to social connections and the attendant norms and trust" (Putnam 1995b: 664–665). This concept was also crucial for the argument of Francis Fukuyama (1995), who saw in it the secret of economic development in South-East Asia.

Fifth, the cross-national comparative research into dominant value orientation, led Ronald Inglehart to propose the notion of "postmaterialist values," apparently emerging in most developed societies during the last decades of the century (Inglehart 1988, 1990). The growing preoccupation with self-realization, harmony with nature, cultivation of tradition, quality of life, health and fitness, personal dignity, peace, human solidarity, metaphysical cravings, and so forth, indicates the shift from "hard" economic interests toward "soft" cultural concerns and commitments. The visible manifestation of this is to be found in the proliferation of "new social movements" (ecological, feminist, pacifist) and new types of communities and associations (Amnesty International, Greenpeace, New Age), finding the bases of integration in new types of common cultural values.

Finally, my own focus on the vicissitudes of postcommunist transition in East-Central Europe has led me to propose the concept of "civilizational competence," by which I mean the complex set of cultural predispositions embracing a readiness for political participation and self-government, work discipline, entrepreneurial spirit, educational aspirations, technological skills, ethical principles, esthetic sensibilities – all of them indispensable for full deployment and consolidation of democratic polity, market economy, and open circulation of thought (Sztompka 1993b).

One may speculate which intellectual and social circumstances have led to the focus on culture, the concern with hidden intangibles and imponderables or elusive moral bonds. Part of the answer may be found in the immanent intellectual tendencies in the discipline of sociology: the exhaustion of "hard" structural or institutional explanations, the challenge of unresolved puzzles, growing intellectual unrest. But perhaps more importantly there are social reasons, having to do with new phenomena and events occurring in human societies and directing the attention of sociologists toward the sphere of culture.

Social origins of the culturalist turn

There is, first, a growing perception of the defects and inefficiencies of some institutional frameworks earlier taken for granted: democratic political regimes, the welfare state, a free market economy. Ungovernability, economic recessions, and social unrest have affected even the most developed and prosperous countries. Barbara Misztal notices "the emergence of widespread consciousness that existing bases for social cooperation, solidarity and consensus have been eroded and that there is a need to search for new alternatives" (Misztal 1996: 3). Looking for deeper causes of troubles under the facade of seemingly faultless institutional designs, sociologists and political scientists hit upon cultural factors.

Second, there is the growing realization that the same institutions may operate quite differently in various societies. Already in the period of postcolonial forced modernization after World War II, the comparative evidence was showing the failure of Western political and economic institutions in some African or Latin American societies, while documenting their considerable success in Asia (Indian democracy, Japanese capitalism, etc.). Similar observations indicate strikingly different fates of immigrants or refugees, coming from various parts of the world, in spite of the common institutional setting in which they find themselves in the country of destination. The levels of their adaptive success vary tremendously (e.g., Koreans and Chinese versus Mexicans or Puerto Ricans in the US). The reason for those disparities was discovered in fundamentally different indigenous cultural milieus, or legacies fit or unfit to new structures.

Third, in the domain of international relations, there is "the increasing sense that culture plays a crucial and neglected role in world politics" (Rengger 1997: 476). The dominant view that international politics is primarily about "real" or "hard" economic interests of countries is undermined by the eruption of conflicts rooted in resentments, hostile stereotypes, prejudices, particularistic identities, even contrasting life-styles, values, and orientations. Divisive forces of religious fundament-alism, ethnic or racial loyalties, and new forms of nationalism seem to manifest themselves particularly strongly in our times.

Fourth, the epochal events of the year 1989 and the collapse of communism, apart from their political and economic implications, also signify a major cultural and civilizational break (Sztompka 1996c). The importance of the cultural dimension of the postcommunist transition first manifested itself in the pervasive experience of obstacles, blocks, barriers, slow-downs, frictions, or backlashes on the path toward democ-racy and the market. Trying to understand the reasons for that "surprise syndrome" (Lepenies 1992) undermining the early enthusiasm and optimism of the reformers, some perceptive observers turned toward hidden cultural factors. Three metaphors used at that time are particu-larly telling. Andrew Nagorski, *Newsweek*'s correspondent for Eastern Europe, has titled one of his first columns after the fall of the Berlin Wall: "The Wall in Our Heads," suggesting that "hard," tangible changes are only the beginning, as the remnants of communist culture and its traces in human mentalities will still haunt postcommunist societies for a long time (Nagorski 1991: 4). Zbigniew Brzeziński, reflecting on the widely expressed aspirations of "joining Europe," introduces a distinc-tion between "joining a European house," and "joining a European home." The house is a "hard" architectural edifice, the home is a "soft" area of intimacy, loyalties, attachments, a place where one truly "feels at home." Joining the framework of common political, legal, and economic institutions is not the same as developing the common cultural milieu. The latter is much more demanding, cannot be legislated, and requires slow, gradual evolution (Brzeziński 1989). The temporal aspect of transi-tion is taken by the third metaphor, that of "three clocks" proposed by Ralf Dahrendorf. In the first book to come out about the "revolutions" in Eastern Europe, he notices the inevitably uneven tempo of reforms at various levels of social life. There is the quickest clock of the lawyers and politicians, who are able to introduce new constitutions and legal regulations almost overnight. There is the much slower clock of the economist, who needs more time to turn the planned, command economy on free market tracks. And there is the slowest "clock of civil society," which measures the speed of changes in the deep realm of cultural heritage (Dahrendorf 1990). The time lag of cultural change is responsible for much of the surprise slow-downs and frustrations that accompany postcommunist reforms.

An example of the culturalist turn: the focus on trust

The current concern with trust is just one aspect of the culturalist turn in sociological theory. It reflects the growing interest in the domain of the "soft" cultural variables, intangibles, and imponderables of social life. But there are also specific reasons why it is trust rather than other "soft" factors that has become the center of rich theoretical debate. The immanent, intellectual attractiveness of the topic may derive from the fact that it has s rich and continuous tradition in philosophy, social and political thought, and ethics, represented by Hobbes, Locke, Ferguson, and others. It has also troubled the classical masters of sociology – Tönnies, Simmel, and Durkheim – as well as contemporary classics such as Parsons or Riesman.

The social relevance of trust

More importantly, there are some unique features of contemporary societies that give particular salience to the problematics of trust. Let us look a little deeper into some relevant aspects of that contingency and uncertainty, which is so characteristic for our times. First of all, the world in which we live is influenced to a growing extent by purposeful human efforts; societies are shaped and reshaped, history is made and remade (by charismatic leaders, legislators, social movements, political parties, governments, parliaments, innovators, discoverers, reformers, etc.). More and more people take active orientations toward the future, and they recognize their agential powers, at least through the electoral procedures, and participation in social movements, political parties, and voluntary associations. "The degree to which our own behaviour, in spite of social dependencies, is thought to have an impact on our future state, has varied considerably in the course of history" (Luhmann 1988: 98). We seem to live in the period in which "the dependence of society's future on decision making has increased" (Luhmann 1994: xii). We have moved from societies based on fate to those moved by human agency. In order to face the future actively and constructively, we need to deploy trust: for example, the politicians have to trust the viability and acceptance of proposed policies, the educators have to trust the abilities of their pupils, the inventors have to trust the reliability and usefulness of new products, and the common people have to trust all those who are involved in "representative activities" (Dahrendorf 1990) acting "on their behalf" in the domain of government, economy, technology, science.

Second, our world has become extremely interdependent. Within every society the differentiation and specialization of roles, functions, occupations, special interests, lifestyles, and tastes has reached immense proportions, rendering "organic solidarity" in the Durkheimian sense more imperative than ever (Durkheim 1964b [1893]). Across various societies the process of globalization has bound them in the network of tightening interlinkages – political, military, economic, financial, cultural. Cooperation – of intra-societal as well as inter-societal scope – becomes a pressing need, a crucial challenge, but also the domain of uncertainties. "The division of labor, though a source of riches, increases vulnerability to others' failures to fulfill their responsibilities" (Clarke and Short 1993: 384). As our dependence on the cooperation of others grows, so does the importance of trust in their reliability. "The ongoing process of global interdependency will only increase the demand for trust as an essential condition for cooperation" (Misztal 1996: 269).

The extreme forms that the division of labor takes, and the great differentiation and segmentation of roles, played at the same time by single individuals vis-à-vis multiple partners in complex role-sets, and status-sets (Merton 1968: 422–438) makes the conduct of role-incumbents less predictable than ever.

The greater the differentiation of system and concomitant proliferation of roles, the more it becomes possible to assign a degree of lability to any particular role (or role-set) and hence the more a certain degree of negotiability of role expectations becomes possible – perhaps even necessary. The greater indeterminacy and the greater negotiability of role expectations lead to the greater possibility for the development of trust as a form of social relations.

(Seligman 1997: 39)

Fourth, social life is pervaded with new and expanding threats and hazards of our own making. "The more technology is applied to nature and society, the more life becomes unpredictable. The complex interactions of technology as they bear upon nature and society create an ever larger number of unintended consequences" (Stivers 1994: 91). Civilizational and technological developments, apart from their uncontestable benefits, have also produced vast possibilities for disastrous failures, as well as harmful side effects (e.g., industrial catastrophes, environmental destruction, climatic changes, civilizational diseases). Our own creations unexpectedly turn against ourselves. "Increasing social and technical complexity elevates the probability that some key portions of the system cannot be safely counted on" (Clarke and Short 1993: 384). Coping with that raised vulnerability in the "risk society" (Beck 1992) requires an enlarged pool of trust.

Fifth, ours is a world of increasingly numerous options. In all domains of life (e.g., consumption, education, labor, leisure) the spectrum of potential choices is vast. The more available options people face, the less predictable are the decisions they will eventually take. This refers equally to ourselves and to our partners. To choose among alternative courses of actions (e.g., to support this or that politician, to consult this or that doctor, to buy this rather than that product, to deposit our money in this rather than that bank) we often have to resort to trust. Similarly, the uncertainty about the actions others will take, when faced with their own pool of multiple options (e.g., which policies the president will choose, which therapy the doctor will prescribe, what price the firm will give to the product, how the bank will invest our money) makes trust an indispensable ingredient of our actions. "Trust becomes increasingly salient for our decisions and actions the larger the feasible set of alternatives open to others" (Gambetta 1988b: 219).

Sixth, large segments of the contemporary social world have become opaque for their members. The complexity of institutions, organizations, and technological systems, and the increasingly global scope of their operations, make them impenetrable to ordinary people, but often also to the professional experts. Who commands a full understanding of global financial flows, stock-exchange fluctuations, computer networks, telecommunications, transportation, or of administrative, managerial, governmental, or military machineries and international bureaucracies? More often than ever before we have to act in the dark, as if facing a huge black box, on the proper functioning of which our needs and interests increasingly depend. Trust becomes an indispensable strategy to deal with the opaqueness of our social environment. Without trust we would be paralyzed and unable to act.

The seventh and related feature of contemporary society is the growing anonymity and impersonality of those on whose actions our existence and well-being depend. The managers of institutions and organizations, operators of technological systems, producers of goods, providers of services are most often unknown to us. We also usually have no possibility of influencing, controlling, or monitoring their activities. They are totally hidden and independent from us, while we are crucially dependent on what they are doing (e.g., we are vitally dependent on the pilots of the plane we fly, on the producers of the medicines we take, on the workers who assembled our car, on the cooks who prepare the food we buy, the tax inspectors who check our returns, on the central bankers who fix the interest rates for our savings, on the telephone operators who connect us with our friends and on postal clerks who expedite our letters – even though we have little chance of meeting any of them in person). On innumerable occasions we have to rely on the efficiency, responsibility, good will of such anonymous "significant others." There is no means of bridging this anonymity gap, but resorting to trust.

The eighth feature is the growing presence of strange, unfamilar people in our environment. Due to massive migrations, tourism, and travel we encounter and are sometimes surrounded by strangers. "The stranger is the representative of the unknown . . . the unknown culturally defined space which separates off the outside from the world of the 'familiar', structured by the traditions with which the collectivity identifies" (Giddens in Beck et al. 1994: 81). To cope with strangers, trust becomes a necessary resource.

Culturalist bias and the career of trust

These are some reasons – intellectual and social, immanent and responsive – for the new wave of sociological interest in trust. As opposed to earlier, psychological approaches that treated trust as a personal attitude, it is now taken most often to be the trait of interpersonal relations, the feature of the socio-individual field in which people operate, the cultural resource utilized by individuals in their actions. Such a culturalist bias in the treatment of trust is evident if we notice that in all six concepts that I have discussed as symptomatic for the present concern with culture, trust appears as a core component.

First, trust is an important dimension of civic culture. As Almond and Verba emphasize, "civic culture" assumes "a widely distributed sense of political competence and mutual trust in the citizenry" (Almond and Verba 1980: 4). Political trust is seen as the reflection of a wider climate of trust obtaining in a society. "General social trust is translated into politically relevant trust" (Almond and Verba 1965: 228). Its presence is an indispensable precondition of a viable political system. Similarly, for Robert Dahl, "a sense of trust forms part of the essential attributes of a liberal-democratic political culture" (Parry 1976: 129–130, commenting on Dahl's [1971] concept of a polyarchy). This belief is widely accepted in later political science literature. "More recently, trust has been taken as key to the 'civic' political culture" (Silver 1985: 52). "The political culture literature argues that the evolution and persistence of mass-based democracy requires the emergence of certain supportive habits and attitudes among the general public. One of the most basic of these attitudes is a sense of interpersonal trust" (Inglehart 1988: 1204).

Second, trust becomes an important aspect of civil society, once the concept is given cultural meaning. That close, solidaristic community of citizens, committed and loyal toward political authority, could not exist without horizontal trust toward each other, as well as vertical trust toward public institutions. It is characteristic that Jeffrey Alexander includes the opposition of "trusting and suspicious" as one of the main dimensions in the "polarizing discourse of civil society" (Alexander 1992: 293).

Third, trust fares as an important, though implicit, dimension of cultural capital. It is an inclusive trust within high-status groups (a sort of class solidarity). The aristocratic pride, the noblesse oblige principle, the "gentleman" model – are just some examples of rules that comprise mutual trust within exclusive communities.

Fourth, trust is a crucial component of social capital. Putnam defines social capital as networks of spontaneous, voluntary associations, pervaded with trust. Participation and trust are seen as mutually dependent: trust emerges from rich associational life, and at the same time facilitates spontaneous recruitment and forming of associations. "The theory of social capital presumes that, generally speaking, the more we connect with other people, the more we trust them, and vice versa" (Putnam 1995b: 665).

Fifth, trust is also linked to postmaterialist values. The concerns with community, solidarity, and interpersonal harmony imply the importance of trust. It is empirically documented by Inglehart and others (Inglehart 1990) that quality of life and subjective well-being are strongly correlated with the presence of generalized trust. Sixth, trust is an ingredient of civilizational competence. It is a prerequisite for political participation, entrepreneurial efforts, readiness to embrace new technologies.

The studies of trust emerge as important fragments of evolving research traditions focused on those and similar concepts. But apart from such indirect approaches, addressing trust in the context of wider cultural problems, it has been addressed directly as a topic of autonomous theoretical interest. Of course the notion of trust is not new, it has ancient origins and has gone through complicated and protracted evolution. "The idea of trust has had a centuries-long intellectual career" (Silver 1985: 52). Extensive accounts of that chapter of intellectual history are provided by Silver (1985), Misztal (1996), and Seligman (1997). In the present book I will abstract from historical roots of the concept to be found in philosophy, theology, socio-political thought, and ethics, and will limit the discussion to those contributions which, during the last two decades, initiated and sustained the new wave of theoretical concern with trust in sociology. It is those ideas that provide the foundation for my attempted synthesis and elaboration, it is their authors on the shoulders of whom I wish to stand. Their work will be referred to constantly as we proceed. Therefore I will list here only the books that I consider most significant for the recent debate about trust.

In 1979 Niklas Luhmann published an influential analysis of trust, in which he related it to the growing complexity, uncertainty, and risk characterizing contemporary society. For the first time, there is a suggestion that trust is not an obsolete resource typical of traditional society, but just the reverse, it gains in importance with the development of modern social forms, becoming truly indispensable in the present phase of modernity. In 1983 Bernard Barber reviewed the manifestations of trust in various institutional and professional domains of modern society, and proposed a useful typology based on the kind of expectations that trust involves, with the category of fiduciary trust being particularly insightful and original. In 1984 Shmuel Eisenstadt and Louis Roniger discovered trust as a core ingredient in patron–client relations, as they appear in various guises from antiquity to modernity. In 1988 Diego Gambetta brought together a number of authors looking at trust and distrust in various settings, from various perspectives, and himself presented the analysis of trust in closed, exclusive communities, like the Mafia. In 1990 James Coleman devoted two chapters of his comprehensive treatment of social theory to the issue of trust, providing the model for analyzing trust as a purely rational transaction, within the framework of rational-choice theory. This avenue was followed in a number of contributions in the nineties by Russell Hardin (Hardin 1991, 1993, 1996) who recently extended the rational-choice framework to the analysis of distrust. In the nineties Anthony Giddens, first himself alone (Giddens 1990a, 1991), and then together with Ulrich Beck and Scott Lash (Beck, Giddens and Lash 1994), approached trust as the characteristic feature of late modernity, elaborating on Luhmannian themes of complexity, uncertainty, and risk. In 1995 the notorious prophet of "the end of history," Francis Fukuyama provided a comprehensive exposition and apology of trust as an indispensable ingredient of viable economic systems, basing his argument on the experience of China, Japan, and other South-East Asian societies. In 1997 Adam Seligman presented an interpretation of trust as a specifically modern phenomenon linked with the division of labor, differentiation and pluralization of roles, and the consequent indeterminacy and negotiability of role expectations.

I have mentioned only selected milestones in the evolving sociological research on trust, and only those that contributed important insights to the general theory of trust. There are also numerous empirical studies of trust in various settings, which do not have immediate theoretical relevance; there are erudite historical accounts of the genealogy of the idea, which illustrate twisted and convoluted roads of human thought. The issue of trust has mobilized the ongoing and expanding research effort of a large number of scholars. This seems the right moment to stop for a while and take stock of the results achieved so far, with an attempt to introduce analytic precision and systematic order, and perhaps by these means moving the problem to a slightly higher level of theoretical sophistication.

2

The idea of trust

Human action and trust

In this chapter I shall attempt a systematic explication of the concept of trust. The argument will develop gradually, step by step, from the most general considerations toward a specific definition of trust and delineation of various types of trust. As trust obviously appears in the context of human actions, the point to begin is with a rudimentary outline of the relevant features of action.

For our purposes the most important trait of action is its orientation toward the future. "All human action occurs in time, drawing upon a past which cannot be undone and facing a future which cannot be known" (Barbalet 1996: 82). All human action is oriented toward the future, because the ends we seek or unintended consequences occurring independent of our will, are always later in time than the means we adopt. There is an inevitable time lag between what we do and what occurs as the intended, or unintended results of our efforts. Thus the results of our action occur when the world is already different than it was when the action actually took place. It is especially true of complex, sequential actions, following several stages, like taking up studies at the university, writing a book, or building a professional career.

In large measure the world changes independently of our actions. It changes for natural reasons (e.g., there is an earthquake, or a flood, or a forest fire), or because of actions taken by other people (e.g., there is a panic and crash at the stock exchange, crowds go to the street to protest against the government, a foreign army enters the country). Both may affect me in important ways (e.g., I may lose a house in an earthquake, or life savings in the fiscal crisis, or family in war). But the world changes also as a response or reaction to our actions. It may change in the way we wanted (e.g., the flowers we planted in the garden bloom in the spring, or the government falls because of revolutionary protests, the president's popularity rises in response to a successful media campaign). It may also change in a different, or even opposite direction to that which was intended (e.g., I make a flirtatious proposal to a woman and find myself in a court of law sued for sexual harassment; I buy a luxurious house to impress others and raise my status, but that provokes a lot of envy and I lose all my friends). The concept of "boomerang response" (Merton and Kendall 1944) grasps nicely that typical predicament of human life.

What the future state of the world will be is always principally unknown, precisely because it does not yet exist. "Social life gets its edge precisely from the crucial and unavoidable fact that the future is unknowable" (Barbalet 1996: 82). There is a perennial epistemological gap. "We cannot gain sufficient knowledge of the future; indeed, not even of the future we generate by means of our own decisions" (Luhmann 1994: 12–13).

Prediction and control

This does not mean that we could not try to predict what the future will bring. We may try to predict both what will happen independently of our actions (in the external world), and what will happen as a result of our actions (as a response to what we do). There are various degrees of such predictions. Sometimes we can predict with practical certainty (e.g., that the sun will set in the evening, or that the soccer ball kicked up in the air by Ronaldo will eventually fall down, or that there will be snow at the Kitzsteinhorn glacier in the Alps in January).[1] In such cases, when we are practically certain about the future, there is obviously no need for trust ("I trust the sun will rise tomorrow" sounds downright stupid). But on many other occasions we may predict only with some degree of probability (e.g., it will rain in Berlin in April; the government will not fulfill campaign promises; an offended friend will accept our apologies). Probability, by definition, leaves a margin of uncertain outcomes, the possibility that our predictions will not be borne out.

Let us notice that in such cases sometimes it makes sense to talk of trust. "I trust that my friend will accept the apologies," or "I distrust the government to fulfill campaign promises" sounds perfectly cogent. But it seems strange to say "I trust there will be sunshine in Berlin at the weekend," or "I distrust the volcano." Intuitively we feel that trust must be vested in people, rather than natural objects or events. Even if we seemingly confer trust on objects, such as saying "I trust Japanese cars," or "I trust Swiss watches," or "I trust French rapid trains," we in fact refer to humanly created systems and indirectly we trust the designers, producers, and operators whose ingenuity and labor are somehow encrypted in the objects. When objects are purely natural, it sounds improper to speak about trust, like in saying "I trust this tree to grow," or "I trust the wind to be strong," or "I trust the earth to give good crops."

Finally we reach a vast category of situations where we cannot make even such probabilistic predictions; the future remains basically uncertain (e.g., I can't know how the passer-by will react when I ask him for directions; I can't know if the driver whom I am overtaking on the highway is not drunk; I can't know if the boom will continue and I will get profits in the future). Such pervasive contingency is a trait of human fate. "We have to learn to live, alert, on the edge of confidence and contingency, aware of but not paralyzed by life's arbitrariness" (Earle and Cvetkovich 1995: 63). To allow us to do that, trust becomes a crucial resource (in our earlier examples, I decide to ask somebody for directions, I dare to pass another driver on the highway, I invest in stocks – only because I deploy some kind of trust). Thus it appears that trust is intimately linked with the uncertainty of the future, as long as that uncertainty is of human and not purely natural provenance.

To make the future more certain, instead of predicting, we may sometimes control the phenomena. Such control also has several degrees. We have complete control over future occurrences when they fall within our coercive or manipulative powers (e.g., I can light my pipe, I can play the CD, I can shut the dog in the closet, I can call a friend on the phone). In such cases, when we are in full control of phenomena, trust is obviously irrelevant. "I trust my prisoner not to escape" sounds absurd. But in other cases, we can only influence phenomena, without absolute certainty of the outcome (e.g., I will probably lessen the chances of a heart attack by exercising systematically; I will raise the chances of promotion if I work diligently; my friend will probably be persuaded to join me for dinner if I insist). In all such cases there is always a margin of uncertainty about the effectiveness of our control. Here it starts to make sense to speak about trust. "I trust my friend will join me for dinner," or "I trust my boss to promote me" sounds proper. But notice that the intuition we articulated earlier applies here too: to speak of trust, the uncertainty of control must refer to people, and not natural phenomena. It would sound strange to say: "I trust the river not to flood the fields."

The relevance of trust applies even more in the third type of situation, when we find ourselves in a condition of helplessness, when we have no control whatsoever (e.g., I have no way to influence the president's decision to raise taxes; I cannot keep the terrorist from exploding a bomb). Here I simply have to resort to trust (I must trust the president's reasons, or the terrorist's moral restraints). Thus it appears that trust is intimately linked to uncontrollability of the future; it comes to our aid when we do not have complete control over future events, as long as those are humanly created.

Actions of others: unpredictable and uncontrollable

All actions occur in the environment, they are oriented toward the world. Part of that is a natural world (important to me when I plant the flowers, or hunt in the woods, or swim in the sea). But the most important part of that is a social world, consisting of other people and their actions (as well as some more persisting sediments of their actions: groups, organizations, institutions, and products of their actions: buildings, roads, cars, TV sets etc.). Trust is not the orientation we would take toward the natural world. It does not sound proper to say: "I trust the rain to fall," or "I trust these flowers to grow," but it is quite normal to say "I trust the meteorologists to predict the rain," or "I trust the gardener to tend for flowers well." Trust belongs to human and not to natural discourse. As we emphasized before, when we trust objects it makes sense only if they are humanly created, because indirectly we trust the people who have created them. This is why we cannot say "I trust the sun to shine," but we can say "We trust the car to run." When we sometimes do use the idea of trust with respect to natural objects or events, we seem meta-phorically to ascribe purposes to nature, as if it were humanized. We link the origins of natural events to some quasi-human agents. It is only the imaginative anthropomorphization of natural forces that allows to to use the discourse of trust with respect to natural events. This happens when we say, for example: "I trust the ancestor spirits to take care of our crops" or "I trust God to stop that epidemic." These are borderline cases that do not invalidate our general claim linking trust exclusively to actions vis-à-vis the human environment.

Thus, let us narrow our focus now, leaving aside the domain of natural events, and considering only social phenomena, the proper domain for trust. Other people and their actions make up the most important environment of our life and those are the crucial targets of our own actions. We have at least to coexist with others, to coordinate our actions with them, and, in more advanced stages of human society, to cooperate with them. The problem with the social environment is that it possesses a particularly large degree of uncertainty and uncontrollability. "We invoke a whole new dimension of complexity: the subjective 'I-ness' of other human beings which we experience (perceive) and understand" (Luhmann 1979: 6). But interacting with others we must constantly formulate expectations about their actions. "All social interaction is an endless process of acting upon expectations, which are part cognitive, part emotional, and part moral" (Barber 1983: 9).

Most often our expectations are weak, as we lack the possibility of precise and accurate prediction of other people's actions. "No one can know how another human being will act in the future" (Dunn 1988: 85). If we had such full possibility of prediction, and strong, certain expectations trust would be irrelevant. But facing other people we often, and perhaps more often than in the case of natural phenomena, remain in the condition of uncertainty, bafflement, and surprise. Part of the reason is epistemological; we simply miss important knowledge. Confronted with others' individual actions we don't know enough about the mechanisms of human conduct as well as about other people's motives, intentions, and reasons. We experience "the opaqueness of others' intentions and calculations," "the fundamental otherness of alter's intentions" (Seligman 1997: 43, 46). This is acknowledged by authors from diverse theoretical schools: "Since other people have their own first-hand access to the world and can experience things differently they may consequently be a source of profound insecurity to me" (Luhmann 1979: 6). "The motivations of those we interact with can be inferred but never known directly and the quality of goods and services we are offered is often unknown or known only approximately" (Kollock 1994: 317).

We must also recognize that others whose behavior matters to us act in interaction with, or under the influence of, large numbers of people, who for them constitute their circles of partners or "significant others" (Mead 1964). Their actions therefore are an extremely complex outcome of those innumerable influences. We cannot grasp them in their unique combination, even if the basic regularities of a single interaction were known.[2]

But perhaps it is not only the lack of requisite knowledge that often prevents us from predicting the actions of others. Without entering into a deeper philosophical debate about determinism, I wish simply to suggest that it may also have something to do with the ontology of human beings. Human action is on many occasions significantly underdetermined. People seem to possess some basic freedom of action, "this disturbing potential for diverse action" (Luhmann 1979: 39), the possibility of always "acting otherwise" (Giddens 1984), showing capriciousness, playing tricks – and frustrating even the best-founded of our expectations. This is what Annette Baier refers to as the "discretionary power of the other" (Baier 1986: 250), and Adam Seligman as the "freedom, agency, and hence fundamental inscrutability of the other" (Seligman 1997: 69). Such underdeterminacy is even more obvious when we are confronted with the collective or combined actions of multiple individuals, whose complex interrelations produce emergent qualities, collective outcomes unexpected from the position of each participant. Some examples of such macro-effects of aggregated micro-behaviors are the fluctuations of demand and supply on the market, booms and recessions, bull and bear periods at the stock exchange, baffling results of political elections, and so forth. Finally, people exhibit what some sociologists label as "reflexiveness." This means that people act on beliefs, knowledge, memory and interpretation of past experiences – and the state of their future knowledge, the beliefs they will hold, interpretations they will entertain and in terms of which they will act in the future cannot be predicted now, before they actually conceive them.[3] People can also reflexively modify the course of their actions on the basis of partial results already achieved; they can introduce corrections, abandon interactions, resign, turn back, and so forth. And to complete the perplexity of the situation, people may through their preventive actions falsify predictions, initially quite sound (self-destroying prophecies), or through their constructive actions make completely unfounded prophecies come true (self-fulfilling prophecies) (Merton 1996: 183–201).

We are in an equally difficult situation trying to control, instead of predict, other people's conduct. It is very rarely that we have full control over others. It is only the extremes of physical coercion that fall under this rubric. In such cases there is no place for trust. If I have complete power I can enforce expected actions, I can coerce others to act as I wish, I do not need to trust them. "Full monitoring and control of somebody's performance makes trust unnecessary" (Giddens 1991: 19).[4] But this occurs very seldom. Most often we lack the possibility of direct, or full control over other people's actions. And then trust becomes centrally important. Trust and freedom are intimately related. "An actor's trust in others presupposes the freedom of action of others" (Barbalet 1996: 79). Trust is a "policy for handling the freedom of other human agents or agencies" (Dunn 1988: 73).

The reason why the others escape our complete control has to do with human consciousness. As even the harshest of tyrants inevitably discovers, by coercion one may subject to full control human physical bodies, but not the thoughts, intentions, imaginations, and dreams. Even in extreme cases of repression, people always have some choice: to submit or resist, to conform or to oppose, to obey or to evade (martyrs, heroes, and saints are also human after all).[5] Thus attempts at full control most often fail. "The more we try to colonize the future, the more it is likely to spring surprises upon us" (Giddens, in Beck et al. 1994: 58).

Hence we routinely find ourselves in a condition of uncertainty about, and uncontrollability of, future actions. We usually cannot know and cannot control what other people will do independently of our own actions, and even more we cannot be sure and cannot completely safeguard how they will react to our actions. Thus, to repeat: "What weighs on all social systems and what all social action must deal with is the unavoidability of an unknown [and, let us add – uncontrollable] future" (Barbalet 1996: 84). "Uncertainty and risk are integral to the human condition" (Short 1990: 181).

Three orientations: hope, confidence, and trust

There are three types of orientations with which we may face that human predicament. The first is hope (or its opposite, resignation). This is a passive, vague, not rationally justified feeling that things will turn out to the good (or to the bad). For example, I hope to be rich some day, or I have lost any hope that inflation will be stopped. Another orientation is confidence (and its opposite, doubt). It is a still passive, but more focused and to some extent justified, faith that something good will happen (or not). For example, reading reports of a criminal trial I have confidence that the court will give a fair ruling in this case (because it has proved to be fair before). Or I doubt in the electoral promises of lower taxes (because I haven't heard of a single political party that would lower taxes after winning an election). "Confidence can be described, therefore, as an emotion of assured expectation" (Barbalet 1996: 76); and doubt simi- larly, as an emotion of assured disbelief.[6] Because in the case of confidence one is not actively involved, but rather passively, contempla- tively observes the situation, it is possible to blame disappointment on others, the regime, the system, the propaganda, the falsified information, the faked credentials, and so forth, but not on oneself. As Luhmann puts it "in the case of confidence you will react to disappointment by external attribution" (Luhmann 1988: 97).[7]

Both orientations discussed so far – hope and confidence – are contemplative, detached, distanced, noncommittal. They fall within the discourse of fate, refer to something happening without our active participation, events we consider only in our thoughts. And yet, most often we cannot refrain from acting – to satisfy our needs, to realize our goals. We cannot just "wait and see." By several circumstances we are made to act, to commit ourselves in spite of the conditions of uncertainty and uncontrollability. Then we have to face risks that things will turn against us – independently of our actions, or as a boomerang reaction to our deeds. "Situations in which we can be taken advantage of are pervasive in every realm of our lives" (Kollock 1994: 317). But nevertheless we have to take the risks, leave the calm security of the discourse of fate, and enter the discourse of agency. William James' term "forced options" adequately describes this challenge (Barbalet 1996: 88). Because in this case we actively commit ourselves, we can no longer blame the others, nor the regime, nor the system, if something goes wrong. We may only regret our actions resorting to "internal attribution" (Luhmann 1988: 97–98).

Trust defined

In situations when we have to act in spite of uncertainty and risk, the third orientation comes to the fore, that of trust. Trusting becomes the crucial strategy for dealing with an uncertain and uncontrollable future. Trust so understood is "a simplifying strategy that enables individuals to adapt to complex social environment, and thereby benefit from increased opportunities" (Earle and Cvetkovich 1995: 38). "Trust is particularly relevant in conditions of ignorance or uncertainty with respect to unknown or unknowable actions of others" (Gambetta 1988b: 218). Then it becomes in fact indispensable. "With a complete absence of trust, one must be catatonic, one could not even get up in the morning" (Hardin 1993: 519). This third type of orientation differs from hope and confidence in that it falls within the discourse of agency: actively anticipating and facing an unknown future.

Acting in uncertain and uncontrollable conditions, we take risks, we gamble, we make bets about the future uncertain, free actions of others. Thus we have arrived at the simple, most general definition of trust: TRUST IS A BET ABOUT THE FUTURE CONTINGENT ACTIONS OF OTHERS.[8] In this account trust consists of two main components: beliefs and commitment. First, it involves specific expectations: "Trust is based on an individual's theory as to how another person will perform on some future occasion" (Good 1988: 33). Placing trust we behave "as if" we knew the future. "To show trust is to anticipate the future. It is to behave as though the future were certain" (Luhmann 1979: 10). Trust refers to the actions of others. Normally I don't place trust in my own actions, I simply do them. It wouldn't sound natural to say "I trust I will brush my teeth this evening" (because I will if I want). The exceptions are those conditions of passion, intoxication, incapability, and so forth, when I lose control over my own will, and appear to myself as somebody else. This may be expressed in saying: "I cannot trust myself not to hit him," or "I cannot trust my driving today," or "I trust I will be able to walk after that surgery." Here I myself become a quasi-other whose actions I endow with trust or distrust.

But the anticipatory belief is not sufficient to speak of there being trust. Trust is more than just contemplative consideration of future possibilities. We must also face the future actively, by committing ourselves to action with at least partly uncertain and uncontrollable consequences. Thus, second, trust involves commitment through action, or – metaphorically speaking – placing a bet. "Trust . . . is the correct expectations about the actions of other people that have a bearing on one's own choice of action when that action must be chosen before one can monitor the actions of those others" (Dasgupta 1988: 51). "Trust is only involved when the trusting expectation makes a difference to a decision" (Luhmann 1979: 24). For example: I trust this girl to be a good mother in the future, hence I marry her (I bet on her); I trust this politician to rule wisely, hence I vote for him (I bet on him); I trust Lufthansa pilots and technicians to prepare the aircraft and fly safely, hence I choose German airlines (I bet on the company); I trust IBM products to perform faultlessly, hence I buy their computer (I bet on the firm); I trust the court to give a fair and just verdict, hence I file a suit (I bet on the institution), and so forth. In all such cases "trust is paid ahead of time as an advance on success" (Luhmann 1979: 25).

In the usage I am adopting in this book, the concept of "distrust" is treated as the negative mirror-image of trust. It is also a bet, but a negative bet. It involves negative expectations about the actions of others (of their harmful, vicious, detrimental actions toward myself), and it involves negative, defensive commitment (avoiding, escaping, distancing myself, refusing actions, taking protective measures against those I distrust). The term "mistrust" will for my purposes refer to a neutral situation, when both trust and distrust are suspended. It means the lack of clear expectations, as well as hesitation about commiting oneself. I use the term "mistrust" to indicate a temporary, intermediate phase in the dynamics of trust-building, or trust-depletion. Mistrust is either a former trust destroyed, or former distrust healed. The concrete qualities of mistrust are path-dependent, related to its alternative origins. It seems that mistrust resulting from the breach of trust, easily leads to full-fledged distrust, whereas mistrust resulting from the withdrawal of unjustified distrust will build toward full-fledged trust much more slowly. This is one of the typical assymetries that we encounter in the processes of trust-building and trust-destroying.

Varieties of commitment

If we look closer we shall discover that trusting may involve three different types of commitment. The first type is involved when I act toward others because I believe that the actions which they carry out anyway will be favorable to my interests, needs, and expectations. Let us call it anticipatory trust. Our earlier examples illustrated this type of commitment: marriage spurred by expected motherly attitudes of the spouse, voting based on expected political wisdom of the candidate, choosing an airline or a computer firm because of its expected relia-bility, going to court in expectation of its fairness. In all such cases we were involved in a bet that others, just doing what they normally routinely do (or should do in their respective situations or roles), will act appropriately to our needs and interests. Notice that such qualities of their actions are independent of our beliefs about them or our actions toward them. They just routinely happen to be good mothers, good politicians, good pilots, to produce good computers, and give fair verdicts. I only recognize those capabilities of others and act upon this knowledge. "It does not imply an obligation on the part of the trusted, who may not even be aware of the trust placed in her" (Hardin 1991: 198).

There are also other sorts of commitments, which are specifically addressed and motivated by the expected response of the others to our placing of trust. Let us call it responsive trust. They involve the act of entrusting some valuable object to somebody else, with his or her consent; giving up one's control over that object and placing it in somebody else's hands, and expecting responsible care. For example, this kind of commitment occurs when I leave a child with a baby-sitter, hire a guard to take care of my house, place my old parents in a nursing home, deposit savings in the bank, and so on. Trust in this specific sense is "letting other persons (natural or artificial, such as nations, firms, etc.) take care of something the truster cares about, where such caring involves some exercise of discretionary powers" (Baier 1995: 105). This is a bet of a specific sort; it is limited to a specific object being entrusted, and it implies a specific, voluntarily accepted obligation to care. It is not enough for a baby-sitter to be usually responsible and caring, she must show these traits in this specific case and not leave my child unattended. It is not enough for the guard to be usually brave, he must not get away when my house is robbed. It is not enough for the nursing house to be well run, it must not ignore the needs of my parents. It is not enough for the bank to be reliable, it must not waste my money in risky investments. As, of course, all such breaches of trust harming the objects entrusted are eminently possible, by entrusting something to others we increase our vulnerability vis-à-vis themselves (Zand 1972: 230). This engenders a specific obligation to meet trust, to live up to expectations expressed by the act of entrusting.

There is a third type of commitment when we act on the belief that the other person will reciprocate with trust toward ourselves. In this case we trust intentionally to evoke trust. This is particularly characteristic for the close, intimate relationships, among family members, friends, and so forth, and is intended to make the bonds even stronger. For example, a mother allowing her daughter to return late in the evening manifests trust in order to be trusted as an understanding and liberal parent. The foreman gives an employee a highly responsible (and well-paid) task so as to be trusted as a good boss. Let us call it evocative trust. Of course, all three types of commitment: anticipatory, responsive, and evocative, may coincide in one act of trusting. Separating them is a little artificial, and is only for analytical purposes.

The commitment accompanying trust has various degrees. We may speak of stronger or weaker commitment, depending on the six kinds of circumstances. First is the range of consequences that an action taken on the basis of trusting expectation will have for ourselves. Consequential commitments are stronger than non-consequential commitments. For example, getting employed in a trusted firm is in this sense a stronger commitment than taking a voyage with a trusted tourist agency; buying a car is a more consequential decision than hiring a taxi. The second factor is the expected duration of a relationship to which we commit ourselves on the basis of trust. Lifelong commitments are stronger than temporary commitments. For example, getting married is in this sense a stronger commitment than going on a date; buying a house has more lasting consequences than renting a room at a hotel. The third factor is the possibility of withdrawal from a commitment, as opposed to the irrevocability of a decision (the "pre-commitment" and "burnt bridges" effect, to be discussed later). For example, it is a stronger commitment to marry when divorce is impossible and infidelity severely sanctioned, than when both are allowed or excused. And it is a weaker commitment to buy in a store that allows you to return the merchandise within five days, than in the one where the purchase is final.[9]

Fourth, the strength of commitment is directly related to the amount of risk: the scope of possible losses incurred by the breach of trust, relative to the probability of incurring such a loss. In this sense, boarding a plane is not a strong commitment even though the loss in the case of a disaster is the highest – our life, because the chances of a crash are very low. It is a stronger commitment in this sense to decide on major surgery; the loss in case of a breach of trust is equally extreme, but the chances of failure are usually higher. It is a stronger commitment to invest the same sum in stocks than in a saving account, because the chances of a loss are greater in the former case. And it is a stronger commitment to invest a million than a thousand, even if the chances of the loss are the same. Fifth, the strength of commitment depends on the presence or absence of insurance or other back-up arrangements against losses in the case of breached trust. It is a weaker commitment to save in a bank with state guarantees, than in an uninsured saving and loans association.[10] It is a stronger commitment to lend money to a friend on his word alone, than to go to a notary public. Sixth, in the special case when we entrust something of value to other people, the strength of commitment depends on the value of that object. Leaving a dog with the neighbors is in this sense a weaker commitment than leaving a child with a baby-sitter. Or in the more measurable domain, lending a car to a friend is a stronger commitment than lending a book (Hardin 1993: 520).

Trust and risk

Trust as defined above is intimately related to risk. "Trust is a solution for specific problems of risk" (Luhmann 1988: 95). Introducing the concept of trust we have already had to refer to risk on numerous occasions, but so far it has been in a vague, undefined manner. Now this crucial correlate of the concept of trust has to be addressed directly and more analytically. In common parlance risk may be used widely to refer to all types of threats, hazards, or dangers. But it may also be used in a more specific sense, applied to a qualified category of threats. The risks we have in mind when speaking about trust are of the latter, more specific sort.

Risk defined

Risk in this specific sense is in many ways parallel to trust. First, it is oriented toward the future. Risk is the unwelcome, threatening future state of the world. Second, the threat may be due to natural reasons, in which case we shall speak of natural risks. For example, there is the risk of an earthquake, or of a comet hitting the Earth. But from our perspective the most important forms of risk refer to the humanly created future, threats due to the actions of other people (personal, social, political, economic risks), for example, the risk of infidelity in marriage, of disloyalty in friendship, as well as the risks of war, economic crisis, crime, and so forth. A derivative category comprises the risks evoked by humanly transformed nature (civilizational, technical risks), for example, the risk of nuclear fallout, ecological disaster, or civilizational diseases. Third, risk implies some uncertainty about the occurrence of a future unwanted state of the world, as well as the at least partial impossibility of preventing such an occurrence. Finally, risk involves agential commitment. "Unexpected results may be a consequence of our decisions, and not simply an aspect of cosmology, an expression of the hidden meanings of nature or the hidden intentions of God" (Luhmann 1988: 96).

Risk is activated by our actions, the choices we make, the decisions we take. We trigger the threats off by acting in certain ways, we make them relevant, threatening for ourselves. There is always a risk of a plane crash, but for me it is actualized, becomes relevant, only the moment I decide to board. There is a risk of a fall on the stock exchange, but it becomes relevant for me only when I decide to invest in stocks. There is a risk of broken marriage, but it exists only if I decide to marry in the first place. There is a risk of pneumonia if one is exposed to the cold, but it touches me only if I choose to swim in the sea in winter. Risks are not just there, rather they are taken and faced. In this narrow sense, risk belongs to the discourse of agency, rather than the discourse of fate. On the other hand, we may speak of dangers when the threat is independent of our actions, coming from without. Whatever I do or do not do, I may die in a nuclear war; whatever I do or do not do, I may get ill in an epidemic. Dangers are passively awaited and at most hoped to be averted or avoided. They belong to the discourse of fate, rather than agency. "The point is whether or not the possibility of disappointment depends on our own previous behaviour" (Luhmann 1988: 98). We may summarize these considerations by defining risk for our purposes as the probability of adversity related to our own actions, due to our own commitments.

Risks of trusting

Placing trust, that is, making bets about the future uncertain and uncontrollable actions of others, is always accompanied by risk (Kollock 1994: 317). This is so because there is always a possibility that those future anticipated actions will be harmful for us, or that our entrusting will be abused or taken advantage of, or that our effort to evoke trust will backfire and produce disdain instead of tightened bonds. "Situations involving trust constitute a subclass of those involving risk. They are situations in which the risk one takes depends on the performance of other actors" (Coleman 1990: 91). Placing trust means suspending, discounting, "bracketing" the risk, acting as if the risk were not existent.

Taking risks may bring many kinds of unwelcome consequences for us. Risk appears in the act of trusting in four different guises. The first-degree risk is the possibility of future adverse events totally independent of our act of trusting: the risk that others will behave badly toward ourselves, or that their conduct will simply disappoint our expectations. For example, the teachers at the school to which I send my child will be good or bad, independent of my decision to choose that particular school (based on my trust in them). The elected politician will be efficient or not, independent of my decision to cast a vote for him in the elections (based on my trust in him). The crews and the ground personnel of a certain airline will operate dependably or not, irrespective of my boarding the plane (as an act of trust toward them). A doctor of medicine will be skilled or not, independent of my choice of her services (based on my trust in her). All of them may be completely unaware of my trust put in them.[11] The risk here is simply the possibility that they will behave otherwise than I expect them to do: teach badly, rule inefficiently, fly dangerously, heal poorly.

The second-degree risk is linked to the very act of trusting. Beyond the risk of the improper or harmful conduct of others, there is a surplus of negative psychological experiences due to our placing trust in somebody who apparently had not deserved it. It may be felt as grief that people are worse than we believe. That can perhaps be a regret that we have trusted someone untrustworthy. It may be shame that we have been so badly wrong. Our discerning and evaluating capacity is brought into question. We may feel ourselves to be fools, or naive, or idealists. We open ourselves to pains of this sort whenever we have high expectations of anybody, and the more so, the higher the expectations, and the stronger the commitment based on them. The disenchantment with a charismatic leader who has embezzled public money, the discovery that our favorite author is a plagiarist, or that our musical idol is a drug addict, are just some extreme examples of this situation. It is indeed a paradox that trust itself, that is, acting "as if" the risk was small or nonexistent, in fact adds another risk, the "risk of trusting." Trust copes with one type of risk by trading it for another type of risk.

The third-degree risk occurs only in those cases when the trustee is aware of and accepts our credit of trust, and is therefore under some moral obligation to meet it. This usually happens in close, intimate relationships, like friendship, love, family ties – where some amount of trust, recognized by the other party, is a taken-for-granted, almost definitional component. It is also present in other types of relationships, when there is an explicit and acknowledged "credit of trust" extended to other people. They are then under some type of self-assumed obligation to meet trust conferred on them, not to disappoint the expectations directed at them. The drama of discovering that a beloved is unfaithful, the sadness of finding out that a friend is disloyal, the repulsion felt when a close business partner cheats on us behind our backs, are all the risks incurred by this kind of trust. It is a surplus of harm beyond other more tangible harms brought about by the trustee's improper conduct.

The fourth-degree risk accompanies the specific case of entrusting some valued object to somebody's voluntary care. Here the risk of breaching trust is much more tangible, and not limited to psychological displeasure. With respect to the entrusted object, "trust involves giving discretion to another to affect one's interests. This move is inherently subject to the risk that the other will abuse the power of discretion" (Hardin 1993: 507). Voluntarily increasing our vulnerability to others by forfeiting control over some valued object, we have to consider the possibility that they will exploit the occasion to their benefit, or ignore obligations incurred by our act of trust.

To illustrate those four types of risk, which may sometimes come together in one act of trust, let me tell a true story. I was teaching as a visiting professor at an American university. A student failed in the written exam. She came to my office in tears claiming that the exam was her last before graduation, that she would lose a promised job and could not afford to study longer, as she had to support two younger brothers in a broken family. She painted all this as a life catastrophe. She put her fate in my hands and offered to write an extended essay, much harder than the exam, over the vacation and send it to my home address in Poland (I was leaving right after the term ended) if only I gave her the minimum passing grade. I accepted the deal, emphasizing that I was granting her an exceptional credit of trust. I chose a topic for an essay she was supposed to write, and even lent her a relevant rare book, which she had promised to send back together with the essay. You may already have guessed the conclusion of the story: she has never got in touch with me and has never sent either the essay or the book. I took four types of risks in this story, all of which unfortunately backfired. I expected that in spite of the failed exam the student was capable of writing a passing essay. There was a first-degree risk that she could not do it, or would do it poorly, so I would not have the expected good essay in my hands. This was not a particularly acute risk in this case, as I could very well do without her essay. But there was also a second-degree, surplus risk of compromising my professional competence as a teacher by not being able to appraise the student's capabilities correctly. It could lead to a feeling of shame, but could also lower my professional prestige if my colleagues in the faculty found out about my credulity. There was also another expectation involved: I believed that she would feel obliged, and recipro-cate the credit of trust vested in her, by writing the essay and sending it to me. To make her aware of that credit and elicit an obligation, I especially emphasized this in our conversation. Apparently to no avail. Here the third-degree risk was involved. It has turned out to be quite painful to recognize that I had trusted a cynical and unfair person, who abused my trust and made a fool of me. I experienced moral disgust, as well as the shame of being a naive sucker. If my colleagues knew that, I could also meet with external sanctions of ridicule or contempt.[12] Finally, I expected that she would take good care of the book I entrusted to her and return it promptly. This specific trust was also breached. I was sorry to have lost the book I lent to her, as it was rare and hard to replace. I felt cheated and victimized. In sum, I paid varied and quite considerable costs for my act of trusting.

Prudent and imprudent risks

By definition, one can never be certain of the outcomes that making the bet of trust will bring. Risk is always present. And yet we may say of some bets that they are prudent, and of others that they are imprudent, depending on the two circumstances: the degree of risk, that is, the chances of winning or losing, and the stakes, that is, the value of what may be won or lost. Let us look from that perspective at the four types of risks distinguished earlier.

Taking the first-degree risk, that is, facing the possibility that quite independently of our own actions, the others' actions relevant for our interests will turn against our expectations or bring us harm, seems to be prudent only if the probability of such an outcome is low, and imprudent if that probability is high. It seems prudent to avoid high risks and commit oneself only if the probability of winning is high. And it seems imprudent to make bets if the chances of winning are low, as well as to neglect the opportunity when the chances of winnning are high. This is right as long as we do not take the stakes into account: the value of the possible goal to be achieved, as well as the value of the goal forfeited, or the costs incurred by not acting. Of course if the risk of trusting is high and the stakes low, it is prudent not to commit oneself, to suspend or withdraw trust. Someone who refuses to buy at a bargain price at the bazaar, and goes instead to a reliable store, behaves prudently, even if the price paid is slightly higher. Similarly if the risk is low and the stakes high, it is prudent to take a risk, and extend trust. Every passenger boarding a plane takes a relatively low risk, and gains a lot of time and comfort compared to other, slower means of transportation. Thus it is prudent to trust the anonymous technicians and pilots preparing and flying the aircraft.

But there are more ambivalent cases. The fear of trusting if the chances of bad outcomes are high may be mitigated by the high value of the possible goal attained if trust is met, as well as the high costs incurred if trust is not placed. Look at the case of a patient deciding on experimental surgery against diagnosed cancer, even if the chances of success are estimated at 10 percent. He takes a risk, trusts the surgeon, because the reward of success – saving life – is extremely high, and the cost of withdrawing trust and not deciding on the surgery is equally extreme – inevitable death.[13] Thus even if the risk is very high, it may be prudent to make the bet of trust, to commit oneself if the stakes of winning are even higher: the goal to be reached is highly desirable or even more so – absolutely vital.

The reverse is also true: even if the risk is low, it may be prudent to withdraw trust and engage in all sorts of precautions if the rare, improbable, and yet possible breach of trust would bring very serious consequences and high costs: in other words, if the stakes of losing are extremely high. Look at the case of airport controls. The unpleasant feeling every passenger experiences passing the magnetic gates and being searched is due to a priori distrust: treating every one as a potential terrorist smuggling weapons. The chance that there will actually be a terrorist in the stream of passengers queuing at the gates is extremely low, and yet trust is withheld from all of them. The possible cost of allowing a terrorist on board would be so high that it justifies the enormous expense and inconvenience of the thorough checks of people and luggage. Or take another example: writing this book on the computer I am now repeatedly making backup copies of the text. It is certainly costly and time consuming, but too much is at stake, if the rare and improbable case of power failure or computer crash were to happen.

In all such considerations the intervening, mediating factor is the subjective estimate of risk, as well as the personal propensity to take or avoid risks. "The perception and evaluation of risk is a highly subjective matter . . . It differentiates people and promotes a different type of risk-seeking or risk-avoiding, trusting or distrusting, individuality" (Luhmann 1988: 100). Also, a peculiar human trait is placing value on risk for its own sake.[14] Some people purposefully seek and enjoy risks.[15] This may substantially modify the calculation of the takes. For the Formula-1 driver the thrill of risk may even outweigh the monetary prize for victory, and make competing a subjectively prudent action in spite of the tremendous risk involved. For the big investor, the risk of playing at the stock exchange may be more motivating than the highly uncertain and problematic profits.

Let us now look at the second-degree risk of psychological displeasure if the expectations involved in our trust are not met. Here we enter a very subjective domain, which differs probably with every individual. There are people highly sensitive to failure of their estimates or predictions, easily blaming themselves, losing their self-esteem as the result of failed trust. Their second-degree risk in every act of trust is relatively high. For them it would seem more prudent to abstain from rash trust-giving, all other considerations being equal. There are also people with stronger self-defenses, able to explain away their failure by various rationalizations, to deflect blame to others, or place it on the circumstances. If they have purchased a proverbial "lemon" from the car dealer, they would blame the breach of trust on faulty information, misleading commercials, bad advice from colleagues – but not on their own credulity. Here the second-degree risk is lower, and hence it would seem more prudent for the people with such a psychological make-up to take those "leaps of faith" involved in trusting a bit less carefully, all other considerations being equal.

In the case of a third-degree risk, which to remind you is linked with the very act of placing trust in full view of the trustee, with the trustee's explicit or implicit acceptance, the new factor in the calculation of prudence is the sheer satisfaction of giving a credit of trust. Like making a gift, it makes one feel magnanimous, generous, and benevolent, and through a reflected glow of the recipient's gratitude raises one's self-esteem.[16] In the case of my untrustworthy American student, I extended trust against strong odds, precisely because of such subjective satisfactions derived from the very act of trusting, whatever the consequences. And this somewhat mitigated the losses due to the eventual breach of trust on her part.

The fourth-degree risk involves entrusting some valued object to another person. This opens up the possibility of abuse and exploitation, perhaps even blackmail by the one now in command of something I value. Prudent trust demands some limitation of vulnerability, leaving some backup options. It seems imprudent to put oneself completely at the mercy of another. This is particularly true if we willingly entrust the highest possible value, namely ourselves, abdicating power of control over our resources, entrusting all wealth, sharing our deepest secrets, opening ourselves entirely to the other person, abandoning all backup insurances. "If part of what the truster entrusts to the trusted are discretionary powers, then the truster risks abuse of those and the successful disguise of such abuse" (Baier 1986: 239). Thus if the possible loss incurred by the breach of trust is very high, it is prudent to build defenses, to limit the entrusted values, to leave oneself some reserves, to construct backup options, to build insurances.

But this principle is not without exceptions. If the possible benefit incurred by entrusting is extremely high, then even a high degree of risk, vulnerability, exposure, may be prudent. Even more so when the very act of unconditional entrusting may turn into a means *per se*, evoking obligation to reciprocate, feelings of gratitude, raising the intimacy of a relationship and in effect safeguarding expected care over the entrusted object, or benevolence toward ourselves (if we abdicated our independence). Mutual love, rewarding friendship, intimate family relations, are good illustrations of this case. If we strive for those, it would be imprudent, and even self-defeating to refuse to open up, to hesitate in granting unconditional trust, to construct defensive insurances. For example, the practice of signing a pre-nuptial financial contract has probably spoilt many marriages, undermining mutual trust, and leading toward divorce. Granted that in such eventuality it saves the partners many troubles, yet the cost of such an escape clause seems too high.[17] Another situation when the unconditional entrusting of ourselves to the care of others may be prudent is seeking help from professionals: doctors, attorneys, and so on. Here it may serve as a good strategy for evoking raised trustworthiness. "Clients who docilely put their fate in the professional's hands may evoke a response that considerably heightens the chances of a favorable outcome ... The feeling of complete responsibility, as complete as that of parent for child, can spur the professional on and inspire a dogged determination to avoid breaching the client's trust at all costs" (Merton, Merton, and Barber 1983: 22). A similar argument is advanced by Giddens, who claims that in the post-traditional society, when trustworthiness cannot be taken for granted, and winning of trust is constantly necessary, it may be prudent to apply the strategy of "active trust": "opening out" to the other, emotional disclosure – even if risky – in order to produce obligation of trustworthiness (Giddens, in Beck et al. 1994: 187).

The distinction of four types of risks was necessary for analytical purposes, but we must again be aware that in real life situations they quite often coincide in various permutations, and hence the evaluation of trustful actions as prudent or imprudent in toto is quite complex, and often ambivalent. Look again at the story of the student who betrayed my trust, not sending back the promised essay, nor the borrowed book. Was I acting prudently, granting her a credit of trust? Of course, *ex post factum*, with the benefit of hindsight, it seems highly imprudent. But we must look at the situation in which I found myself preceding the betrayal. The first-degree risk, that she would not be able to write the essay, was relatively high given her earlier academic performance (low grades and failing the exam). But the stakes were quite low: I did not really care about reading her essay, so the cost of possible unfulfillment of my expectation was negligible. Thus from this perspective trusting was still prudent.

The second-degree risk of shame that I overestimated her abilities, which is not appropriate for an experienced teacher, could easily be mitigated by indicating that teaching at the Summer School (as was the case) I knew her only very briefly, had no access to her earlier academic record, and was possibly misled by a colleague who praised some of her earlier work done for him. Thus from this perspective also the psychological cost was low, and hence my decision prudent.

The real psychological distress came only as the result of a third-degree risk. I was feeling cheated, made a fool of, and disgusted by contact with a clearly dishonest person. Of course personal levels of tolerance for liars, traitors, and crooks are variable. Mine happens to be quite low, so I was very upset. Knowing myself, I should have estimated that the third-degree risk of being betrayed was too high, and should have been more hesitant in conferring the credit of trust. From this perspective I was not behaving prudently. The peak of my imprudent conduct came with neglecting the fourth-degree risk, and entrusting a valuable book to someone I did not know. Here the chance of a loss was most tangible, and as it referred to the rare volume I needed, should have been weighted more seriously.[18]

Now, just considering those four dimensions of risk together, we can reach a verdict. It seems that on balance I acted imprudently, the trust was not warranted, and I paid a fair price for my mistake. At least, such is my subjective self-evaluation, confirmed by the solemn decision not to make that kind of gesture again. This gives occasion to another reflection, namely that rules, codes, and regulations may sometimes embody the collective wisdom about the average trustworthiness of people. Were I following the university regulations scrupulously, no case like that could occur. The regulations forbid that kind of arbitrary trust, demanding instead objective exams, tests, and checks of all kinds. They assume that even if exceptions existed, it would still be more prudent to act as if all students were not entirely trustworthy.

Risk society

Risks of all sorts, including risks of trusting, have certainly been a universal and eternal feature of human society. But in our time the pervasiveness and scale of risks seems to grow. There arises the "inevitability of living with dangers which are remote from the control not only of individuals, but also of large organisations, including states; and which are of high intensity and life-threatening for millions of human beings and potentially for the whole of humanity" (Giddens 1990a: 131). To be more specific, according to Giddens the "risk profile" of high modernity is set apart from earlier experiences, both objectively and subjectively; there is both stronger actual presence of risk, and stronger perception of risk than ever before.

Objectively, there is first the universalization of risk: the new possibility of global catastrophes jeopardizing everybody irrespective of class, ethnic, and power positions (e.g., nuclear war, ecological destruction). Then there is the globalization of risk: extension of risk environments over large segments of the human population, touching large masses of people (e.g., financial markets reacting worldwide to political upheavals, military conflicts, price increases of oil, corporate takeovers, etc.). Next, there is the institutionalization of risk: the appearance of organizations having risk as the principle of their operation (e.g., investment markets or stock exchanges, gambling, sports, insurance). Finally, there is the reflexiveness of risk: the emergence, or intensification of risk as unintended side effects or boomerang effects of human actions (e.g., ecological dangers as resulting from industrialization; crime and delinquency as outcomes of faulty socialization and collapse of the family; new so-called "civilizational" diseases as produced by work patterns or lifestyles typical of modernity). Another objective risk-enhancing condition typical of modern society and obtaining extreme forms in late modernity is noticed by Seligman: "Risk became inherent to role-expectations when, with the transformation of social roles and the development of role segmentation, there developed a built-in limit to systematically based expectations" (Seligman 1997: 170).

Subjectively, there are additional factors making the experience of risk more acute. First, there is stronger sensitivity to threats and dangers, due to the disappearance of magical and religious defenses and rationalizations. Then, there is the more common awareness of threats, due to rising levels of education. Finally, there is the growing recognition of the limitations of expertise and repeated faults in operation of "abstract systems" (Giddens 1990a: 131): those complex, huge, impersonal technological arrangements whose principles of operation are not fully transparent to ordinary people, but on whose reliability everyday life depends (transportation, telecommunications, financial markets, nuclear power plants, military forces, transnational corporations, international organizations, mass media, provide good examples). People have to learn to use them and to depend on them. "Now there exists a kind of risk fate in developed civilizations, into which one is born, which one cannot escape with any amount of achievement" (Beck 1992: 41).

The theorists of high or late modernity picked up this theme, introducing the concept of a "risk society." Coined originally by Ulrich Beck, "this concept designates a developmental phase of modern society in which the social, political, economic and individual risks increasingly tend to escape the institutions for monitoring and protection" (Beck, Giddens, and Lash 1994: 5). In effect we witness "the return of uncertainty and uncontrollability" (p. 10). And even more, there appear new forms of uncertainty – "manufactured uncertainty" or "techno-scientifically produced risks" – as an unintended effect of our main ambition of "colonizing of the future" (Giddens 1991: 114; Beck 1992: 18). The attempts to construct the future release unforeseen consequences: "In the risk society the unknown and unintended consequences come to be a dominant force in history and society" (Beck 1992: 22).

It is due to that central trait of modernity that risk becomes so important and finds strong reflexes at the level of social consciousness. "Many aspects of our lives have suddenly become open, organized only in terms of 'scenario thinking', the as-if construction of possible future outcomes" (Giddens in Beck et al. 1994: 184). "Industrial society is skidding into the no man's land of uninsured threats. Uncertainty retains and proliferates everywhere" (Beck et al. 1994: 12). "The notion of 'risk' is central to modern culture" (Beck et al. 1994: vii).

And this relates to the growing significance of trust, as a means of taming risks and countering uncertainties. The link was already perceived by Luhmann: "One should expect trust to be increasingly in demand as a means of enduring the complexity of the future which technology will generate" (Luhmann 1979: 16). This is also emphasized by Giddens: "With the development of abstract systems, trust in impersonal principles, as well as in anonymous others, becomes indispensable to social existence" (Giddens 1991: 120).

3

Varieties of trust

The targets of trust

Making bets of trust, we direct them at various objects, the targets of trust. What are those objects? Our definition indicates that ultimately we direct trust at "contingent actions of others."[1] But those "others" come in various guises, and their actions display various degrees of complexity.

Primary targets

There are several primary targets of trust. The most fundamental are other persons (actors), full-fledged individuals with whom we come into direct contact. Some authors consider "interpersonal trust" to be a paradigmatic type, with all other types put under the common label of "social trust," as only derivative (Earle and Cvetkovich 1995). They argue that only interpersonal trust involves face-to-face commitment, as opposed to "faceless commitments" toward other social objects (Giddens 1990a: 88). Supposedly this spatial co-presence of partners entails some unique primordial quality of interpersonal trust, which sets it apart from other forms of trust. But in my view, behind all other social objects, however complex, there also stand some people, and it is the people whom we ultimately endow with trust (sometimes we are acquainted with them, but we may also imagine them, have some information about them, obtain second-hand testimony about them, etc.). For example, when I trust Lufthansa and decide to fly with them to Tokyo, it implies that I trust their pilots, the cabin crew, the ground personnel, technicians, controllers, supervisors, and so forth. I don't need to meet all of them in person to have some image of them, drawn from various sources (including their suggestive commercials, stereotypes of German precision and efficiency, references from friends, etc.).

So the difference between interpersonal trust and social trust is not so striking and fundamental. There are in fact gradual, expanding, concentric circles of trust ("radius of trust" – to use a phrase of Fukuyama [1995]), from the most concrete interpersonal relations, toward more abstract orientation toward social objects. The narrowest radius covers trust in the members of our family, pervaded with strongest intimacy and closeness. Then comes trust toward people we know personally, whom we recognize by name, and with whom we interact in a face-to-face manner (our friends, neighbors, coworkers, business partners, etc.). Here trust still involves a considerable degree of intimacy and closeness. Modern technologies, and particularly TV, produce an interesting variety of that: virtual personal trust. Idols, celebrities, pop-culture heroes, famous politicians, seem to be known to us personally and intimately. Passing them in the street we can hardly control the urge to greet them or to smile, as if they were friends or good acquaintances. The wider circle embraces other members of our community, known at most indirectly, by sight, and directly only through some individual representatives (inhabitants of our village, employees of our firm, professors at our university, members of our political party). The widest circle includes large categories of people, with whom we believe we have something in common, but who are mostly "absent others" (Giddens in Beck et al. 1994: 89), not directly encountered, and constructed as a real collectivity only in our imagination (our compatriots, members of our ethnic group, of our religion, of our race, of our gender, of our age cohort, of our generation, of our profession, etc.). Here trust in concrete persons shades off imperceptibly into trust in more abstract social objects. I share the view of Bernard Barber: "we may usefully think of these various kinds of trust as existing not only between individual actors but also between individuals and systems – indeed, even between and among systems" (Barber 1983: 18).

Thus at the borderline between interpersonal trust and social trust there are social categories (understood as pluralities of persons sharing certain common traits). For example, trust or distrust may be targeted on gender (I trust men and distrust women), or age (I trust the elderly and distrust the young), or race (I trust white people and distrust blacks), or ethnicity (I trust the French and distrust the Turks), or religion (I trust the Catholics and distrust the Muslims), or wealth (I trust the poor and distrust the rich), and so forth. Needless to say, this form of trust is often pervaded with stereotypes and prejudices.

The next, more abstract and "social" objects of trust are social roles (understood as ways of acting typical for specific positions). Independent of the concrete incumbents, some roles evoke prima facie trust. Mother, friend, doctor of medicine, university professor, priest, judge, notary public – are just some examples of the trusted personal roles, or offices of "public trust." And there are other roles, and related positions, which imply a priori distrust. The bazaar merchant, used-car dealer, tax-collector, money-changer, prostitute, secret agent, spy, provide good examples.

The definition of some roles as trustworthy or not may of course differ across various societies, and in different historical moments. If there is widespread corruption, then public officials, police officers, politicians may fall into the class of the a priori distrusted. If there is a widespread practice of cheating the customers, then all merchants, or taxi-drivers, or construction workers will be treated with initial distrust. If the media are biased, heavily censored, involved in indoctrination and propaganda, then all journalists, TV anchors, radio newscasters may be distrusted.[2] My research in Poland at the end of the nineties shows such roles as the medical doctor, the lawyer, successful businesspeople, the university professor, the professional soldier at the top of the hierarchy of trust, while politicians take the lowest position. The marked difference from the communist period is the new association of trust with financial status. The monetary criteria typical for a capitalist system have elevated private businesspeople from a low, distrusted position to high ranks in the hierarchy of trust, while at the same time it has pushed down university professors (obviously not so successful financially) from the top rank to much lower, medium levels of the hierarchy.

The next abstract object of trust is a social group (understood as a plurality of persons kept together by specific social bonds). An example may be a football team, as viewed by the fans (I trust Real Madrid, and distrust Dynamo Kiev); the cabinet, as viewed by the citizens (I trust Tony Blair's government as strongly as I distrusted Margaret Thatcher's); the student group, as seen by a professor (I trust my UCLA class more than my Krakow class), a work brigade, as seen by a foreman (I trust the painters more than the electricians in my car-assembly plant), an army platoon as seen by the general (I trust the artillery more than the tanks under my command), and so on.

An even more abstract case is the trust directed at institutions and organizations (understood as specific structural arrangements within which actions and interactions take place). The school, the university, the army, the church, the courts, the police, the banks, the stock exchange, the government, the parliament, the industrial enterprise, and so forth, are typical objects for this type of trust. The amount of trust that people vest in various institutions differ among societies, it also undergoes changes in time. For example in Poland, due to its long history of foreign domination and oppression, the army and the Catholic Church, considered as the embodiments and depositors of national struggle and continuing identity, have always stood at the top of trusted institutions. But as my research shows, after the revolutionary changes of 1989, we can observe the advancement of new democratic institutions – the Constitutional Court, the Ombudsman – to high positions in the trust hierarchy, as well as the relative demise of the Catholic Church, no longer so important in its unifying role.

An interesting variant of trust in institutions may be called procedural trust. It is trust vested in institutionalized practices or procedures, based on the belief that if followed they will produce best results. A good example is trust in science as the best method for reaching the truth. Or picking out more concrete illustrations from the domain of science, trust in peer review as the best way to assure high quality of publications (Barber 1990), or trust in test exams as the most objective means of evaluating students. Other examples may be taken from the political realm: trust in the democratic procedures (elections, representation, majority vote, etc.) as the best ways to satisfy the interests of the largest part of the population and to reach the most reasonable compromises among conflicting interests. Or trust in the due process of law, as the best means to reach a justified, balanced verdict. In the area of the economy, one may mention trust in the competitive market as the means of safeguarding the best and cheapest products and services. Or the trust in deregulation and lifting of trade barriers, as leading to the same beneficial effects. Of course, distrust may also be directed at such procedures. Monopoly is distrusted because it is seen as harmful for the customers, inviting higher prices. Granting state concessions to industrial firms is distrusted because it easily generates corruption. Oral exams at the university are distrusted as being more stressful and less objective than tests, or written essays.

The next important category of objects endowed with trust is technological systems ("expert systems" or "abstract systems" in Giddens' terminology). As Giddens defines them, they are "systems of technical accomplishment or professional expertise that organize large areas of the material and social environments in which we live today" (Giddens 1990a: 27). We live surrounded by them: by telecommunications, water and power systems, transportation systems, air-traffic control systems, military command networks, computer networks, financial markets, and so forth. The principles and mechanisms of their operation are opaque and cryptic for the average user. We usually take them for granted, do not even notice their pervasive presence. And we have learned to rely on them, to the extent that their failure looks like a catastrophe.[3] "Trust in the multiplicity of abstract systems is a necessary part of everyday life today" (Giddens in Beck et al. 1994: 89).

The more tangible targets of trust are various products and utensils that we purchase and use. We routinely deploy this kind of trust in everyday life. Trust in this case may refer in a general way to goods of a certain type ("Cornflakes are healthy"), or to goods made in a certain country ("Japanese cars are highly dependable"), or in a more concrete fashion to products of a certain firm ("I buy IBM only"), or even creations of a specific author ("If this is by Le Carré it will surely be an exciting book").[4]

The most abstract objects of trust are the overall qualities of the social system, social order, or the regime. We have this kind of trust in mind when we speak of the existential security, that is, "confidence in the continuity of their self-identity and the constancy of surrounding social and material environments of action" (Giddens 1990a: 92), viability of the social order, strength of a society, functionality of a political or economic regime, and so forth. For example, we could say: "America is a great society," "Democracy is the only equitable regime," "Market reforms in postcommunist societies are irreversible." In all these cases we express trust toward a general system.

The concept of a systemic trust seems close to the notion of legitimacy. Following Weber's distinctions we may say that charismatic legitimacy presupposes personal trust (or at least, what we are calling virtual personal trust: the seeming intimacy and emotional ties with quite distant persons), legal legitimacy presupposes institutional trust (or its special variant, procedural trust). But in the case of traditional legitimacy, no form of trust is necessarily presupposed. Traditional legitimacy does not *per se* imply trust of any kind. This is so because tradition, as long as it prevails, may substitute for trust. It replaces trust with the sanction of ancient and eternal routine. In this way tradition reduces uncertainty and contingency – preconditions for the salience of trust. When tradition stops playing a major role, as in "post-traditional society," trust becomes crucial. "The whole institutional apparatus of modernity, once it has become broken away from tradition, depends upon potentially volatile mechanisms of trust" (Giddens, in Beck et al. 1994: 90).

In my view, the various types of trust reviewed above – personal,

categorial, positional, group, institutional, commercial, systemic –
operate according to the same logic. Most importantly, behind all of
them there looms the primordial form of trust – in people, and their
actions. Appearances notwithstanding, all of the above objects of trust
are reducible to human actions. We ultimately trust human actions, and
derivatively their effects, or products. Thus, in the case of systemic trust,
we expect beneficial actions of our fellow citizen as well as the agents of
various institutions and organizations, making up the fabric of our
society. In the case of institutional trust – say, in the government – we
trust those who have constructed its constitutional frame, those who
actually perform governmental functions, and those who monitor and
supervise their performance (members of constitutional courts, tribunals,
parliamentary committees, free media, the Ombudsman, and ultimately
the electorate, etc.). In the case of commercial trust, we trust the actions
of designers, constructors, and producers, or those who supervise
production (by means of quality control, standardization, industrial
norms). In the case of technological trust, we trust those who design
expert systems, those who operate them, and those who supervise the
operations (e.g., pilots, air traffic controllers, and technicians). In the
case of group trust, we expect certain actions from all, or most, members,
as well as the agents acting on behalf of a group as a whole. In the case of
positional trust we expect certain beneficial actions, from all or at least
most of those who play certain roles. In the case of categorial trust, we
expect some actions from all, or most, representatives of a certain
category. Finally, in the case of personal trust, we expect certain actions
from a particular partner.

Secondary targets

So far we have been dealing with primary objects of trust, those targets
toward which we direct our bets of trust. But there is also an important
category of objects to be called the secondary objects of trust, which
become the targets only derivatively, in the process of placing and
justifying trust toward primary objects. In deciding on our bets of trust
we often rely on second-hand cues. An important type of those are
testimonies of experts, witnesses, reliable sources, authorities, referring to
the credibility, or trustworthiness of the objects on which we consider
placing our primary trust.

To take them seriously, to rely on them, we must trust them. Hence,
those sources of information about trustworthiness of other objects
become themselves the objects of trust. "Most of what we know, or think

we know, about science and history, rests on belief in various authorities, and on our trusting what we read and are told, and not on anyone's personal verification" (Malcolm 1988: 286). The problem we face is often the choice of right witnesses, sources, or experts: "since there are no super-experts to turn to, risk calculation has to include the risk of which experts are consulted, or whose authority is to be taken as binding" (Giddens in Beck et al. 1994: 87). For example, in the domain of science the "peer review" by judges, referees, and reviewers is a standard procedure for determining trustworthiness. But this requires that reviewers themselves be trusted. "A great deal obviously depends on the trustworthiness of these peer evaluators of scientific contributions; they must be both competent and fiduciarily responsible to the welfare of science" (Barber 1990: 143).

Such secondary trust, providing foundation for our primary trust, may appear in many guises and at multiple levels in our generation of trust. There may be characteristic "pyramids of trust." Let us look at two examples: I trust the American pianist Van Cliburn to give a great concert (and hence I buy the ticket), because I know he has graduated from the Juilliard School at New York which is famous for being highly selective; he has also won the main prize at the reputable Tchaikovsky competition in Moscow; I have also read a good review by the critic I trust, in the *New York Times*, the newspaper I trust, and the pianist's recordings were produced by the Deutsche Grammophon Gesellschaft, the firm I trust; and my friends tell me he is great, not to speak of all those anonymous crowds that go to his concerts, who cannot be dismissed as all being so badly wrong. Or take another example: I buy the new Le Carré spy novel because I have read a lot about him in my favorite journals, because I trust the publisher, and my friend tells me it is the best of his books so far, and besides it is a bestseller, which means that other readers have endowed it with trust and they cannot all be mistaken. Pyramids may also appear in the selection of experts: I trust this expert because he is employed by the consulting firm I trust, teaches at the famous university I trust, and so on.

Another indirect cue to trust is the existence of various "agencies of accountability," which elicit or enforce trustworthiness of the objects of primary trust. They provide insurance of trustworthy conduct, by putting pressure (facilitating, controlling, or sanctioning) on persons, roles, institutions, or systems that are the targets of our primary trust. Such agencies of accountability include: courts, police, controllers, standardizing agencies, licensing bodies, examination boards, editorial committees, juries of various prizes, consumer organizations – supplementing (or substituting for) the direct trustworthiness of the objects of primary trust, with indirect implications of accountability. But to raise my trust in the primary objects, thanks to the presence of such agencies of accountability, I must first of all trust that they will control and enforce fairly and efficiently. "Enforcement agency itself must be trustworthy . . . If your trust in the enforcement agency falters, you will not trust persons to fulfil their terms of an agreement and thus will not enter into that agreement" (Dasgupta 1988: 50).

There is the special category of such institutions keeping the government and the whole political regime accountable. Some are internal: the autonomous media ("fourth state"), the constitutional court, the Ombudsman, the parliamentary watchdog committees, the opposition. Some are external: international organizations (UN, IMF), jurisdiction of international tribunals or agencies accepted by treaties (the Hague's International Court of Justice, the Strasbourg tribunal, the European Commission). All such agencies providing accountability must themselves be trusted, in order to lend some of their trustworthiness to the realm of politics.

Targets of trust combined

The numerous types of trust based on the variety of objects on which trust is conferred, are not mutually independent. Just the reverse, there are certain systematic relationships between trust vested in some objects and trust vested in other objects. Let us select some interesting cases for a brief discussion. The first is the relationship between personal and positional trust. If trust attaches to a certain social role (position), then it extends to every incumbent. But the personal trust vested in incumbents is not irrelevant for preserving, enhancing, or diminishing positional trust, and even converting itself into trust for the whole institution. For example, when Karol Wojtyla, the Bishop of Krakow, was elected as Pope John Paul II, he was taking a position of established high trust (at least for the huge community of Catholics), and hence was raising his personal trust through the incumbency of the office. But due to the personal charisma that he brought to the office, he has greatly enhanced trust in the papacy during his pontificate, and will leave the institution greatly rejuvenated. As a counter-example, think of the priest who is appointed to the local parish, inherits part of the traditional positional trust, and then destroys his personal trust by immoral conduct and abuse of parishioners. As a consequence the trust vested in the position itself, and perhaps even in the whole institution of a church, will suffer enormously.

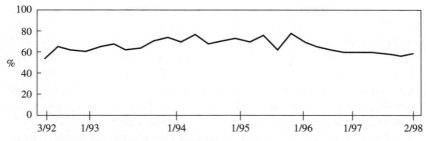

Diagram 1: Trust in the Ombudsman

Personal trust may also elevate initially low positional trust, and even spread to the whole institution. The new democratic institutions in postcommunist Poland – the Constitutional Court and the Ombudsman – have attained high levels of trust mainly because they were under the leadership of two eminent and widely trusted lawyers: Andrzej Zoll and Ewa Letowska, whose outstanding work was widely recognized.

There was a similar situation in case of the Ministry of Labor in the Polish postcommunist government when it was led by a highly trusted hero of the democratic opposition, Jacek Kuron. The reverse mechanism operates equally well: distrust in politicians (e.g., because of their tainted communist past, or current abuses of power) may extend to the offices they occupy, then to the whole government, and finally even to the political regime as such. Similarly, if judges are not trusted (because they are corrupt or biased), the distrust easily spreads to the courts, and even to the whole judiciary.

But there may also be cases when such extensions and transfers of trust and distrust do not occur. People may make in their minds quite rigorous distinctions between personal, positional, and institutional trust. For example: distrust may be limited to personal qualities of politicians, without undermining trust in democracy. People believe that "all politicians are crooks," and yet they go to vote. How come? This is because they trust that democracy, through elections, is still the best system for getting rid of bigger crooks and for promoting lesser crooks. Also during the term of office, through the existence of opposition, it is seen as the best way to prevent bad or incompetent rulers from doing too much damage (Benn and Peters 1977: 307). In the reverse direction, trust in democracy and its institutions need not convert itself into trust for politicians. Rather, as shall be argued in detail in chapter 7, trust in democracy is quite consistent with constant looking at the politicians' hands.

Turning now to institutional trust, it may be observed that various domains of such trust may mutually lend trust to each other. Some may operate on "borrowed trust." For example, it is quite common for trust in the viability of the economy to translate itself into trust in political authorities. This is perhaps the explanation for the growing rate of trust in government that we observe in Poland at the end of the nineties, when the economy is in a phase of boom. There may be other transfers of trust as well. In the case of medieval monarchy or presentday Islamic states, trust in religion lends itself to trust in political rulers. Or in the case of communist regimes, they have attempted to build trust toward themselves on the trust in science, invoking "scientific socialism" as their erstwhile base. In a similar way the Church of Scientology invokes the trust in science, hoping to extend it to the domain of religion.

Finally, considering systemic trust (in the regime, viability of society, existential security), we see that it relates very closely to several other types of trust. It may be considered as a combined effect of institutional, technological, and commercial trust: the belief that institutions, technological systems, and products are dependable, reliable, and functioning smoothly. In this way trust in institutions, technological systems, and products builds up toward systemic trust. Trust and distrust may be directed at specific targets; we shall then speak of "targeted trust." But it may also take the shape of a more generalized orientation toward a variety of objects; we shall use the term "diffused trust" for this case. The diffusion of trust or distrust from one level to another happens quite commonly, because trust as well as distrust are contagious. In many cases trust seems to spread out from above toward lower levels, and distrust, from the bottom upwards.

For example, if there is a systemic trust in the social order, then most probably we shall also discover institutional trust in specific economic, political, judicial, and educational arrangements. This will further expand downwards toward concrete positions and roles within institutions: of a judge, attorney, minister, manager, professor. And eventually it will be reflected in a personal trust for Mr. X, a parliamentarian, or Mrs. Z, an attorney at law. The higher the level of objects endowed with trust, the more expansive trust becomes, embracing all lower levels. The reverse mechanism sometimes operates in the case of distrust. When distrust appears it has a tendency to expand upwards, from more concrete toward more general levels. Take an example: we spot an episode of corruption, or malpractice, or nepotism, in the conduct of people we have trusted. We lose personal trust in Mr. X or Mrs. Z. But this easily expands upwards, producing positional distrust. We start to think in a stereotyped way: that all lawyers are crooks, all politicians corrupt, all doctors incompetent. That may in turn lead to institutional distrust directed at the whole segment of social life: there is no fair justice, medicine kills, politics is rotten, schools produce morons. Eventually a systemic distrust may appear targeted on the supposedly decaying social order: "This rotten system must collapse," "Democracy cannot work," and so forth. We can see that trust is a "fragile commodity": "If it erodes in any part of the mosaic it brings down an awful lot with it" (Dasgupta 1988: 50).

For a given actor, as well as for a given target, there is always some balance of trust and distrust of a more specific or diffused sort. For example, there may be a bias toward interpersonal trust and against any form of social (public) trust: a person may trust family and friends, and distrust the police and the politicians. There may also be preferences within the same level of objects: a person may trust doctors but distrust priests; trust trains but distrust airlines; trust the parliament but distrust the government. Even more concretely, there may be different orientations toward different objects of the same type: a person may trust John, but less so Julie, and still less so Frank, totally distrusting Mary; or he may trust the liberal party, rather than the social-democratic party, and completely distrust the radical right; or he may trust Lufthansa but less so Continental Airlines, and completely distrust Air Africa. The balance of trust and distrust for a given agent is always very complex and sometimes ambivalent.

Looking at it from the side of the target, from the perspective of the trustee, there is an equally complex balance of trust and distrust received. Sometimes the unraveling of that balance may be important. For example, for a politician it may be important to find out what is the level of trust, and how trust giving or trust withdrawal are distributed among various groups of supporters or opponents. The knowledge of the specter of political support or rejection may be crucial for election campaigns, fund raising, and so forth. Similarly for the producers or marketers it may be important to find what is the level of trust in a given product, and how it is distributed among the consumers. Marketing research often addresses this question, as the answer is very important for the promotion of a product: targeting specific groups of consumers, reassuring those who trust, and converting those who distrust.

The substance of trust

We have seen that the bet of trust may be directed toward various objects. But the next question must be faced: what is the content of the bet, what kinds of expectations are involved? The most important distinction is between the expectations engendered by the very act of trusting or entrusting, and the expectations that are prior to the act of trusting or entrusting. Let me explain. If I lend a friend a sum of money, placing trust in him, I expect a number of things. The minimum expectation is that he will return the money, pay his debt in time. The maximum expectation is that he will extend loyalty and trust toward myself, for example lending me money when I find myself in need in the future. To generalize from this example, the expectation of reciprocity implied by the act of trusting may take two forms: the expectation of returning the good entrusted, and the expectation of mutual loyalty and trust. Both expectations may appear together, as in the example above, when I expect a friend to be solvent but also loyal and trusting. But suppose I am lending money not to a friend, but to a client who pays interest. Then the expectation of reciprocity takes only the weaker form: that the client will return the debt plus interest. Finally, suppose that I am giving (and not lending) money to my daughter. I do not expect to receive money back, but I do expect reciprocity: I count on her loyalty and trust toward myself, which may take many forms, from telling me her secrets to taking care of me when I get old.

These examples have illustrated the first case, namely when expectations are engendered by the very act of trusting. But there is the other case, when expectations refer to the conduct of the target that is quite independent of the act of trusting. For example: I board a Lufthansa plane because I expect the German airline to be safe, punctual, and comfortable. I base my bet of trust on such expectations, but the reliability of the airline is not affected in any way by my act of trusting. They are reliable, whether I trust them or not. I would have got the same service, even if I had boarded in a totally distrustful mood, frightened to death and complaining that my firm has not placed me on British Airways, which I really trust. Or to take another example, I consult a doctor of medicine, because I expect him to be competent and caring. These virtues have nothing to do with my act of trusting. If he is a good doctor, I would get the same treatment even if I had completely distrusted him, coming for consultation only because there was no other doctor in the vicinity.

Obviously, both types of expectations – of reciprocity and of benign conduct – may appear together in one bet of trust. For example, if I place a large sum of money in the bank, I expect the bank to be efficient, to invest the money properly, to provide easy access to my account. I base my bet of trust on expectations of reliable professional services. But I also expect the reciprocity: getting my money plus the interest back when I want to, and to be trusted by the bank with a good credit line when I need it, as a mutual favor of trust to the faithful, trusting depositor.

Varieties of expected conduct

Let us focus now on expectations of benign conduct, independent of acts of trusting. There is a whole variety of them, which can be arranged along a sort of scale: from the least demanding to the most demanding expectations, and respectively from the weakest, least risky bets, to the strongest, most risky bets of trust. First, we may expect only some instrumental qualities of actions taken by others: (a) regularity (orderliness, consistency, coherence, continuity, persistence), for example, I expect the bus to run on schedule; (b) reasonableness (giving grounds, good justification for actions, accepting arguments), for example, I expect scholars to prove their claims; (c) efficiency (competence, consistency, discipline, proper performance, effectiveness) (Barber 1983: 14), for example, I expect the manager to raise the profits of the enterprise. Expectations of type (a) are rather safe, because the probability that most agents will behave regularly, rather than randomly and chaotically, is relatively high. Expectations of type (b) are more risky, because people are not always reasonable, sometimes behaving in an emotional, spontaneous, arbitrary manner, and refusing to give reasons for their actions. Expectations of class (c) are most risky, because there is quite a sizable proportion of inefficient, incompetent, and negligent agents. Thus to expect efficiency and competence is a relatively strong bet of trust, as for example many voters find to their dismay, once their political favorites take office. In general, when trust is based on instrumental expectations, we shall refer to it as instrumental trust.

The second class of expectations is even more demanding. We may expect some moral qualities of actions performed by others: (a) we expect them to be morally responsible (i.e., engaging in principled, honest, honorable conduct, following some moral rules, showing integrity), for example, I expect the politician not to embezzle public funds; (b) we expect them to be kind, gentle toward ourselves, treating us in a humane fashion, for example, I expect the priest not to ridicule or to humiliate me when I confess my sins; (c) we expect them to be truthful, authentic, straightforward, for example, I expect my girlfriend to tell me with whom she went to dinner yesterday;[5] (d) we expect others to be fair and just (applying universalistic criteria, equal standards, due process, meritocratic justice), for example, I expect the boss to pay me for additional work. Generally speaking, betting on the moral virtues of others is more risky than believing in their basic rationality. The category of moral agents is certainly narrower than that of rational agents. But within the class of moral expectations there is also the gradation of bets. Expectations of type (a) are least risky: some moral principles are usually observed, and totally amoral and dishonest people are a minority in any population. Expectations of type (b) are more demanding, and hence risky, because there is quite a contingent of brutal, despotic, and harsh individuals. Expectations of type (c) may be frustrated even more easily, as lying and cheating are quite common human vices. And expectations of type (d) seem most difficult to be met, as the number of biased, unfair, unjust, abusive, or exploitative actions seems quite considerable in every society. In general, when trust is based on moral expectations, we shall speak of axiological trust.

We may also make the strongest bets, and expect from others what Bernard Barber called "fiduciary" conduct and defined as "duties in certain situations to place others' interests before our own" (Barber 1983: 9). This category is exemplified by: (a) disinterestedness (i.e. acting without consideration of one's own interests or even against such interests), for example, I expect the teacher to stay after hours to explain some point I don't understand; (b) representative actions (acting on behalf of others, displaying concern for the welfare of others, serving their interests), for example, I expect the trade union to fight for my higher wages; (c) benevolence and generosity (caring, helping, protecting, expressing sympathy, sensitivity to the sufferings of others), for example, I expect my friend to defend me against false accusations.[6] This is the strongest, most risky bet because the probability that most people will be disinterested is low, and that they will take on representative duties, and engage in altruistic help is even lower. The category of truly caring actors is narrower than that of rational and even of moral actors. When trust is based on fiduciary expectations we shall speak of fiduciary trust.

A reverse logic operates in the case of distrust. The scale is symmetrically opposite. Thus, to suspect that others will not exhibit disinterested, fiduciary care is a rather safe bet. Hence fiduciary distrust is the least risky, and relatively weak bet. After all we cannot expect too much, "people are just human," as the saying goes. It is a stronger form of distrust to suspect others of being immoral, unfair, unjust. Axiological distrust is more risky, and hence it entails a stronger bet. After all, not all people are crooks. And instrumental distrust underlies the strongest, and a rather risky bet. It is bordering on paranoia to expect all others to be irrational or outright mad.

Trust as relative to expectations

The great variety of expectations that can be involved imply that the content of trust is extremely variable. Speaking about trust, we must always specify: trust to do what? Absolute trust is a rarity. "Only a small child, a lover, Abraham speaking to God, or a rabid follower of a charismatic leader might be able to say 'I trust you' without implicit modifier" (Hardin 1993: 507). Most often trust is relative. "Trust is a three-part relation: A trusts B to do X.[7] Typically, I trust you to do certain kinds of things. I might distrust you with respect to some other things and I may merely be skeptical or unsure with respect to still other things. To say 'I trust you' seems almost always to be elliptical" (Hardin 1993: 506).

There is another relativization, too. Expectations involved in trust are congruent or incongruent with the nature of objects toward which trust is directed. Specific expectations fit to specific objects, and do not fit to others. It seems obvious to expect care from a mother (but not necessarily from a competitor in business), or help from a friend (but not necessarily from a stranger in the street), or competence from a pilot (but not necessarily from a patient in a hospital), or reasonableness from a professor (but not necessarily from a child). Similarly it seems natural to expect justice from a court (but not necessarily from a tax collection agency), cost-efficiency from an industrial firm (but not necessarily from a museum), generosity from the charitable foundation (but not necessarily from a bank), fair play from a football team (but not necessarily from a street gang).

My own research has provided ample corroboration for this type of relativization. When asked about the expectations necessary for granting trust to the government, instrumental considerations were dominant: 47.9 percent of the respondents indicated efficiency, and 44.2 percent – competence. Honesty and moral integrity received only 38.5 percent of indications. With reference to courts of law, the axiological considerations came to the fore with 79.9 percent emphasizing fairness. When asked about trust toward the Catholic Church and its institutions, the respondents switched toward fiduciary expectations: 64.3 percent indicated disinterested help for the needy as the criterion of their trust. Among social roles as targets of trust, administrative officials were expected to be competent (55.1 percent), efficient (48.1 percent), and reliable (44.7 percent). Business partners were expected to be reliable (69 percent), honest (44.4 percent) and truthful (25.3 percent). High axiological and fiduciary expectations are directed toward neighbors: 76.7 percent expect help from them, and 74.4 percent – honesty.

Thus expectations of a specific sort seem to be bound to specific positions (roles) and institutions. There seem to exist normative rules prescribing how the incumbents of a position or employees of an institution should act. The sets of such rules attaching to specific positions make up social roles. The network of rules regulating the operation of an institution makes up its "charter." We are justified in expecting a person or institution to act in a specific way if that way of acting is prescribed by normative rules. We expect the mother to care, because caring is a component of a mother's normative role. We expect the social worker to give help, because this is a component of a social worker's social role, similarly as in other "helping professions" (Merton et al. 1983). We expect the business firm to be efficient, because profit seeking is a normatively accepted goal of such an institution. And we expect the football team to play fair, because fair play is a crucial normative component of the institution of sports.

People often adjust their trusting expectations to social roles, rather than to persons. As people usually have multiple roles, with different expectations accruing to each, they may be trusted in one capacity and distrusted in another. For example, it seems that for the role of a president, what counts for the citizens is competence and efficiency, rather than impeccable honesty and integrity. In this case the voters deploy instrumental trust, rather than axiological trust. Some years ago, apparently following this logic, Polish voters elected a skillful and brilliant political operator, with a somewhat dubious communist past and a record of recent lies (Aleksander Kwasniewski), in preference to the champion of all polls measuring axiological and fiduciary trust, the hero of oppositional struggle, and an utterly honest, humble, and caring person (Jacek Kuron).[8] Asked immediately after the elections about their image of the new president, 89 percent of the respondents emphasized his intelligence, 75 percent his competence, 57 percent determination in reaching goals, and only 33 percent his honesty (CBOS Bulletin, No. 4/ 1996: 26). Similarly, the American public obviously does not care about the dubious moral standards of their president, Bill Clinton, as long as he proves efficient and successful as a politician. "We don't care what he does in his bedroom as long as he is a good leader," is the dominant tone of the letters to the editors of *Time* magazine in the wake of the Lewinsky affair.

But not all roles are so one-dimensional. There are roles that include multiple, and even mutually incongruent, ambivalent expectations. The famous example analyzed by Robert Merton is the "detached concern" of the medical doctor, who is normatively expected to be coldly profes-

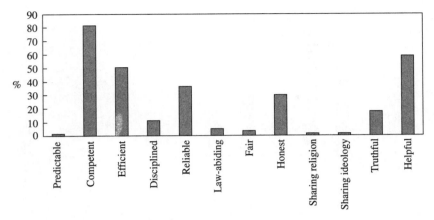

Diagram 2: Expectations relevant for doctors of medicine

sional and technically efficient, but at the same time to manifest warm care, sympathy, and help toward the patients (Merton 1976: 68). Trusting a doctor we usually expect both. This doubles the risk of our bet, because we shall feel that our trust was breached if the doctor meets only one type of expectation (she operates brilliantly but does not care about our pain, or she is concerned with all our family problems but prescribes the wrong medication). In my research this ambivalence was quite clear: 82.4 percent trust doctors if they are competent, but at the same time 59.6 percent are ready to trust if they express sympathy and helpfulness.

A similar interesting ambivalence came out in my research, with respect to the institution of the army. Instrumental expectations of efficiency (70.7 percent of indications) and discipline (41.2%) naturally dominate, but fiduciary expectations of help also attain a high level (24 percent of indications). Perhaps it is due to the fact that the army in peacetime sometimes fulfills some social services, like the rescue of victims in case of natural disasters, supporting police in fighting crimes, and so forth.[9]

Once the expectations are normatively prescribed, the persons or institutions become accountable for their actions. The breach of our trust becomes synonymous with normative deviance. The villains may expect sanctions for their improper conduct, which by the same token disappoints our trust. Their trustworthiness is monitored and enforced, which adds plausibility to our bet of trust, and lessens the risk of frustration. As Barber puts it: "Effective organizations create a set of monitoring, auditing, and insurance arrangements to guarantee maintenance of competence and to forestall or compensate for failures of fiduciary

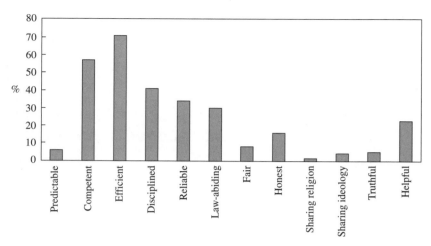

Diagram 3: Expectations relevant for the army

responsibility" (Barber 1983: 22). On the other hand, when our expectations do not coincide with such normative prescriptions (role demands, or organizational demands), then our bets of trust are more risky and open to disappointment. For example, it may happen that our boss is a caring person and will give us personal help to solve a family problem, but there is no obligation on his part to do so, and hence no sanctions will meet him if he doesn't (provided we are not in Japan, where corporation mores may demand this sort of care). Similarly it may happen that our neighbor has good medical experience, but to consult her in the case of illness would be very risky, and if the advice turns out to be disastrous, no "malpractice suit" will be possible. In general, we significantly raise the risk of our bets of trust if we direct incongruent expectations toward targets that are not normatively obliged to meet them.

The types of expectations linked with trust depend not only on the targets, but also on the characteristics of the trusters. Probably there are some personality traits predisposing to "hard" expectations of an instrumental sort, focused on efficiency and competence, and other personality traits that predispose to "soft" expectations of the axiological and fiduciary sort, focused on honesty, fairness, benevolence, and help, across all kinds of targets.

There are social differences in this respect as well. My research in Poland has shown significant gender differences: women tend to emphasize "soft" expectations, and men "hard" expectations ("Efficiency" is indicated as the main criterion of trust by 19.7 percent of men and only 9.1 percent of women, "Fairness" by 36.4 percent of women, and 29.5 percent of men, and "Readiness to help" by 60.8 percent of women, and 50.3 percent of men). This is most likely due to stereotyped demands of gender roles which, in a relatively traditional country like Poland, encourage the focus on "soft" qualities from women, and on "hard" qualities from men.

There are also similar differences in emphasis among occupational roles. Compare a foreman in a factory who would expect skills and efficiency ("hard" traits) from trusted workers, and the local priest who would expect honesty and truthfulness ("soft" traits) from the parishioners. The explanation of this is simple, and it invokes the cultural demands included in respective roles.

The social categories in stratification hierarchies also differ markedly. My research shows that the affluent and those employed in high-level jobs tend strongly to emphasize "hard" criteria, whereas the poor, those employed in low-level jobs or those unemployed, put emphasis on "soft" criteria (e.g., "Competence" is indicated by only 3.6 percent and "Honesty" by as much as 55.4 percent among the poor, and correspondingly by 2.7 percent versus 52 percent among the unemployed). Similarly in educational hierarchies, highly educated people seem to stress "hard criteria," whereas those who have only low-level education put emphasis on "soft" criteria (e.g., "Competence" is indicated by 5.1 percent of uneducated people, and 22 percent of highly educated people, while "Truthfulness" is indicated by as much as 36.1 percent of uneducated and 26.8 percent of highly educated people). This moralistic orientation of the lower strata is confirmed by the responses to another set of questions. The claim that "In Poland, we witness a universal moral decay" is accepted by 42.9 percent of the poor, and only 24.4 percent of the rich; 49.5 percent of the unemployed, and only 23.7 percent of the elites; 41.8 percent of the uneducated, and only 19.5 percent of the highly educated. The possible, but only hypothetical, explanation is that people who fail in the success race, ignore or discount the importance of criteria that are due to achievement (as most of the "hard" criteria are; after all one becomes competent or skillful through hard effort), and emphasize those that are based on ascription (most of the "soft" criteria; after all one simply "happens" to be honest and truthful or not). This may be a case of rationalization: not basing estimates of trustworthiness on expectations that they themselves do not meet, and would not like to be applied to themselves ("I am a poor, and simple guy but you may trust me, as I am honest and truthful").

Three dimensions of trust

To complete our account of the concept of trust, we must determine the ontological status of the category: where are the bets of trust actually located, in which domain of reality? There are three answers to this question, which we shall not consider as competing, but rather as complementary, adding together to the complex three-dimensional status of trust.

Trust as a relationship

The first answer says that trust is a quality of a relationship. Even though it is initially a unilateral expectation and unilateral commitment, eventually it always results in a relationship: direct or indirect exchange. It is a direct exchange when the act of placing trust evokes reciprocity, that is, results in returning an entrusted object, or paying back with mutual trust. For example, getting back my money plus enjoying the trust of a person whom I had entrusted with a credit, is a direct reward for my trust vested in that person. But there may also be an indirect exchange, when trust is a projected orientation toward others, whose actions are important for me, but who are not aware of my trust and respond only unwittingly by acting in ways that meet my expectations, by satisfying my needs, or realizing my goals. For example, reliable, efficient, just operation of institutions, organizations, and regimes provides an indirect reward for my trust vested in them.

The relational dimension of trust is addressed by the rational-choice theory (Elster 1989; Coleman 1990; Hardin 1991, 1993, 1996). The basic premise of the theory is that both the truster and the trustee are rational actors, attempting to maximize their utilities (the goals realized, benefits achieved, profits obtained minus costs incurred), by rational calculations taking into account the available information. Their relationship takes the form of an exchange, or a game in which each partner is driven by such rational calculations, and takes into account the similar calculating rationality of the other. This is "an account of trust as essentially rational expectations about the – mostly – self-interested behavior of the trusted . . . Trust [is seen here] as encapsulated interest" (Hardin 1991: 187).

A specific quality of exchange involving trust is the presence of basic uncertainty or risk (i.e., principally incomplete information about the partner's future actions). As Luhmann puts it, "Trust is only required if a bad outcome would make you regret your action" (Luhmann 1988: 98), that is, when the possible failure would bring losses. In such conditions of risk, placing trust is guided by two main rules. The first is the maximalization of utility under risk: "If the chance of winning, relative to the chance of losing, is greater than the amount that would be lost (if he loses), relative to the amount that would be won (if he wins), then by placing the bet he has an expected gain; and if he is rational, he should place it" (Coleman 1990: 99). The second is the minimalization of loss in a risky situation. We could paraphrase Coleman to read: "If the chance of losing, relative to the chance of winning is greater than the amount that would be won (if he wins), relative to the amount that would be lost (if he loses), then by abstaining from the bet he has an expected gain; and if he is rational, he would withdraw trust."

The crucial problem for the truster, under this account of trust, is the lack of sufficient information concerning all relevant aspects of the situation: the probabilities of winning or losing hinging on the overall trustworthiness of the trustee, or the estimate of the potential gain and potential loss, made even more difficult by the incompatibility of scales by which various gains and losses can be measured and compared (e.g., how one can compare the regret, shame, or "loss of face" caused by the partner's breach of trust, with the potential monetary gain if trust is met). "This requires the individual, at minimum, to engage in various processes of information acquisition and integration" (Earle and Cvetko-vich 1995: 28). Perhaps the most complex and difficult estimate requiring various sorts of information has to do with trustworthiness of the person or social object that we consider as the target of trust. "Often the least well known of the three quantities involved in making a decision about whether to place trust is the probability that the trustee will keep the trust" (Coleman 1990: 102). For example: if I deposit money in the bank, it is relatively easy to calculate the interest I will receive, but the real question mark is the solvency of the bank and the probability of its collapse. This may be countered by insurance of the deposits, but it implies trust in the viability of the insurance provider, with the same problems of estimating trustworthiness reappearing at another level.

The single relationship is only the smallest building block which, combined with others, produces more complex networks of relationships involving trust or distrust (the "systems of trust," as Coleman [1990] calls them). They acquire some emergent properties due to the interaction effects, cross-cutting and overlapping, of multiple lines of trust. One interesting case is mutual trust. This does not only mean that there is trustworthy conduct on the side of the trustee, that the trustee simply meets the expectations of the truster, but that the trustee mutually extends trust toward the truster, expecting trustworthiness on the truster's part, who is now obliged to meet trust if the relationship is to continue. Each partner is simultaneously a truster and a trustee (Giddens 1991: 96). This creates a strong, mutually amplifying bond of trust. "Each person now has additional incentive to be trustworthy" (Hardin 1993: 506). Similar dynamics operate in the case of the mutual distrust. It is not only that I suspect my partner of wrongdoing but my partner directs similar suspicion at me. Each of us is distrusting and distrusted at the same time. Protective measures taken by each of us – distancing oneself from the other, avoiding interaction, limiting communication – enhance the feeling of threat from each other, at the same time curbing access to possible contrary evidence (limiting visibility of possible trustworthy conduct). As a result mutual distrust escalates through a vicious loop of growing alienation and suspiciousness. The exception to that scenario occurs in situations of normatively regulated distrust, when rules of the game allow and even condone mutual suspiciousness. The examples of such adversarial setups would include: bluffing at poker, bargaining at an Arab bazaar, appearing as defense counsel and prose-cutor at a court of law. Distrust is kept within the acceptable or prescribed limits and therefore does not produce escalation of mutual suspicion.

Trust and cooperation

The most complex systems of trust appear in the situation of coopera-tion. "The importance of trust derives directly from the nature of human beings as social animals who can only satisfy most of their needs by means of coordinated and cooperative activities" (Benn and Peters 1977: 279). People most often act in the presence, and in connection with, the actions of many others. Cooperation occurs when acting together, collectively, they aim at some common goal, which cannot be attained individually by each of them. In such situations the success of each depends on the actions taken by all others. This significantly enhances the uncertainty and risk, as this is multiplied by the number of partners, each of whom is a free and principally unpredictable agent. Therefore, trust acquires particular importance. Trust is the precondition for cooperation, and also the product of successful cooperation. As some authors put it, "trust is a lubricant of cooperation" (Dasgupta 1988: 49), or "trust is the emotional basis of cooperation" (Barbalet 1996: 77). Conversely, distrust destroys cooperation. "If distrust is complete, cooperation will fail among free agents" (Gambetta 1988b: 219).

In the situation of cooperation, trust means a set of bets directed at each of the partners, whom I expect to fulfill their parts of the job (I trust Jane, and Mark, and Helen, and Frank to do their task well). As each of the partners makes such a set of bets toward each other, the network of mutual trust becomes extremely complex. Over and above those individual, cross-cutting lines of trust, there is also a generalized trust vested by each in the whole cooperating group ("this is a fine group of dependable, skilled partners"). And on top of that, there is even more abstract trust in the organizational regimes of coordination, supervision, or leadership that safeguard smooth cooperation ("this group is well-organized and wisely managed").

Because the success of each requires the contribution of all, the cooperative situation, apart from having all the normal types of risks involved in interpersonal relationships, creates a new type of risk: that others (all others, some others, or in some cases even a single other) will defect and make the efforts of the rest futile. The risk is significantly raised when the goals to be achieved by cooperation have the character of public goods, eventually beneficial to all independent of the degree of their contribution (the winning of the World Cup in soccer brings fame and money to all players and not only those who scored, the success of a democratic revolution brings freedom to all citizens and not only the revolutionaries). Then each member of the cooperating team may be tempted toward freeriding, lessening the effort, or defecting altogether, while counting on others to attain the goal. This practice, ultimately self-defeating, may yet prove beneficial in the short run, and therefore elaborate measures are devised in cooperative situations to counter the risk of freeriding (organizational controls, distribution of incentives, etc.). Let us look at various cases of cooperation, and try to disentangle the complex networks of trust appearing there. Considerable differences will be due to the different character of cooperative tasks undertaken. Sport provides a good pool of examples. Thus our first case is the national tennis representation in the Davis Cup, or the team of gymnasts participating in collective events at the Olympics. They are in a situation akin to Durkheim's "mechanical solidarity" (Durkheim 1964b [1893]), or one that micro-sociologists call "coacting" or "additive" tasks (Ridgeway 1983: 290–291): each player performs identical tasks, taking turns, but literally not together, and each has to perform perfectly in order for the team to win. Every player trusts others to be good and not to make their own effort futile. Instrumental trust is present. Being trusted by teammates produces a strong obligation to excel. The sum of those multiple, cross-cutting lines of trust produces a generalized climate or atmosphere of trust, which we label metaphorically as team spirit, or group morale. As all coaches know, its emergence is a crucial precondition for success.

A similar case outside of sports is the group of workers shoveling snow in the street. Each performs the same job as the others, but parallel to the others, in their presence, actually together. Their efforts add to a common goal. Each trusts the others to do their share, not necessarily to excel, but just to contribute at some accustomed level of efficiency. Again, instrumental trust is involved. The bets of trust are not very risky, as there are ample opportunities for immediate monitoring, and mobilizing collective sanctions against the free riders.

A rather different case is provided by a football team. This falls close to Durkheimian "organic solidarity" (Durkheim 1964b [1893]), or "interacting tasks" in modern terminology (Ridgeway 1983: 291). There is a division of tasks, players are involved in different actions and the success of the team depends on their smooth execution and coordination. Each player trusts the others to do their special tasks properly: for example, the goalkeeper depends on good blocking by the defendants, the scoring player depends on good passes of the ball, and so on. Instrumental trust is again at stake here.

Typical work groups, brigades, task forces, committees, and juries operate in a similar manner. Pronounced division of labor produces strong ties of dependence, and trust appears as a precondition of effective operation. In some of them purely instrumentral trust appears (e.g., in the brigade assembling a car, where every worker has to count on the competent and efficient labor of the others); in some other groups axiological trust may be needed as well (e.g., in juries where each member has to trust the moral integrity and fairness of the others).

Our last case is the Himalayan expedition. In dangerous team sports, the dependence of members on each other goes far beyond the efficient execution of tasks. In the face of maximum risk I trust others not to abandon me, to support me, to help me, even to risk their lives to save me. Axiological and fiduciary trust is crucial. Also there develops a particularly strong attachment to the team as a whole, which is seen as the necessary support for survival. Climbers are ready to forfeit their own comforts and satisfactions for the sake of the team. "In an organization with a high morale it is taken for granted that they will make small sacrifices, and perhaps even large ones, for the sake of the organization" (Banfield 1967: 87).

From the area outside of sports a comparable example is the team of surgeons performing a complex operation. All three kinds of trust are present there: instrumental, axiological, and fiduciary, and only in their combination is successful cooperation possible. Another example is the army unit. In battle conditions, with this maximum level of threat, the high morale, attachment to the group, and responsibility toward other soldiers, become crucial for success. High trust of the instrumental, axiological, and fiduciary type seems a prerequisite for battle effectiveness. "The amoral familist does not win battles. Soldiers fight from loyalty to an organization, especially the primary group of 'buddies,' not from self-interest narrowly conceived" (Banfield 1967: 88).

Trust as a personality trait

A different approach to trust treats it as a personality drive, a quality of a truster rather than of the relationship between the truster and the trustee. This is typical of the psycho-social perspective. A number of authors assume that there is "basic trust," or the "trusting impulse," or fundamental trustfulness (Giddens 1991; Wilson 1993), which appear as products of successful socialization in the intimate, caring climate of healthy families. This propensity to trust may later be enhanced by happy life experiences with well-placed, mutual, reciprocated trust. Once it is implanted, basic trust becomes emotionally flavored. Barbalet includes it among basic "social emotions": "confidence, trust and loyalty are emotions which constitute the bases of social life" (Barbalet 1996: 75).

A trusting impulse may be specific or general; it may refer to a particular category of people, or it may embrace all people. In the latter case it is often linked with such general, diffused orientations toward the world as optimism, openness, activism, future orientation, achievement orientation, and the like.

The trusting impulse operates exclusively toward other human beings. Therefore to paralyze the trusting impulse it is enough to dehumanize, to reify the target of trust, to purge it of its human traits: individuality, identity, dignity, autonomy. Zygmunt Bauman argues that this was a strategy used in the Holocaust against the Jews, who were ideologically and authoritatively defined as parasites or weeds, but not humans. Toward such objects the impulse of trust (or sympathy) could not appear. Hence there were no inhibitions against the most brutal, massive extermination of them (Bauman 1988). Chong follows this argument: "SS brutalized and humiliated their prisoners by withholding food, sleep and privacy and enforcing group punishments in order to take away their self-respect and individuality . . . This made it much easier to control the inmates" (Chong 1992: 704). This effect occurred not only because the prisoners' resistance was broken, but because the oppressors were released from any pangs of conscience. The same strategy is taken in religious wars, ethnic cleansing, and other forms of discrimination and persecution based on differences of ascribed identities.

Trust as a personality disposition is the second dimension of trust, complementary with respect to trust as a relationship. The presence or absence of basic trust is a modifying factor in the calculation of risks and costs, leading to the granting or withdrawal of trust toward various objects. It is independent of any rational considerations, sometimes may support rational estimates, but sometimes may run against rational cues. The neglect of such psychological biases toward or against trust reduces the ability of rational-choice theory, at least in its orthodox version, to deal adequately with trust. It seems to forget that calculating rational agents are also full-fledged persons, often emotional and irrational as well.

Trust as a cultural rule

The orthodox versions of rational-choice approach seem also to forget that the decisions to trust or distrust occur in the pre-existent cultural context, where normative rules push toward or away from trusting. Looking at trust as a cultural phenomenon is the domain of the cultural approach, unraveling the third dimension of trust. From this perspective, trust appears as neither a calculated orientation, nor a psychological propensity, but a cultural rule. It is located among the "social facts" *sui generis* in the sense of Durkheim (Durkheim 1964a), or at the level of purely "social reality" in the sense of Lewis and Weigert (1985). It is the property of social wholes, rather than relationships or individuals. If the rules demanding trust are shared by a community, and perceived as given and external by each member, then they exert a strong constraining pressure on actual acts of giving or withdrawing trust. They may significantly modify rational calculations, as well as inherent propensities to trust.

The rules of trust refer to those who give trust, as well as to those who receive trust; trusters and trustees. There are normative obligations to trust and there are normative obligations to be trustworthy, credible, and reliable. One locus of both types of obligations are social roles, demanding specific conduct from their incumbents. Such normative obligations are role-specific. There are social roles that refer to trusters and include a normative imperative to trust others. This is true of "helping professions" (see: Merton et al. 1983): the doctor of medicine, the defense counsel, the social worker, the priest, and so forth. There are other social roles that refer to trustees and place strong emphasis on trustworthiness (the demand for meeting trust, i.e., acting reliably, morally, caringly). For example, university professors are expected to be truthful and responsible for their words, judges to be fair and just in their verdicts, football referees to be impartial. The more general rule of "noblesse oblige" demands exemplary conduct from those who have attained high positions in the social hierarchy, usually endowed with trust.

There are other rules that refer to the special case of entrusting valuable goods to others. They define a strong obligation of the trustee to take good care of the entrusted object, or to return it in proper shape. For example, a person entrusted with the secrets of another is normatively expected to keep the secret. The rules of "privileged communication"[10] strictly forbid the attorneys, doctors, priests, and journalists to reveal information obtained in secrecy. Or, to take another example, a babysitter is strongly expected to take good care of a child. Similarly, a nursing home is held responsible for the well being of the inmates. The hospital is expected to give the best treatment to patients. The strength of such and similar normative demands may be judged by the repulsion and severe sanctions that meet those who breach this kind of trust: the doctor who neglects the patient, the babysitter who harms the baby, the priest who reveals the secret obtained at confession, the parents who sexually abuse the child.

Some social roles include an expectation, or even a demand, to distrust. This is the case of border guards, police at the airports, customs duty officers, ticket controllers, public attorneys, or prosecutors at court. They are expected to exercise suspicion as a professional duty. There are other roles that allow distrust as a normal attitude. For the buyers at an Arab bazaar, it would be improper not to bargain, which entails an assumption that the merchants usually cheat, inflating the initial price. For the poker player it would be against the rules of the game to manifest trust toward the opponent. The norms of distrust sometimes assume pathological forms in bureaucratic organizations; they become the components of bureaucratic culture. For example, for the tax collector the client appears as guilty, or neglectful, or cheating almost by definition.

Finally, there are also some social roles that assume untrustworthiness. Nobody would expect the spy to be truthful, caring, or reciprocating trust. It is one of the demands of the job to be able to obtain trust from others, and yet it is normal, accepted conduct to breach it by cheating, hiding, lying, "building cover," outwitting others.

All those are role-specific rules of trust. But there are also more diffuse expectations to trust or distrust, which become pervasive in some societies at some periods of time. Francis Fukuyama makes a distinction between high-trust societies (cultures), in which he includes several countries of the Far East, and low-trust societies (cultures), in which he includes some countries of the West (Fukuyama 1995). Robert Putnam and Richard Stivers complain about the demise of the high-trust American culture of the nineteenth century, and the emergence of the "culture of cynicism" in our time (Putnam 1995b, 1995c, 1996; Stivers 1994).

In cultures of trust, some rules may be very general, demanding diffuse trustfulness toward a variety of objects, and expressing a kind of certitude about the good intentions of others, implied by overall existential security. There may also be more specific rules, indicating concrete objects as targets of normatively demanded trust or distrust. Object-specific cultural trust or distrust is often embedded in stereotypes and prejudices. "You should not trust anybody over 30," or the reverse: "You can only trust elderly people," "Don't trust the Russians," but "Trust the French;" "Buy American," but "Don't buy Chinese products."

There are also culturally diffuse rules demanding and enforcing general trustworthiness. Medieval guilds, firms with long tradition, famous corporations, gold and diamond dealers, elite newspapers and journals, and established publishing houses put great emphasis on fulfilling the obligations and meeting the trust of their clients. The "pride of the profession" or the "honor of the firm" become general normative guidelines embracing various sorts of activities.

Once the trust culture emerges and becomes strongly rooted in the normative system of a society, it becomes a powerful factor influencing decisions to trust, as well as decisions to meet or to reciprocate trust taken by many agents, in various social roles, and in many situations.

4

Foundations of trust

Three grounds for trust

According to our definition, trust is a bet on the future contingent actions of others. All people sometimes have to make such bets toward some others; but some people make such bets more often, while other people are more hesitant. In some societies people are more ready to grant trust, in other societies they are suspicious and distrustful. On some occasions people decide to grant trust, and on other occasions to withhold trust. And even when they grant trust, sometimes they make more risky and demanding bets, and sometimes they make only weak bets avoiding risk. "The potential truster's decision is nearly always problematic – to decide whether or not to place trust in the potential trustee" (Coleman 1990: 96). "There are obviously some cases which call for trust and other cases which call for distrust" (Luhmann 1979: 86). And, let us add, some cases which call for one kind of trust, and other cases which call for another.

In this chapter we shall inquire into various clues – reasons, predilections, and rules – which make people grant or withdraw trust, and choose specific type of trust. Such grounds for trust are never conclusive nor foolproof; they never give complete certainty about the correctness of the decision. Trust always remains a bet with a chance of losing. "The clues employed to form trust do not eliminate the risk, they simply make it less. They do not supply complete information about the likely behaviour of the person to be trusted. They simply serve as a springboard for the leap into uncertainty" (Luhmann 1979: 33).

Based on our earlier distinction of three dimensions of trust – relational, psychological, and cultural – we shall look for grounds of trust in those three directions. As far as trust is a relationship with others, granting trust is based on the estimate of their trustworthiness. Trust in this case may be considered as the reflected trustworthiness of others, their trustworthiness as subjectively entertained in the judgment of the trusting agent. Here the grounds for trust have an epistemological nature: they come down to certain knowledge, information obtained by the truster about the trustee. Such knowledge may be true or false, right or wrong, correct or incorrect. The probability of well-placed trust rises with the amount and variety of true information about the trustee. Without such knowledge trust is blind and the chances of breach of trust are high.

But trust is not only a calculating relationship, but also a psychological propensity. Trustfulness may incline people to grant trust, and suspiciousness to withhold trust, quite independently of any estimate of trustworthiness. The origins of trustfulness or suspiciousness are not epistemological. They have nothing to do with knowledge about the partners of future engagements. Rather they are derived from past history of relationships pervaded with trust or distrust, primarily in the family and later in other groups, associations, and organizations. They are the traces of a personal history of experiences with trust, petrified in the personality of the trusting agent. It is genealogy, and not epistemology, that is at stake here, and in this case it is individual, biographical genealogy.

Similarly, it is a genealogical foundation of trust, but on a different scale, when we are encouraged to trust or distrust by the surrounding cultural rules. We may submit to the constraining pressure of culture and follow cultural demands about granting or withholding trust, quite independently of the estimates of trustworthiness, or of our innate propensities to trust. The culture of trust may provide sufficient presssure toward trusting others, while the culture of distrust may evoke distrustful behavior. But cultures are not God-given; they are sediments of the historically accumulated collective experience of a given society, community, or social group. Thus in this case the grounds for trust also have a genealogical character, but collective and historical, rather than biographical, genealogy is now at stake.

We have identified three grounds on which decisions to grant or withhold trust may be based: reflected trustworthiness, agential trustfulness, and trust culture. Now we have to look more carefully into the ways in which those three foundations of trust determine the bets that people make.

Reflected trustworthiness: primary trust

Certainly the most important and most common ground for trust is the estimate of the trustworthiness of the target on which we are considering whether to confer trust. We are typically involved in various kinds of "trust ratings" (Coleman 1990: 185), and as a result attain some level of "cognition based trust" (McAllister 1995: 25).

The information that we use in such estimates, and which often we actively seek before making our bets, falls into two distinct categories. Some have to do with the immanent traits of the trustee, features that the trustee may be said to "possess" (e.g., somebody is honest, or some institution is efficient). Here we may speak of primary trustworthiness. Some other kinds of information have to do with the context in which the trustee operates, the external influences that may bear on trustworthiness (e.g., there is a rigid supervision in the factory, which allows me to trust the workers not to lower quality; there is a strong enforcement of contracts, which allows me to trust my business partner not to cheat me). Here we may speak of derived trustworthiness.

Reputation

There are three bases on which we determine the primary trustworthiness of targets: reputation, performance, and appearance. Let us discuss them in this order. Reputation means simply the record of past deeds. The persons or social objects (institutions, organizations, regimes) on which we consider conferring trust usually have been around for some time. "Rarely is it the case that exchanges requiring trust are ahistorical single instances" (Good 1988: 33). We might already have been engaged with them earlier and therefore possess direct experience of their meeting or breaching our trust. We may possess good first-hand knowledge about their conduct toward other people, and again their meeting or breaching of trust. Or we may have second-hand information about them, based on stories, testimonies, evaluations, or credentials given by others.

The knowledge relevant for our decision to trust depends on the type of trust being considered. Sometimes it will refer simply to past conduct of the same sort as the one we expect in the future (e.g., "Was she previously honest?" if we consider marriage; or "Was that corporation previously efficient?" if we consider investment; or "Did that politician take wise decisions in the past?" if we think about voting for someone in an election). Sometimes it will refer to past cases of meeting trust (e.g., "Did that person previously pay debts in time?" if we consider lending money, or "Was my friend known for keeping secrets?" if I want to confess to something shameful I did). Sometimes it will refer to past occasions of reciprocating trust (e.g., "Does this bank give easy credits to its faithful depositors?" if we consider the possibilty of being in financial need in the future; or "Was that business partner ready to delay payment to his contractors before?" if we intend to delay his payments in the future). Thus there are reputations for reliable, trustworthy conduct, for meeting trust, and for reciprocating trust. Each in its own domain signifies that an individual or an institution can be "counted on" (Wilson 1993: 231).

Independent of the substance of past deeds, there is one crucial meta-characteristic that is taken into account in estimating reputation. This is the consistency of the past record, a certain unity of conduct over time. For example, it may be consistent lifestyle, or a principled way of life, when dealing with people. Similarly it may be persistent policies, continuous growth, or steady profits, when dealing with an institution. It is crucial to know if a person or an institution have "always" behaved in a trustworthy manner. This allows us to assume that breaching of trust would be "out of character" or "out of line" (Giddens 1991: 82); something not to be expected. This is what we mean by personal integrity, or dependability of the institution. In short: the better and longer we are acquainted with somebody, and the more consistent the record of trustworthy conduct, the greater our readiness to trust.

How do we acquire all that relevant knowledge? Sometimes we can assess reputation directly, by reference to our own observations and memories. We usually have prolonged and intimate knowledge of our family members, close friends, neighbors, coworkers, long-term business partners. We may also have long acquaintance with the school or university where we have spent many years, or the enterprise where we have been employed for a long time. We may have continuously used the products of a certain firm, have been buying cars of a certain make, wearing a certain brand of shirt, or patronizing a certain hotel chain. In all these cases we have relatively reliable first-hand grounds to estimate reputation. But most often we deal with people or social objects whom we do not know directly or continuously.

Then we have to rely on various credentials. One type of these are second-hand testimonies referring to reputation: stories, biographies, accounts by witnesses, CVs, résumés, publication lists. They give a straightforward account of reputation. Sometimes we use more subtle, implicit signals of reputation. One of these is the continuous line of achievements as a proof of some permanent virtue of the trustee, relevant for our placing trust (e.g., the sheer fact that the firm is old, has operated say since 1907 is an indicator of its trustworthiness – how otherwise could it have stayed in business?; or the fact that an author has published ten books with good publishers tells something about her reputation –

they could not be all that wrong to accept her repeatedly for publication).
Another clue is practicing in highly selective professions, or employment
in prestigious firms or corporations (e.g., being a medical doctor,
working for IBM, teaching at Harvard). Still another is membership in
exclusive groups and associations, admitting members through rigorous
meritocratic selection (e.g., learned societies, academies of arts and
sciences, boards of corporations, "halls of fame," elite clubs). In such
cases there is an implicit assumption that admittance was based on the
high reputation of a member, subjected to careful scrutiny by competent
gatekeepers. There are also encapsulated credentials: diplomas, academic
degrees, professional licenses, medals, prizes. Here we assume that those
who have granted them reviewed carefully the reputation of the laureate.
Finally there is a very special case of credentials based on trust extended
earlier by other people. If somebody, or some institution, is known to be
trusted by others – and especially "significant others," the people whose
judgment I treat seriously – I am ready to imitate that trust, and consider
the target trustworthy without considering any other cues. In this sense
trust is contagious. The bandwagon effect in elections provides an
example of this situation, when I join my ballot – a token of trust – to the
majority. A similar mechanism operates in the case of famous celebrities
or idols, of products that are known as bestselling, performances that are
sold out, and the like. Here the assumption is that fame and popularity
are achieved through exceptional deeds, as testified by the masses of fans,
followers, readers, theatregoers who could not be so totally wrong about
the exceptional achievements of their heroes. For example, it seems
reasonable to buy a bestseller, without reading any reviews before, as
those millions of earlier readers could not have been so terribly mistaken.
The sheer fact of being a bestseller provides sufficient credentials. No
wonder advertising so often invokes this fact, as the ultimate reason for
purchase.

Some new forms of credentials appear with emerging technologies.
Since the Internet has become a widely used resource, there is a new
practice in the academic community of checking on the credibility of
newly acquainted professional colleagues, or authors of recently read
books, by looking at the catalogs of the Library of Congress, or the
British Library, and searching for their bibliographies. Similarly there
are often individual biographical pages to consult. Huge professional
databases collect easily available information on millions of individuals.
This trend will inevitably grow, in spite of some legal doubts concerning
the protection of privacy and personal data.

The emphasis on certain credentials as particularly reliable clues to reputation is culturally specific. Which credentials count differs from culture to culture, and also from period to period. Some societies attach more significance to titles, diplomas, medals, and other symbolic marks of distinction. This is usually the case in traditional, elitist societies, with steep hierarchies of social rank or prestige. Other societies, more democratic and egalitarian, pay more attention to popular fame, visibility in the media, and a mass following.

Similarly there is a cultural, and perhaps also a personal, variation of sources on whose opinions people depend. For example in research carried out in Poland in 1995 concerning the sources from which people obtain information and judgments about parliamentary candidates, 23 percent of the respondents indicated family members as those whose opinions are taken most seriously; 12 percent rely on friends, neighbors, and colleagues from work; 12 percent on the mass media, and 2 percent on Catholic priests (CBOS Bulletin No. 11/95: 13). In the case of political candidates the credentials are obviously most important, as direct acquaintance is necessarily limited. Only 10 percent of the respondents relied on their own observations of candidates' performance.

All clues of trustworthiness may be abused and subjected to manipulation: "the trustee may engage in actions explicitly designed to lead the potential truster to place trust" (Coleman 1990: 96). This is particularly common in cases of reputations that can be purposefully constructed,[1] trimmed, presented selectively, purged of shameful events, and infused with self-aggrandizing fabrications, and therefore can mislead even direct observers. Even more easily indirect credentials can be falsified (e.g., fake diplomas may be obtained, "man of the year" titles purchased, medals of honor counterfeited, etc.). A specially vicious case is the emergence of closed, well-knit "mutual admiration societies" devoted to the collective building of fake reputations for the whole group, which benefits each member and is therefore not challenged by anyone. An example from the domain of science would be an academic faction, where each member writes wonderful reviews of the research done by another, and can expect the same in return. This raises the visibility and reputation of the whole group, and adds a bonus of being a member of a reputed group to the individual reputations of each member.

When the appraisal of reputation is based on second-hand testimonies, or indirect credentials, there is a peculiar shift of trust. We have to assume the reliability of such clues, which means that we have to trust their sources (e.g., the biographers, witnesses, story-tellers, licencing agencies, prize committees, publishers, the wider public). We have referred to those earlier as secondary targets of trust. Addressing them, we make supplementary bets of trust as the validation of our beliefs about the trustee's reputation, which in turn is taken as the foundation for our main bet of trust. Using anonymous sources of information as credentials creates particularly serious problems. The complete anonymity of the Internet makes the trust given to the sources of personal information extremely problematic. The exceptions are highly reputable institutions opening their files to Internet users, like the Library of Congress or the British Library in the case of bibliographic search. This supplementary trust may often be breached. This is an additional reason why the bet of trust, even when based on seemingly solid grounds, is still only a risky and uncertain gamble.[2]

Reputations may be quite specific, limited to one area of activity, one particular role, one sort of conduct, one capacity (e.g., a person may have a high professional reputation but a low socializing reputation among friends, a student may have a high reputation as an athlete but a low academic record, an attorney may have a reputation for defending criminal cases rather than appearing in civil suits). But there may also be generalized reputations, spreading from one field of activity to another, from one role to another, from one capacity to another. In such cases trust is based on reputation not directly relevant for the expectations involved, but assumed to be important nevertheless (e.g., an efficient boss of an industrial enterprise is chosen to run the country as a prime minister,[3] on the assumption that organizational and managerial talents are most important for leading the government, or an accomplished athlete is made a manager of a corporation[4] on the assumption that self-discipline, persistence, and will power are crucial for the executive position). Such transfers of reputations, and consequently of trust, from one domain to another are based on an implicit theory of human personality, namely that:

people have consistent personalities and traits and that their behavior is driven by them. Either they are a certain way (e.g., honest, fair, selfish, etc.) or they are not. We also think that certain combinations of traits go together. We suppose honest people to be generous and to possess other positive traits; and bad people to be bad through and through.   (Chong 1992: 695)

Why do we care so much about our reputations? Because, to put it metaphorically, "reputation is a capital asset" (Dasgupta 1988: 62). It is a sort of investment, a resource which allows us to elicit from others some other valuable assets, among them, their trust and all that goes with it. As we argue in detail later, to be trusted is usually gratifying in itself, releasing our actions from constraints, allowing them more spontaneity and innovativeness. But it may also bring other benefits conditional on trust, for example, getting employed, being promoted in a job, being accepted for marriage, obtaining a credit at the bank. Reputations, while always cherished, are particularly valuable if they are recognized by the people we care about or depend on, by our "significant others."[5] The "most significant" others, with whose opinions we are most concerned, are the partners in continuing, long-lasting relationships, intended to go on in the future. Here building or preserving reputation is a rationally justified strategy. "Although short-run costs are incurred, our long-term interests are nevertheless better served by developing and protecting our reputations than by not doing so" (Chong 1992: 683). "Future expectations, generally based in ongoing experience, contribute much of the force that binds in a trusting relationship" (Hardin 1991: 190).

Sometimes reputation, and trust built on that, may quite literally "pay," making it possible to raise the price of our services or our goods. Peter Kollock describes such a case:

The prices buyers were willing to pay for goods from a particular seller and the rush by some buyers to complete a trade with particular sellers seemed to be sources of information for other buyers – if other buyers were eager to trade with seller X, then perhaps they should be too. In this way sellers who established a reputation for selling high quality goods could demand a premium for their goods because of the identity they had established for themselves.

(Kollock 1994: 337)

This mechanism, which I propose to call a "Bloomingdale's effect,"[6] and which obviously applies not only to sellers but to producers, where it could be called an "Armani effect,"[7] is partly responsible (together with purely snobbish motivations, sensitiveness to fashions, etc.) for the readiness to pay exuberant prices in famous stores for goods of famous brands.

Earning a reputation is an arduous and protracted process. Once earned, it is a precious and "fragile commodity" (Chong 1992: 699) which must be constantly guarded and cultivated. "Once one reaches a certain prestige level, one must work hard to preserve the status that has been attained by not letting down one's guard in this new rarefied environment" (Chong 1992: 694). High reputation adds to the visibility of actions, and invites more scrutiny and control by means of more demanding standards. This is grasped by the principle of "noblesse oblige." In the research carried out in Poland in 1996, people were asked if they would judge the politicians more harshly than their colleagues from work, if both committed the same misdemeanor. For the abuse of office for private material benefits, 82 percent would condemn politicians stronger than common people; 74 percent for violating border duties, 72 percent for evading taxes, 70 percent for telling lies, and 67 percent for getting drunk (CBOS Bulletin, April 1996: 5). Applying it to the domain of science, and considering the cases of Nobel laureates, Merton argues that "there is no repose at the top" (Merton 1973: 442).

Trust rooted in reputations requires an equal effort of permanent confirmation. "Trust accumulates as a kind of capital which opens up more opportunities for more extensive action but which must be continually used and tended and which commits the user to a trustworthy self-presentation, from which he can only escape with great difficulty" (Luhmann 1979: 64). Reputation, and the trust that goes with that, constitute a kind of pre-commitment, obliging an individual to behave impeccably also in the future. In spite of its value it may also become a burden.[8] "Our biographies therefore constrain the actions that we can take in our lives" (Chong 1992: 696). Reputations and trust, so hard to earn and preserve, are incomparably easier to lose. "A serious slip-up by a person may have a disproportionate effect on people's impressions of his or her whole character and may cause an otherwise exemplary life to be tarnished irreparably" (Chong 1992: 699). This is just one case of the typical asymmetry between building and losing trust.

Performance

The second category of clues taken into account in the estimate of trustworthiness goes under the label of performance. Performance means actual deeds, present conduct, currently obtained results. The past is suspended, "bracketed," and one focuses on what the potential beneficiary of trust is doing now. This is, of course, a much less reliable clue than reputation, because it does not allow for a judgment as to whether trustworthy performance is continuous, typical, and "in character." Extrapolation from presently observed episodes of conduct to the future, and basing trust on that, is much more risky than extrapolation of long and consistent trends.

But there are quite common situations when reputational data are unavailable: the records of the past actions are missing or purposefully hidden. There are other situations when past performance is not considered as an asset in granting trust at present. For example, in professional tennis, getting a seeded position at a tournament is based only on recent results as reflected in a position on constantly updated ranking lists, and not on past achievements, even if great.[9] There may also be cases when earlier reputations may be considered as principally improper for granting or withdrawing trust. For example, on purely medical grounds, an earlier perfect record of health is deemed irrelevant for airline pilots, who have to undergo periodical tests checking their current condition. Similarly some countries require that tests for a driving license be repeated after a certain number of years. Such exclusion of past data from consideration may also occur on ideological or political grounds. For example, when the first Polish democratic government after the collapse of communism in 1989 took a firm decision to disregard the earlier involvement of politicians, professionals, scholars, and so on, in the former communist regime, and trust them with jobs, governmental positions, and management roles exclusively on the basis of actual commitments (which became known as the "policy of the thick line," cutting the present off from the past, as opposed to the strategy of rigid "decommunization" applied in some other Eastern European societies), the criterion of performance became the only acceptable one, by political choice.

Evaluation of performance makes use of various methods. There are exams of all sorts at schools and universities. Faculties' achievements are reviewed from time to time by rectors' committees. There are various tests and checks for applicants considered for a job. There are trial periods of employment. There are various sorts of competitions, where people test themselves in comparison to others, with sports providing the most salient examples. Industrial products are submitted to stringent trials before they are put on the market.[10] Performance of corporations is measured by share prices on the stock exchange. Governments are appraised by looking at growth rates, unemployment rates, and inflation levels.

Such indicators of performance are never totally reliable, as they are always open to manipulations. It is easiest in the case of statistical measures.[11] But certainly fraud is possible in other cases. To mention just the best-known examples: drugs in sports may be used to raise the levels of performance momentarily over the normal standard, referees may be corrupted, football matches intentionally lost for huge money. In another area, industrial trials may be fake, standards of quality stretched. At schools, written exams may invite cheating and oral exams may produce arbitrary grades, tests may be skewed, and graders biased. In general, if aware of being evaluated, people may put up a show of exemplary performance, efficiency, generosity, caring, even heroism, which has nothing to do with their everyday conduct, but is intended to impress another and win trust (get employed, get promoted, get elected, pass the exam, persuade somebody to marry them, make the client purchase the car, and so on).

Appearance

The third type of cues that are used to estimate the trustworthiness of others are their appearance and demeanor. We say of some people that their looks "exude trustworthiness," and of others that they look suspicious. It depends on a large number of external features: physiognomy, body language, intonation, readiness to smile, hairdo, dress, ornamentations, jewelry. Some of these features may be esthetically rewarding or repulsive, evoking spontaneous, emotional trust or distrust. Some, like smiling or an aggressive posture, have a biological rationale. Some have symbolic value indicating wealth, social rank, power, and by implication trustworthiness (designer clothes, famous labels worn on display, brand watches, luxurious cars, etc.).

In general, among those external characteristics there are three that seem to provide the central cues to trust, indicators of underlying personality, identity, and status. One of these is dress (Giddens 1991: 62). A special case of that are uniforms (of soldiers, police officers, doctors carrying their stethoscopes, often useless in the era of computer scans), which make their carriers easily and immediately recognizable as trustworthy partners. Another important cue is bodily discipline, control of the body, health, fitness, as well as cleanliness and neatness. We tend to trust people who show such a control: who are more orderly, neatly dressed, groomed, clean, and look healthy and fit (Giddens 1991: 57). The third type of cues include civility, good manners, self-restraint in everyday conduct, which are taken as the signals of trustworthiness in more important matters. "As confidence tricksters know, many superficial aspects of personal presentation can quickly lead to conclusions about the nature of another person's beliefs and sentiments. On first seeing someone, we immediately classify that person according to age, sex, and many other social categories" (Good 1988: 45).

All these are superficial, externally observable signs relevant for trust. But trust depends not only on how we look, but also on what we have. The car we drive, the house we own, the area we live in, the furniture and gadgets we display in our living room and kitchen, all those may serve as indicators of trustworthiness. Finally, trust depends also on who we are, due to our ascribed, given statuses independent of reputation or performance (the latter gained by achievement). Those may be inferred from our appearance, and include race, ethnicity, gender, age. The link

between such ascribed features and trust is usually mediated by stereotypes and prejudices (e.g., you cannot trust the blacks, Gypsies are
deceitful, women are cunning, youngsters are not dependable).

Which features of appearance and demeanor are taken as signals of
trustworthiness, and which evoke suspicion, is always relative to the
truster, as well as the context in which the evaluation takes place (e.g.,
for the punk, a well-dressed businessman does not look trustworthy, and
vice versa; a neatly clad swimmer on the nudist beach certainly looks
suspicious, equally so as the naked streaker in the city street). There
seems to be a general rule dealing with such relativization of cues, which
indicates the importance of similarity: "People tend to trust others who
are similar to them and to distrust those who are dissimilar from them"
(Earle and Cvetkovich 1995: 17). This applies to external looks (punks
trust punks, and elegant businessmen other businessmen), age (teenagers
trust other teenagers), gender (women trust women), race (blacks trust
blacks), and so forth. The possible reason is that "we are merely better at
predicting the behavior of those most like ourselves" (Hardin 1993: 512).
Not able to predict the future conduct of those who are different from us,
we react to such uncertainty with suspicion. An extreme case of that is
xenophobia, a priori distrust of strangers.

So far we have discussed appearance and demeanor as traits of
persons. But they also refer to more complex social objects. For institutions they become relevant in two ways. First, all institutions are visible
through their agents, their employees, but particularly those who have
direct contact with clients, patrons, or customers; to put it metaphorically, those who work at the "gates" of the institution. Bank tellers,
salespersons, travel agents, waiters, judges, senators are the visible
embodiments of banks, stores, travel offices, restaurants, courts, and
governments. It is not by accident that such institutions attach great
importance to the dress, uniforms, neatness, civility, comportment,
politeness of their representatives. Through such external cues they can
enhance trust, so crucial for their operations. But second, institutions
also take care of the appearance of their premises: picture galleries and
marble halls in banks, the architectural wonders of department stores or
shopping malls, luxuriously designed shop windows, glass construction
of car dealerships, plushy interiors of restaurants, monumental government buildings – all are intended to suggest reliability and trustworthiness. It is also obvious how important the sheer appearance of products
(design, color, wrapping, display) is for eliciting consumer trust, and
raising sales of various products.

Nobody was more perceptive than Erving Goffman in spotting the possible manipulations with appearance and demeanor; the purposeful "presentation of self," building artificial "fronts," arranging the "stage," and using various "props" in order to seduce others into trusting (Goffman 1959, 1967). Cues of this kind are obviously easier to fake than reputations or performance.[12] This is perhaps why there are so many self-help books, courses of instruction, and even whole schools devoted to teaching the proper appearance and demeanor as the means for eliciting trust.

Estimating primary trust

We have reviewed three types of cues taken by people in estimating the trustworthiness of others, as the ground for granting trust. All three – reputation, performance, and appearance – require obtaining some knowledge, acquiring some information about the potential targets of trust. This may be easier in some conditions and more difficult in others. One general regularity seems to indicate that closeness, intimacy, familiarity open access to relevant information, and also diminish the chances of manipulation and deceit. Luhmann points out that "the familiarity of the trustee is undoubtedly a vital factor" (Luhmann 1979: 33). And Hardin stresses the importance of close, "thick relationships" in substantiating trust (Hardin 1993: 510).[13] The causal link is the raised visibility of conduct under such familiar and intimate conditions. "To the degree that members of a society are visible to one another in their performance of social roles, this increases the scope and decreases the cost of both monitoring and sanctioning activities" (Hechter and Kanazawa 1993: 460–461). For example, the authors argue that the secret of Japanese high-trust culture is to be found in the visibility of every individual in the life-world: in the family, at work, at leisure, and so on (Hechter and Kanazawa 1993: 481). To attain familiarity and visibility, a dense network of groups, communities, voluntary associations, and friendship circles, providing opportunities for personal contacts, seems necessary.[14] For the feeling of familiarity and visibility of more abstract social objects, when direct contact and appraisal is impossible, open communication becomes central. In the case of public institutions, organizations, officials in public roles, expert technical systems, they may be made more transparent, and therefore seemingly familiar, by easily accessible mass media, publications, open informational policy. Such arrangements provide arenas for mediated, vicarious contacts and open the world of institutions and organizations to closer scrutiny. By implication, anonymity and, distance breed distrust, as they block access to relevant information and prevent judgments of trustworthiness. Perhaps the often noticed symptoms of pervasive distrust in the "lonely crowd" or "society of strangers" typical of modern, urban society, may be at least partially credited to such lack of visibility.

A new area where the dilemmas of anonymity as limiting trust appear particularly strongly is the Internet. Anonymity of communications and transactions is at its peak.[15] And this raises the factor of risk. As an article in the *International Herald Tribune* puts it: "The borderless anonymity of cyberspace makes transactions over networks more suspect than contracts signed in a local office or purchases made in a Main Street emporium" (*IHT*, June 22, 1998, p.11). To address this problem companies are allocating huge funds for developing security measures, among them proofs of identity through digital signatures and certificates, complex methods of encryption, "fire-walls," and intrusion detection systems. This is intended to restore the feeling that individuals and organizations know with whom they communicate and are doing business. The business community recognizes that, as in all business, there is no e-business without trust. And hence to the question "How much is trust worth?" posed in the title of the *IHT* article, they respond that it is priceless. As Lou Gerster, the chairman of IBM puts it: "Our job is to make sure that when people and enterprises go to the Internet, they never have to pause to say: 'Is it safe?'" (*IHT*, July 22, 1998, p. 11). The risk will never be eliminated completely, but anonymity must be reduced to the levels acceptable for any "normal" transactions, not to block the tremendous commercial potential of the Internet.

Another important factor influencing estimates of trustworthiness is the clarity of criteria, unambivalent standards of achievement, unambiguous comparative scales. Various domains of social life differ significantly in this respect. It is relatively easy to determine reputation or performance in sports, where in most disciplines the results may be precisely measured, or winners in competitions clearly established. But in an occupational or professional field, it is much more difficult. Take the academic profession as an example. Is the measure of excellence to be found in the number of publications, or perfection in teaching? Is the number of publications relevant, or rather the quality? But how to determine the latter: by looking at the reputation of the publishers, or the tone of reviews, or the number of citations? And how can excellence in teaching be determined: by student evaluations, or faculty committees? All those are contestable solutions, provoking unending debates. Of course, it is even harder to find common, generally acceptable criteria when we move to the domain of arts, literature, and music. The appraisal of institutions moves the difficulties to an even higher level, because the appraisal of their trustworthiness usually requires simultaneous consideration of various scales of achievement, and the scales are most often incommensurable. Is it more important for the government to be influential in international relations, or to safeguard economic growth? Or is it more important to curb inflation, or to lower unemployment? Or for the university, is it more important to conduct innovative research or to provide high quality education? Or is it more important to teach large masses of students or to cultivate an individualized curriculum and personal care of professors over an elite student body?

Apart from visibility and clarity of criteria, some competence is needed to perceive and interpret the cues of trustworthiness. People must pay attention and be sufficiently discerning to make good use of various cues, assuming they are available. It is relatively simple and easy when dealing with the everyday conduct of family members, friends, or close acquaintances. It is more demanding, and requires considerable discerning competence, to determine the trustworthiness of products, especially on the modern, extremely diversified and rich consumer market.[16] But when dealing with occupational or professional activities, the components of reputation, standards of performance, measures of achievement are not self-evident. It is impossible for ordinary people to estimate directly the reputation and performance (and hence trustworthiness) of professionals, experts, specialists, scientists, technicians, athletes. Here other grounds for trusting become more important: indirect opinions of trusted authorities (reviewers, juries, referees), or the presence of controlling agencies enforcing professional standards. It requires even more competence to estimate the trustworthiness of more abstract social objects: banks, courts, technological systems, stock exchanges, governments, regimes. "Increases in complexity decrease the possibilities of familiarity on which individual trust rests" (Barbalet 1996: 80).

So far, we have treated three types of cues to trustworthiness – reputation, performance, and appearance – analytically and separately. But in actual estimates of trustworthiness, people often take all three, or various combinations of them, into account, sometimes arranging them in a preference order. When we try to determine the trustworthiness of a politician, a teacher, a doctor, a student, a priest, an airline pilot, a driver in the traffic, a fiancé, or a friend, we get involved in many different types of considerations. Similarly, when we appraise various institutions, technical systems, consumer products, regimes, we employ certain types of cues, or even various concrete cues, and disregard others.

Let us first look at a concrete example of such a complex, multidimensional estimate of trustworthiness. I have recently taken part, as an examiner, in the qualifying tests to the "Invisible College," a highly selected, elite group of Polish undergraduates, who receive tutorial help, financial support, and other privileges until graduation. The idea is to fish out the best of the best, and to invest in their personal development, in order to create an intellectual elite in the future. Considerable trust is needed to commit present resources for such a distant goal. Therefore estimates of trustworthiness are especially careful. First, there is a long written questionnaire that attempts to reconstruct the candidate's reputation: results at schools, all kinds of extracurricular activities and interests, including sports, art, and associational and political activism. There is also a request that the candidates submit three one-page essays on various, freely selected topics. This is to appraise their written performance. Finally, the candidates are asked to attach three letters of recommendation from their earlier teachers or leaders of extracurricular activities. This is to check credentials. To make the estimate more objective, the questionnaires, essays, and letters of recommendation are evaluated by five judges, and their scores averaged. Then there is a second stage: oral interviews, with the preselected group of those who ranked highest through the questionnaires. Again, these interviews are evaluated by five judges who attempt to corroborate the reputational accounts, as well as check the oral performance, by asking a number of challenging, problematic questions. It is also an occasion for observing the appearance of the candidate: manner of speaking, body language, assertiveness, and so forth. The final result of this procedure is the selection of approximately one among twenty-five candidates (last year twenty were admitted out of around 500 taking the tests). This example describes a particularly complex and careful estimate of trustworthiness, because both the risk and stakes are considerably high. But both in similarly complex, and in many simpler situations there are some general regularities that guide people in their judgments.

First of all, people make distinctions about the kind of trustworthiness relevant for various potential objects of trust. They ask: trustworthy, but for what, for what kind of future activities? This relates to our earlier distinction of role-specific congruent and incongruent expectations. For example, what people expect of a good president is efficiency, organizational talents, leadership abilities, that is, mostly instrumental qualities. What they expect of a good supreme court justice is moral integrity, honesty, impartiality, that is, mostly axiological qualities. What they expect of a famous philanthropist is disinterestedness and generosity, that is, mostly fiduciary qualities. Therefore in the reputation, performance, or appearance of those people they look for relevant information, and ignore other information. For example: Americans continue trusting President Clinton in spite of some grave moral doubts concerning his relationships with women. But they were ready to deny trust to Supreme Court Justice Clarence Thomas, accused of similar moral misdemeanors. They would probably withdraw trust from George Soros, in the unlikely case that he were found to be selfish and greedy. But they would most likely excuse Lee Iacocca, the famous corporate executive, for the same weakness of character.

Sometimes there are peculiar trade-offs: a famous scientist is trusted in spite of disorderly conduct, disheveled appearance, forgetting appointments, and always being late; a great composer is forgiven excessive love adventures; a rock star is excused for taking drugs. It is only in the rare cases of charismatic heroes, idols, or saints that people demand multidimensional, "rounded" trustworthiness; being effective, moral, and caring at the same time, and confirming those expectations in all domains of life.

An interesting case of a cue of an ascriptive sort, not related to any achievement, but nevertheless taken into account in the estimate of reputation, is the factor of luck. If the soccer player, the Formula 1 driver, the broker at the stock exchange, the attorney at court, have a reputation for bad luck, the best of skills and commitment may not be sufficient for high trustworthiness. The coach will probably not put the player on the team, the driver will be kept in the pits, investors will not entrust their money to this broker, and clients will not enlist this attorney's services. This is because in such specific occupations, having good luck is widely recognized as a necessary, additional competence, however elusive it might be.

There are not only differences in the emphasis attached to various dimensions of trustworthiness, but significant patterned differences in the choices of concrete types of cues. First, some cues are considered generally more relevant than others, when dealing with different objects. For example: as we already indicated, performance may be more important than reputation for an athlete; appearance may be more important than reputation and even than performance, for a pop musician; for the university professor, reputation weighs more than appearance; when selecting a car, wise buyers pay more attention to acceleration than to body color.

Second, there are some situational or historical factors that raise the importance of some cues and lower the importance of others. One of the unexpected findings of my research on trust in postcommunist Poland was that people almost completely ignore the person's political and religious orientation, when deciding to place trust (look at diagrams 2 and 3 in chapter 3). I suspect that it might be due to the peculiar situation of a society oversaturated with official ideology, and overcommitted to the Church as a defense against authority during the communist period, which is suddenly liberated from those two forces, and therefore over-reacts, treating them both as entirely anachronistic. Another similar explanation would indicate that formerly much ideological and religious fervor were not authentic, but rather were playing instrumental roles in controlling the society (through ideology), or defending the society against such control (through religion), and as a result both ideology and religion are no longer treated as authentic commitments saying anything important about the person supporting them.

Third, there are cultural differences in emphases put on various cues. "The specific attributes of persons who are viewed as powerful or credible can be expected to differ from culture to culture" (Earle and Cvetkovich 1995: 15). As indicated earlier, reputation counts perhaps more than performance in traditional cultures, whereas appearance becomes significant in modern mass culture. There are cultures that pay special attention to symbolic credentials (diplomas, titles), and others that disregard them. There are cultures that attach great importance to physical fitness and health, and others that look at such features with indifference or aloofness.

Finally, there are personal, idiosyncratic differences in applying certain cues. "People do vary in the values they consider important when dealing with other persons or institutions" (Earle and Cvetkovich 1995: 29). Individuals attach different importance to various attributes of trust-worthiness, because of their personal predilections, various accumulated experiences, and the like. Some are "taken with" appearances; other have a more inquisitive frame of mind, and demand full knowledge of reputation, some are skeptical and only convinced by the performance they actually witness, believing only what they "see for themselves"; some are more suggestible, conformist in following the judgments of others, and for them credentials of fame, idol status, titles, diplomas become crucial; some are more snobbish than others and some may even adhere to the perverse "snobbishness of anti-snobbishness."

Contextual cues: secondary trust

The trustworthiness of various objects of trust may be due not only to their immanent qualities – reputation, performance, or appearance – but also to some features of the external context in which their actions take place. There are some contextual conditions that make the actions of persons or institutions more trustworthy, independent of any other characteristics they might have. We shall speak here of derived trustworthiness. And we shall distinguish three types of contextual conditions, most relevant for enhancing trustworthiness: accountability of the trustees, pre-commitment, and trust-inducing situations.

Accountability

Accountability means the enforcement of trustworthiness, or more precisely the presence of agencies monitoring and sanctioning the conduct of the trustee, or at least potentially available for such monitoring and sanctioning if the breach of trust occurs. Let us compare two cases. I buy a Rolex watch from somebody selling it in the street. It soon turns out that it is a valueless fake made in Hong Kong. My trust, a bit naive to be sure, was breached, but I cannot do anything about it, I do not even know the seller. Now imagine that I buy my Rolex at an auction at Sotheby's, and it turns out to be broken. My claim to get my money back will most likely be met, but even if it is not, I am not helpless. I can always resort to litigation, and recover my money at a court of law. In the first case the anonymous seller was not accountable, his trustworthiness, if any, was entirely intrinsic, not enhanced by any enforcement. In the second case the seller, highly reputable anyway, was made even more trustworthy by its potential accountability before the law. The courts, the police, the consumer protection agencies, citizen defense committees, ombudsman, standardization boards, stock exchange commissions, and so forth, are the formal agencies of accountability, to which the trusters may refer when their trust is breached. But accountability may also be provided by informal groups. Look at one more case: I lend money to a friend. Of course we do not sign the contract, nor go to the notary public. It would be improper between friends, and could even cause offense. Unfortunately the friend refuses to give my money back. I cannot go to court, and yet I am not entirely helpless. I can disclose this outrageous breach of trust to a group of our mutual friends. Their open denouncement of the dishonesty, and the threat of expulsion from the group, may do the job: my friend will apologize and return the money. Other similar informal agencies of accountability would include the family, neighbors, coworkers, fellow students, and teammates.

Accountability enhances trustworthiness because it changes the trustee's calculation of interests, it adds an extra incentive to be trustworthy, namely to avoid censure and punishment. "You can more confidently trust me if you know that my own interest will induce me to live up to your expectations" (Hardin 1991: 189). "You trust someone if you have adequate reason to believe it will be in that person's interest to be trustworthy in the relevant way at the relevant time" (Hardin 1993: 505). And this is precisely the case when accountability is present. Therefore "it is to the truster's interest to create social structures in which it is to the potential trustee's interest to be trustworthy, rather than untrustworthy" (Coleman 1990: 111).

Thus, from the perspective of the trustee, accountability means that it would be harder not to meet trust, or to breach trust, because it would not go undetected and unpunished. And from the perspective of the truster, it makes it easier to place trust, or entrust some valuable good to the trustee. Accountability dampens inhibitions to grant trust and encourages a more open, trustful attitude, because it provides the truster with a kind of insurance against possible losses, a backup option against potential breaches of trust. "Creating institutions that help secure trustworthiness thus helps to support or induce trust" (Hardin 1996: 28). For example: it is easier to trust business partners to deliver the goods, if there is an enforceable contract signed by them at the public notary's office; it is easier to trust fellow musicians in the orchestra not to botch the tune, because of the towering presence of the "maestro" who will enforce good performance if needed; it is easier for the department store to trust customers with access to open shelves, when there is the visible presence of blinking cameras, security guards, and magnetic gates.

The sheer presence of the agencies of accountability is not enough to make the trustee accountable. Those agencies must be able to act effectively with respect to the trustee. If they can't, all benefits of accountability are lost: the trustee is not encouraged to keep trust, and the truster is not encouraged to extend trust. The courts may well be there, but neither the seller of the Rolex in the street, nor my dishonest friend, need to worry. They do not fall under the effective jurisdiction of the courts, and transactions are not enforceable.

What are the conditions that make the agencies of accountability effective with respect to a given trustee? Or to put it in the opposite way: which factors make a trustee effectively accountable? Some personal factors have to do with characteristics of the trustee, and some structural factors with the special organizational arrangements safeguarding effective accountability. The most important among the personal conditions is non-anonymity. The strongest asset of the street-seller of Rolex watches, allowing him to cheat the buyers with impunity, is his anonymity. "Anonymity releases inhibitions and gives people license to act in a fashion that they otherwise would not" (Chong 1992: 701). You cannot hold somebody responsible if you do not even know who he is, and where he is to be found. On the other hand, Sotheby's auction house has well-known and long-established identity and location. There is no problem with going back there, and demanding money, or suing the firm at court, if necessary. Clear identity (location, address) is the precondition for accountability.[17]

The other important personal characteristic is dependence on the jurisdiction of the agencies of accountability, or to put it otherwise, being vulnerable to their influence. For example, in most cases one has to be a citizen of a certain country to face suits at its courts, under its laws. Foreigners are much more likely to escape that threat. Perhaps this explains why typical sellers of Rolexes in the streets come from foreign countries. And perhaps it is why we usually trust our compatriots more. Similarly, one has to be a religious believer, and a member of the Church, to put oneself under the jurisdiction of God, and consider the prospect of confession or even the loss of grace, when breaching somebody's trust. Perhaps it is because they are in this sense constantly accountable before a watching and all-seeing God that religious people seem to us more trustworthy. It was the atheist Voltaire who noticed that: "I want my attorney, my tailor, my servants, even my wife to believe in God, because then I shall be robbed and cuckolded less often" (Wilson 1993: 219). And current research seems to validate this view: "Evidence has begun to accumulate that in the inner city, church-going males are less likely to commit crimes than are others of the same economic status" (Wilson 1998: 30). "The practice of religion has a high correlation with family stability, communal activity, and charitable contributions; and a low correlation with suicide, depression, drug addiction, alcoholism, and crime" (Himmelfarb 1998: 10).

The third crucial personal trait of the trustee is the possession of resources that may be treated as a collateral or insurance of obligations. A large variety of resources may play this role: a permanent job with a salary, a bank account, real estate ownership, collection of jewelry or paintings, a luxurious car, and so forth. The point is that all such valuables may be sequestered if necessary to satisfy our claims. Nothing of the sort can threaten the poor, unemployed, or homeless. There are certain measures people take to escape this kind of accountability. One is the establishment of a company with limited liability. Another is signing pre-nuptial contracts excluding marital community of estate. And a rather more illicit move is to place money at a secret account at some offshore bank. The price of those strategies is of course lowering one's trustworthiness.

Apart from the individual traits of the trustees, there are some structural arrangements that people resort to in order to raise their trustworthiness, or the trustworthiness of their partners. The most important of those is the legally enforceable contract. "When we have to trust strangers in important matters, we commonly prefer to bind them through contracts under law" (Hardin 1991: 190). The contract not only safeguards meeting trust in its specific domain (e.g., supplying some goods, or returning debt), but also by raising the trustworthiness of the trustee facilitates more open relationships pervaded with trust in other domains, not explicitly regulated. It provides a border security of a whole field of activities, which then can proceed more freely. "The contract or audit may protect the relationship against the worst of all risks it might entail, thereby enabling the parties to cooperate on less risky matters" (Hardin 1996: 52). To make contracts more binding, partners use various additional measures. It was Max Weber who demanded a written form of contract in properly functioning bureaucracy. Even more rigid forms involve notaries, witnesses, swearing before God, making blood oaths, and so forth.

An example of a more specific arrangement raising the trustworthiness of certain social roles, is the principle of privileged communication (known in the legal profession as "attorney–client privilege"). This has two edges: it forbids anybody to coerce lawyers, doctors, priests, and journalists to reveal information obtained in a professional capacity, or entrusted to them as a secret, but it also forbids those professionals to spread such information of their own will, under heavy legal sanctions or strong condemnation of their professional communities. This gives a twofold guarantee to anybody sharing secret information with such professionals, thus making them immediately more trustworthy in this respect, and therefore eliciting trust. In the case of attorney–client privilege, the recent ruling of the US Supreme Court explicitly extended it beyond the death of the client. The Justices have stated: "It has been generally, if not universally accepted for well over a century that attorney–client privilege survives the death of the client" (*IHT*, June 26, 1998, p. 10). And the rationale for that is obviously increasing the trust of clients toward their attorneys. The American Bar Association argued in a brief for the Court that "an end to the privilege would cast a chill over their clients' talks with lawyers" (*IHT*, July 27, 1998, p. 10).

A similar mechanism operates in the case of malpractice suits in the medical profession. The very knowledge that such suits are legally available makes every doctor more trustworthy, and allows patients to extend trust more freely and openly. For example, if doctors advise complex surgery, the assumption will be that they know what they are doing, and that apparently the risk is not too high. Then the patient will more easily decide to have the operation.

In the consumer market, the very existence of consumer protection organizations, or consumer magazines and catalogs, which give objective estimates of quality and comparative reviews of various goods, increases the trustworthiness of producers. The consumer may assume that producers, aware of the public screening of their products, will put more effort into raising the quality and lowering the price. This effect on trust is independent of the actual use of such consumer advice, similarly as one does not have to file a malpractice suit in order to feel more secure when such suits are available.

With reference to consumer products, another trust-building strategy is giving extended guarantees and advertising it widely. It has a two-fold impact on the trustworthiness of the product and the readiness to buy it. First, it gives an assurance of having the product replaced or repaired, in the potentially possible case that it is defective or breaks down. But even more, it gives a strong intimation of high quality, on the assumption that it would be against the company's obvious self-interest to produce bad quality products and pay for all those replacements and repairs.

Different reasoning is linked with the practice of recalling potentially defective cars. The firm that does it sends the triple message to all future buyers: the negative one, that it sometimes produces defective cars, but much more importantly two positive ones: that even if defects happen they do not go undetected, and that the firm really cares about the consumers, going to all that length of recalling, and paying the very high costs of the operation. The strength of the positive messages outweighs the negative one considerably, and therefore the strategy raises overall trustworthiness, elicits trust, and earns more buyers.[18]

Pre-commitment

A special case when accountability, and therefore trustworthiness, is increased by the decisions and actions of the trustee, may be selected for separate discussion under the heading of pre-commitment. This is a situation when, metaphorically speaking, people are willingly binding their hands, or burning bridges. To be more precise, pre-commitment means that trustees purposefully change the context of their own action, making it more rigid and demanding, and forfeiting the usual degree of freedom.

Look at some examples. In the state of Louisiana, the law allows for the "covenant marriage," in which couples forfeit their right to no-fault divorce (Himmelfarb 1998: 20). This makes their contract more binding, as it eliminates the normal, easy possibility of a divorce, without going into the protracted and complex procedure of proving guilt. The partners willingly and purposefully change the legal context in which their relationship will be operating. The fact that the partner proposes or accepts this legal solution, indicates stronger determination to make the marriage lasting, greater seriousness of purpose, perhaps a higher degree of love. Hence, pre-commitment makes the partner more trustworthy.

It is interesting to note that the existence of such an option in the legal system changes the context of trustworthiness for all marriages, and not only those that choose the exceptional form of "covenant marriage." For any partner who does not want to choose that option, trustworthiness is lowered, as it immediately raises the question why the spouse is afraid to do it: is the possibility of a divorce already contemplated, isn't he or she serious, doesn't he or she love me enough? The "normal" marriage is immediately a bit suspect, if the more "serious," stronger binding form of marriage is available. For example, during communist rule, two kinds of marriages were available in Poland. One was a civil ceremony in front of a state official, legally mandatory for the validity of the union. The other was a church ceremony, irrelevant from the point of view of the state, but in a country of more than 95 percent Catholics, considered as the only "real thing" and gone through additionally by the majority of couples. If somebody chose to have the civil marriage only, in that context it immediately looked suspect, and threw a bad light on the trustworthiness of the spouses. This explains why even high communist party officials were secretly taking marriage oaths in churches, sometimes being driven for this purpose to some secluded village.

An exactly opposite arrangement to the "covenant marriage" is the pre-nuptial financial contract suspending the normal rights of the partners to the common estate. This immediately lowers the trustworthiness of the partners, and makes the bond weaker, for at least two reasons. First, it is like a vote of no confidence; it sends a signal that the partner who proposes it does not trust the other, does not envisage a lasting union, perhaps is already thinking about divorce. Hence he or she is not trustworthy enough for the other's complete and unconditional commitment. From the very beginning the marriage is tainted by nagging suspicions, and the self-fulfilling prophecy may easily start to operate. Second, a contract of that sort obviously makes divorce much easier, so there is even greater likelihood that it will sooner or later end in this way.

The fact that the law allows pre-nuptial financial arrangements changes the context for all marriages, and not only those that choose that option. But the impact is exactly opposite than that in the case of pre-commitment. The fact that it is not chosen, when it is available, increases the trustworthiness of the partners, as it shows mutual confidence, a stronger determination to make the marriage lasting, making divorce more difficult. But because pre-nuptial contracts are the exception rather than the rule, forfeiting them and following the normal, taken-for-granted procedures will not have such a strong effect on trustworthiness, as taking the exceptional form of "covenant marriage," and forfeiting normal future options. The meaning and message carried by the decision are incomparably stronger in the latter case. The general lesson to be drawn from this example is the importance of the context in which the obligations are incurred, for the trustworthiness of the partners. The same obligations have different value from the perspective of the partners, if more demanding commitments are possible but not taken. Another example, from a different area, is the initiation through pre-commitment practiced in juvenile gangs, or criminal organizations. New members are required to steal something, or even to kill somebody. This raises their trustworthiness because first, it proves the seriousness of their aspirations to belong, and second, because it changes their legal situation as guilty of crime, binding them stronger within the criminal group which they now vitally need for escape and protection.

Situational facilitation of trust

After discussing various aspects of accountability, we have to look at the other source of derivative trust, the character of the situation in which the truster and the trustee find themselves. There are some features of the setting in which the relationship takes place, that exert general facilitating or constraining pressure on the trusters to grant or withdraw trust, because they raise or lower the prima facie trustworthiness of the trustees. First, trust is generally easier to come by in close-knit, small, intimate communities as opposed to anonymous urban crowds. This is due to two important traits of such communities. On the one hand, the members are mutually visible, and this very fact, quite independently of any agencies of accountability, enhances motivation toward conformity, preventing breaches of trust. "To the degree that members of society are visible to one another in their performance of social roles, this increases the scope and decreases the cost of both monitoring and sanctioning activities" (Hechter and Kanazawa 1993: 460–461). The authors analyze the example of Japanese society which, "despite its rapid industrialization and economic development, seems to have maintained a level of global order characteristic of pre-industrial, gemeinschaft-like societies" (Hechter and Kanazawa 1993: 485). They notice that "the lives of the Japanese are under almost constant supervision by other members of their groups, making individuals visible and therefore accountable for their behavior" (Hechter and Kanazawa 1993: 468). This surveillance by others is carried out at school, at work, in company housing, through neighborhood associations, and so forth. This provides an encouragement to meet or reciprocate trust: "members comply with these extensive obligations because their behavior is highly visible" (Hechter and Kanazawra 1993: 486).

There is another related trait of such well-knit communities: high density and intimacy of relationships, infused with intense emotions, a high degree of interdependence, and continuing, long-lasting existence. Durkheim speaks of "moral density" of groups (Durkheim 1964b), and Blumstein and Kollock describe such conditions as "close relationships" (Blumstein and Kollock 1988: 469). Early tribes, the nomads, peasant villagers, and also Arab merchants and gold and diamond dealers provide examples of such communities. When people are implicated in such dense, intimate networks, they are "horizontally constrained" to keep trust. If one cheats another, the rest will intervene, in defense of the easy, free flow of interactions beneficial for all. A merchant who cheats a customer may expect sanctions from other merchants who will not want to spoil the trustworthiness of a firm, or the wider market network, which brings benefits to all. Aware of those mechanisms, people may feel more secure and trustful dealing with such communities. In the case of gold or diamond dealers, the customers may risk transactions more easily.

To encourage trustworthiness in settings different from tight communities, those two features of communities – visibility and closeness – are sometimes purposefully simulated by special technical or organizational measures. Some of those focus on visibility. Bright lights are installed in public parks or crime-infested streets.[19] Instead of closed offices, the employees of some corporations sit in open compartments in full view of all the others. At American universities, professors usually keep the doors of their offices open to the corridor. At the White House, all conversations and proceedings are taped. After a wave of excesses at soccer stadiums, some cities have introduced name badges, providing obligatory identification of fans. All these and similar measures are aimed at eliminating anonymity and secrecy, which usually lower trustworthiness. Some other measures focus on closeness and intimacy. In some ethnic communities in the United States, for example, among Korean grocery merchants, and Chinese or Italian restaurateurs, there is a practice of employing close relatives within a firm, or doing business only with friends. In this way informal networks of kinship or friendship, which engender strong bonds of trust, are superimposed above formal organizational structures.

The next situational factor influencing the trustworthiness of others, and hence the readiness to grant trust, is the sacred quality of the setting in which the relationships take place (in the wide Durkheimian sense of the sacred [Durkheim 1965]). It is a common knowledge that one is much less likely to get robbed in a church than at the subway station, or to get beaten at the Philharmonic than at the soccer stadium. Some places, due to their sacred or quasi-sacred character, create psychological inhibitions for potential violators. Maybe a similar psychological mechanism is responsible for the surprising, and often noticed fact, that orderly, neat, clean, elegant parks or streets are much less often vandalized than those that are abandoned, neglected, and dirty. Another kind of occasion where sacredness also seems to operate, eliciting trust and trustworthiness, are religious or patriotic demonstrations, bringing together huge crowds of emotionally aroused people. I vividly remember two cases of this sort, in which I happened to participate. One was the celebration of the American Bicentennial in 1976, in New York, at the Battery Park, with several millions present. Another was Pope John Paul II's first pilgrimage to Poland in 1979 with a mass at an open field at Krakow gathering over two million people. On both occasions I was amazed by the unusual closeness, friendliness, help, care, sympathy, well – trust – that people were expressing toward each other. And some objective indicators supported that impression: in both cases the police statistics showed a much smaller, rather than larger, number of crimes or misdemeanors, in spite of apparently greater opportunities. Even the criminals seem to have become more trustworthy, due to the climate of sacredness.

Finally, there are quite special circumstances where trustworthy conduct is self-enforced. I have in mind the situations when the breach of trust threatens the villain automatically with very serious sanctions, even without the intervention of any enforcing agency. The best example is provided by driving in traffic. Were it not for the hard fact that speeding, or overtaking on the hills, or driving on the wrong side of the road, are quite often immediately punished by crashing the car and killing oneself, orderly traffic would probably be impossible, and the police would be unable to help. Morally responsible drivers are certainly a minority, and to count on their discipline, fairness, or care would be suicidal. It is the self-policing mechanism, appealing to the egoistic interest in self-preservation, that makes most drivers trustworthy, and makes it possible to drive in the streets at all. The traffic police are needed only for that contingent of untrustworthy drivers without imagination, or without the instinct of self-preservation, or with excessive confidence in their skills and luck, who cause accidents. On a different scale, similar self-policing mechanisms operate at crowded skiing slopes, where breaching the trust of other skiers, and violating some simple rules, often ends in broken legs or arms, if not worse.

Both types of estimates of trustworthiness that we have discussed so far, primary and derived, are taken prior to placing trust. They refer to expected trustworthy conduct, meeting the future expectations of the truster. The estimate is based on a number of cues – personal or contextual – but precedes our placing of trust, which has not yet taken place. Those are, in fact, estimates of potential trustworthiness. But there are occasions when we undertake continuous, or repeated, estimates based on the trustworthy response to our earlier placing of trust, the meeting or reciprocating of trust by the trustee in earlier exchanges. Here we estimate future trustworthiness as the extrapolation of earlier conduct of the trustee vis-à-vis ourselves. For example, if my business partner has always returned debts in time, I am ready to lend him money again. If a friend has never revealed my secrets before, I am ready to tell her a new secret. Trustworthiness accumulates, builds up in the relationship on the basis of earlier, consistent episodes of meeting obligations and returning trust. Trustworthiness is here continuously and directly tested by past conduct toward myself, related to my placing of trust, and not simply by displaying reliability, efficiency, competence, fairness, and so forth in dealings with other people.

We are usually ready to trust more those whose trustworthiness has been tested before in relation to ourselves, for example, our proven friends, tested business partners, favorite authors of books, car makers who didn't fail us before. This is the strongest cue to trustworthiness, a kind of meta-cue we use, over and above all the other cues discussed above. Of course this cue, like all others, is not foolproof, as the assumption of consistency and continuity in human conduct is not always borne out, and formerly trustworthy partners may one day breach our trust. And also, like all other cues, it may be subject to cynical manipulations eliciting our trust precisely in order to abuse it. One example would be the spy in the army befriending his commander, and proving his loyalty and trustworthiness on many occasions, only to prepare the ground for the final single feat of huge betrayal. Another, more mundane, illustration is the poker player drawing a naive partner into the game by raising stakes and losing several times, only in order to prepare the final "kill."

The situation of prolonged, repeated contacts with the trustee is the exception rather than the rule. Most often we do not have the chance to apply this strong meta-cue of consistent trustworthiness toward ourselves. Then we have to start from scratch, decide on the first occasion, a priori, whether to grant or to withdraw trust to partners never tested before. This is why most often we have to resort to reputation, performance, appearance, accountability, and trust-evoking situations, to ground our bet of trust.

Trusting impulse

The estimate of trustworthiness in all its forms provides epistemological foundations for trust. But there is also another way in which trust can be grounded. This is a genealogical foundation of trust, to be found in some earlier sequence of circumstances. This occurs when trust is not so much target-driven via reflected trustworthiness, but rather agency-driven via trusting impulse, or context-driven via the trust culture. In the latter cases trust emanates from specific personal predilections, or normative imperatives.

It is commonly assumed that trustfulness is a personality trait. "Readiness to show trust is dependent on the systemic structure of personality" (Luhmann 1979: 5). There are various terms used to refer to the psychological propensity to be trustful. Wilson speaks of "moral impulse" (1993), Giddens of "basic trust" (1991), Hardin of "capacity for trust" (1993), Fukuyama of "innate sociability" (1995). It follows a long sociological tradition of looking for some pro-social components of human nature, started by Simmel (1971: 23–25) with his notion of "sociation," or Durkheim with the concept of "expressive solidarity." The contemporary approach prefers not to consider such traits as genetically obtained, innate, and immutable, but rather as learned tendencies due to a particular run of life experiences. "High capacity for trust is a by-product of fortunate experience" (Hardin 1993: 524). And, at least since the days of Freud, with the confirmation of considerable recent research, particular importance is attached to the events of early childhood. "Everything we have learned in the last decade about the future of children suggests that the course is largely set in the earliest years . . . The human personality emerges early; if it is to be shaped, it must be shaped early" (Wilson 1998: 28–29, 34).

It may be hypothetically assumed that the trusting impulse derives primarily from life experiences related to trust. Theoretically they may have to do with meeting or breaching trust in the beneficial conduct of others, with reciprocating or abusing the acts of entrusting some valuable goods, and with repaying through mutual trust rather than reacting with suspicion. And also various forms of trust may be at stake: instrumental, axiological, or fiduciary. During early socialization in the family, it is the intimate, warm, and tender fiduciary trust coming from the parents – caring, helping, sympathizing – that initiates the formation of the trusting impulse. "Children are not raised by programs, governments, or villages; they are raised by two parents who are fervently, even irrationally, devoted to their children's well-being" (Wilson 1998: 29). The trust that matters is the instinctive, vague, not yet articulated expectation of such fiduciary conduct from the parents. There is no entrusting yet, as the child does not yet recognize, nor has command over, external valuable objects that could be given up.

During the next stage of upbringing, new forms of trust manifest themselves in peer groups, play circles, game teams, street gangs, neighborhoods – those natural primary groups that surround the growing child. The content of trust also embraces axiological expectations, of fair play, keeping secrets, being loyal. And as the ideas of possession or ownership, and the definitions of what is valuable, emerge, the practices of entrusting something to others appear (be it a ball, a doll, or a bicycle), and related expectations of reciprocity slowly crystallize.

Perhaps the slowest to emerge are instrumental expectations about competence, efficiency, reasonableness, which start to dominate only in the occupational sphere central for adults. At all these stages, the emerging varieties of trust may be met or breached, rewarded or violated. If typically and consistently met, the trusting impulse slowly roots itself in the personality. If commonly breached, the trusting impulse may never shape itself, or it may become suppressed, intimidated, or paralyzed. The most devastating effects for the impulse to trust are brought about by the decay of the family. From the common shortage of time for family care, early initiation to the pathologies of adulthood, traumas of the parents' separation or divorce, through the neglect of children in one-parent households, to the extremes of child sexual abuse by trusted parents – this is the rising scale of traumas that result in a learned incapacity to trust. The trusting impulse becomes replaced with inherent suspiciousness, obsessive distrust, and alternative pathological developments in the social realm of juvenile gangs, organized crime, the Mafia, and so forth. "There is a natural, universal human impulse toward sociability, which if blocked from expressing itself through legitimate social structures like the family or voluntary organizations, appears in pathological forms like criminal gangs" (Fukuyama 1995: 338).

Trust culture

In the same way as the trusting impulse is a product of biography, the trust culture is a product of history. The ideas of innate cultures, national character, and so forth, are either completely discredited or entirely historicized. Cultures are seen as deriving from the collective and shared, or individual but typical experiences of the societal members over long stretches of time. In the words of Fukuyama: "Culture is not an unbending primordial force but something shaped continuously by the flow of politics and history" (Fukuyama 1995: 211). Or as Wilson puts it, "Cultures grow up out of the countless small choices of millions of people" (Wilson 1998: 35). Sometimes, one may add, they also emerge as the result of purposeful reforms or revolutions. One track of cultural emergence is from below, via the actions of ordinary people. It goes briefly from instances of certain action, through spreading of common "practices," to codification in normative patterns. Another track is from above via the actions of people such as charismatic leaders, heroes, prophets, saints, idols, innovators. It leads briefly from the phrasing of a rule, through its exemplary applications, spreading of usage, to encoding as expected universal practice. In effect, culture acquires certain persisting, lasting qualities as the sedimentary traces of earlier practices in collective memory, social awareness, axiological conscience, manifested by means of values, norms, symbols, codes, institutions, organizational forms, patterns of discourse, and so forth. The emergence or "morphogenesis" of culture has been vigorously studied for some decades now (Archer 1988; Sztompka 1991a), and even though the process is not yet completely understood we may venture some initial guesses about the origins of trust culture, leaving the detailed discussion of this process to chapter 6.

Trust culture in the sense introduced in earlier chapters is a system of rules – norms and values – regulating granting trust and meeting, returning, and reciprocating trust; in short, rules about trust and trustworthiness. Trust culture accumulates and codifies into rules those prevailing, lasting experiences with various types of trust. If the dominant and continuing results of the bets of trust are positive, and occur in various domains of social life, a generalized rule to trust may appear. More specific rules of trust respond to varied experiences with various kinds of trust. Thus if anticipative trust, merely involving expectations about the actions of others (occurring independently of the act of trusting), turns out to be commonly met, the normative encouragement for optimistic predictions will emerge. Or if the entrusting of valuable objects to others normally leads to the return of those goods (or their equivalents), the encouragement for such faith in others will be present. Or if the extending of trust usually evokes mutual trust, it may turn into a rule prescribing evocative trust, as a means of obtaining trust for oneself. The rules may also deal, more specifically, with various substantial types of expectations: instrumental, axiological, or fiduciary. And they may also be selective, dealing only with some domains of social life, or even exclusively some objects, with respect to which experiences with trust have turned out to be positive. For example, during the communist period in Poland it was considered right to exhibit trust in the private domain – toward family members, friends, acquaintances; and improper or even shameful to extend trust to the public domain – toward the regime, the ruling party, the government, political elites, administrative officials, police, and so forth. Usually there also occurs a deeper differentiation of normatively prescribed trust among concrete positions, roles, institutions, and organizations. In Polish conditions, even though those institutions were located in the shameful public domain, the army was to be trusted much more than the police, the parliament more than the communist party; and although those persons were located in the acceptable private domain, family members were to be trusted more than acquaintances at work, and friends more than neighbors.

The appearance of trusting impulses in individuals, and trust culture in wider societies, provides the grounds of trust, quite independent of any estimates of trustworthiness. Genealogical justification of trust supplements epistemological justification. Most often both are present together. It is rarely that people act just on the impulse of trust, or blindly follow a rule demanding trust, without any consideration of trustworthiness: of reputation, performance, appearance, accountability, and situational constraints of those on whom they consider conferring trust. It is equally rare – or perhaps impossible – to find people acting as perfectly rational calculators of trustworthiness, free from any personal predilections or cultural pressures. The trusting impulse and trust culture enter into the complex causality in an individual act of trust, as important factors skewing the rational calculation in favor of placing trust. When the trusting impulses and culture of trust are common, making bets of trust gets much more probable, sometimes even in spite of doubts about trustworthiness. Of course all this is symmetrically true for the opposites of the trusting impulse and trust culture, the inherent suspiciousness and the cultural syndrome of distrust. Their emergence makes distrustful actions much more probable, sometimes even against all evidence of trustworthiness.

Among the three dimensions of trust, and the three foundations on which bets of trust rest – reflected trustworthiness, the trusting impulse, and trust culture – the cultural level is relatively neglected in the earlier research and theory on trust. And our discussion leads to the conclusion that it is precisely cultural rules that may play a powerful role in codetermining the degree to which trust or distrust prevail in a given society, at a certain historical moment. To understand great variations in this respect among contemporary societies, as well as to explain the historical shifts in the intensiveness of trust or distrust occurring in time, it would not be enough, and in fact would even be tautological, to invoke differences in trust cultures. Cultures of trust, or cultures of distrust, cannot be treated as givens: as independent, explaining variables. Rather we must look at them as problems to be explained, and try to locate the social conditions, as well as the causal processes, which generate them. This is the task we shall undertake in chapter 6. But first we have still to attend to the general problem of the consequences or functions that trust in all its forms may have in social life.

5

The functions of trust

In our discussion so far there has been an underlying, implicit assumption that trust is something good, to be sought, whereas distrust is something bad, to be avoided. Sometimes this assumption is made explicit. Let us look at some typical statements: "Trust is a social good to be protected just as much as the air we breathe or the water we drink. When it is damaged, the continuity of the whole suffers; and when it is destroyed, societies falter and collapse" (Bok 1979: 28). "Trust is an integrative mechanism that creates and sustains solidarity in social relationships and systems" (Barber 1983: 21). "Trust underlies order in civil society – allows mutual dealings (both business-like and personal) among formally free persons" (Silver 1985: 56). "A nation's well-being, as well as its ability to compete, is conditioned by a single, pervasive cultural characteristic: the level of trust inherent in a society" (Fukuyama 1995: 7). "Any long-range attempt at constructing a social order and continuity of social frameworks of interaction must be predicated on the development of stable relations of mutual trust between social actors" (Seligman 1997: 14).

Such an idealization of trust is too simple to be true. More detailed scrutiny is needed, and several questions must be asked: Is trust always good and distrust always bad, are various types of trust equally good or bad, and finally – good or bad for what? In this chapter we shall attempt to identify the social functions of trust and distrust, and to determine the functional balance of positive and negative effects that those phenomena have for social life. It will become obvious that any statements about the functions or dysfunctions of trust need double relativization. First, epistemological relativization, as the functional balance will be completely different if trust is grounded or not in sound estimates of trustworthiness (e.g., it is certainly good to trust honest people, but is it equally good to trust crooks?). And second, ethical relativization, as trust may be beneficial for the whole society, or only for some limited segments of society, against the other segments (e.g., it seems good to trust fellow citizens, but is the trust within criminal gangs something to be praised?).

General functions of trust

But before we turn to the relativization of functions, we must specify what functions in general could be at stake. What are the general functions of trust, meaning by that, the consequences that it has for the functioning of social life? Three distinctions are necessary. First, we must look separately at the functions of giving trust (placing trust, granting trust, entrusting something, etc.), and at the functions of meeting trust that has been received (confirming trust, returning what was entrusted, reciprocating with mutual trust). Second, we must look separately at the personal functions for the partners taking part in the relationship, and the social functions for the wider society (community, group, etc.) within which the relationship takes place. Finally, we must distinguish personal functions significant for the truster from those that trust plays for the trustee.

For the partners

Speaking most generally, endowing others with trust evokes positive actions toward those others. Trust liberates and mobilizes human agency; releases creative, uninhibited, innovative, entrepreneurial activism toward other people (Luhmann 1979: 8). The uncertainty and risk surrounding their actions is lowered, and hence "possibilities of action increase proportionally to the increase in trust" (Luhmann 1979: 40). We are more open toward others, more ready to initiate interactions, to enter into lasting relationships with them. For example, "belief in the benignity of one's fellow citizens is directly related to one's propensity to join with others in political activity" (Almond and Verba 1965: 228). And interactions with those whom we endow with trust are liberated from anxiety, suspicion, and watchfulness, and allow for more spontaneity and openness. We are released from the necessity to monitor and control every move of others, constantly to "look at their hands." "Moral order is based on self-restraint, binding oneself in 'covenants.' But in effect – it enlarges the 'freedom to' – capacity to release goals, and extends mutual benefits" (Silver 1985: 57). Consequently our conduct becomes more innovative, departing from careful routines. The overall level of our mobilization, activism, and freedom is raised. In some cases (of entrusting or evocative trust) there may also be an additional bonus: our trust may be reciprocated by mutual trust, and then we shall enjoy all the benefits of being trusted (to be discussed shortly).

Exactly opposite consequences are brought about by distrust. We are hesitant to initiate interactions (and therefore may forfeit important opportunities), carefully check all our moves (and therefore remain constantly "on guard"), and follow safe routines (avoiding any innovations). The overall level of mobilization, activism, and freedom is lowered. In some cases we may also expect mutual distrust, with all the harmful effects that it brings. "As confidence declines, people develop a sense of defensive pessimism to protect themselves against further risk and vulnerability . . . They are likely to have relatively closed minds and to react as if they have concluded that their partner is not truly concerned about them or the relationship. Positive behavior by the other will be viewed with suspicion" (Holmes and Rempel 1989: 214).

But trust has positive consequences not only for its givers, but for the recipients as well. "It is important to trust, but it may be equally important to be trusted" (Gambetta 1988b: 221). Being endowed with trust provides a temporary suspension of normal social constraints and inhibitions: such persons, roles, organizations, and institutions obtain a "credit of trust," a temporary release from immediate social monitoring and social control. This leaves a wide margin for non-conformity, innovation, originality, or to put it briefly – freedom of action. "The placement of trust allows an action on the part of the trustee that would not have been possible otherwise" (Coleman 1990: 97). There is one additional benefit: being visibly trusted by some may be an argument for others to grant trust too. Thus receiving trust raises one's trustworthiness in other transactions (e.g., when I buy a book because it is a bestseller, I follow the trust granted by thousands of earlier readers. With each additional reader the trustworthiness of a book is raised. Or if I know that most of my friends keep money in that particular bank, I am more ready to deposit my money there. The bank's trustworthiness is raised by each credible depositor). Obtaining a credit of trust with a bonus of raised trustworthiness is equally important for a politician, a scholar, an athlete, a medical doctor, a journalist, but also for institutions: the army, the police, the government. Exactly opposite consequences are caused by being distrusted. It binds one's hands through constant vigilance and controls of the other party. It pushes toward safe, defensive routines and avoidance of "sticking one's neck out." It deprives one of needed goods that are withheld and not entrusted. In general it leads to a reduction of activeness, isolation, and preventive hostile conduct.

For the wider community

Trust has important functions, not only for partners but also for wider communities (groups, associations, organizations, etc.) within which it prevails. First of all, it encourages sociability, participation with others in various forms of associations, and in this way enriches the network of interpersonal ties, enlarges the field of interactions, and allows for greater intimacy of interpersonal contacts. In other words it increases what Emile Durkheim called the "moral density" (Cladis 1992: 196), and what modern authors describe as "social capital" (Putnam 1995a, 1995b, 1995c), "spontaneous sociability" (Fukuyama 1995: 27–29), or "civic engagement" (Almond and Verba 1965: 228). Next, trust favors the spread of communication and overcomes the syndrome of "pluralistic ignorance" (Allport 1954) preventing spontanous collective action. Third, trust encourages tolerance, acceptance of strangers, recognition of cultural or political differences as legitimate – because it allows them to be perceived in a nonthreatening manner. In this way trust bridles expressions of inter-group hostility and xenophobia, and civilizes disputes (Parry 1976: 129). Fourth, the culture of trust strengthens the bond of an individual with the community (the family, the nation, the church, etc.), contributes to feelings of identity, and generates strong collective solidarities leading to cooperation, reciprocal help, and even the readiness for sacrifice on behalf of others. Fifth, when the culture of trust is present transaction costs are significantly lowered and chances for cooperation increased (Offe 1996: 10). To put it briefly, "when there is trust there are increased possibilities for experience and action" (Luhmann 1979: 8).

On the other hand, distrust erodes social capital, leading to isolation, atomization, breakdown of associations, and decay of interpersonal networks. Second, it closes the channels of communications, leads to isolation of societal members, and contributes to "pluralistic ignorance" (Allport 1954). Third, it mobilizes defensive attitudes, hostile stereotypes, rumors, and prejudices, as well as downright xenophobia. Fourth, it alienates and uproots an individual, inciting the search for alternative, often illicit identities (in gangs, the Mafia, deviant subcultures, etc.). Fifth, through a sort of halo effect, the diffuse culture of distrust is apt to expand toward interpersonal dealings as well as relations with outsiders. In both cases the transaction costs due to the necessity of constant vigilance are significantly raised and the chances of cooperation hindered. "People who do not trust one another will end up cooperating only under a system of formal rules and regulations, which have to be negotiated, agreed to, litigated, and enforced, sometimes by coercive means . . . Widespread distrust in a society, in other words, imposes a kind of tax" (Fukuyama 1995: 27–28).

Let us turn now to the possible reactions of the partners, which follow our placing of trust. Depending on the character of trust the partners may react with confirming the predictive trust, returning the entrusted good, or reciprocating evocative trust. For those who give trust, having their trust met allows them to reap all the benefits expected by the bet of trust. If their predictions come true, the actions prove effective (e.g., if I voted for the government expecting it to lower the taxes, and it does lower taxes, I get what I wanted). If the entrusted goods are taken care of and returned, I cash on intended gain (e.g., if the bank invested the deposited money wisely and brought me good profit, I obviously benefit more than keeping cash at home). If the evocative trust intended to produce mutual trust is indeed reciprocated, I benefit from being trusted and all that goes with that. In all these cases I also obtain two extra bonuses. First, I have the psychological satisfaction of making good bets, which raises my self-esteem, and inclines me to be more trustful in the future. Second, I enlarge my personal pool of those targets (persons, institutions, firms, products, etc.) that have proved to be trustworthy, and who therefore may be trusted in the future. Conversely, if our trust is breached it brings losses of resources committed in placing trust (actions taken on wrong expectations prove futile, goods mistakenly entrusted are lost). There is also a psychological distress of being so badly mistaken, with possible lowering of self-esteem. The only consolation is that we may know better in the future, being warned against a given partner and potentially able to avoid future losses.

Meeting trust has also discernible functions for the trustee. Most importantly it increases trustworthiness, which may bring more benefits in future transactions (e.g., the government may be re-elected, the store visited again, the bank receive more deposits, and the friend told more secrets). On the other hand, breaching trust may bring short-term benefits (e.g., getting extra profit by cheating the customer), but destroys trustworthiness for the future, and closes the chance of future beneficial transactions (no more calls from that customer, and possible spread of bad reputation as well). In some cases when trust is backed, "insured" by institutions of accountability, it may also bring costly sanctions (liability, litigation, retribution). Thus in general it is highly dysfunctional.

The situations when trust is generally met – confirmed, returned, or reciprocated – are functional not only for the partners but for the wider society. It produces a feeling of order and security, and fosters cooperation. As it provides gratifying experiences with trust, it may lead to raised trustfulness, and contribute to the emergence of the culture of trust.

Relativization of functions

These are the general functions and dysfunctions of trust. But is their meaning always unequivocal? Is it good to trust against reason (as in the blind, naive trust toward vicious dictators). Or is it good to reciprocate by extending mutual trust to somebody who cynically fakes trust toward myself only to benefit from my trust (as in that pseudo-Gemeinschaft pattern of personal concern exhibited by some salespeople). We can immediately see that the functionality or dysfunctionality of trust is relative to its epistemological foundations: the trustworthiness of the target.

Functions relative to trustworthiness

To put it simply: it is functional to trust the trustworthy, and it is equally functional to distrust the untrustworthy. Let us unpack this condensed formula. When we trust those who are trustworthy there is a good chance that our trust will be met[1] and that both ourselves as well as our partners will reap all the benefits of trusting, being trusted, having one's trust met, and meeting trust. "If the trustee is trustworthy, the person who places trust is better off than if the trust were not placed" (Coleman 1990: 98). "Where there is trust that is justified, there are increased possibilities for experience and action" (Hardin 1993: 512). On the wider social scale it leads to all the beneficial consequences of repeated gratifying experiences with trust, including the emergence of the culture of trust.

When we distrust those who are untrustworthy (as judged by our best knowledge of their bad reputation, weak credentials, poor performance, etc.) we have an equally good chance that our negative bets will be borne out. Distrust in such a situation involves "rationally based expectations that technically competent performance and/or fiduciary obligation and responsibility will not be forthcoming" (Barber 1983: 166). Therefore it is more prudent for us to eschew contact, distance ourselves, or if interaction is unavoidable, at least to protect ourselves by close monitoring and control of the other's conduct. In this way we insulate ourselves against untrustworthy conduct and its dangers. Let me give some examples of the functionality of distrust, which is a less intuitive case than the functionality of trust. Somebody who has been divorced five times does not qualify as a dependable marriage partner. If an airline has a bad record of crashes, passengers will be reluctant to use it. If the government has a long record of repressiveness or inefficiency, it can hardly expect to be re-elected. Somebody who is obviously intoxicated would not be trusted to drive a car. And when the quality control at a certain car factory is known to be negligent, one is rightly reluctant to buy its products. In all such cases distrust leads to defensive measures, by avoiding contact, cutting off any relationships, and if that is not feasible, raising vigilance, scrutiny, and attempts at direct control of the other. It may also mobilize backup insurances of controlling agencies against the partner (e.g., making deals in the presence of witnesses, certified by a notary, demanding independent collaterals of debts, resorting to litigation). By raising the costs of harmful conduct the justifiably distrusted partners may thus be pushed toward more cooperative, trustworthy behavior.

Now we may give a brief formula for dysfunctional trust: it is equally dysfunctional to trust the untrustworthy as to distrust the trustworthy. The idealization of trust as uniformly good breaks down here: "Trust can finally be stupid and even culpable. Merely trusting *per se* obviously need not help in managing complexity well – it could lead to dismal results, including quick destruction" (Hardin 1993: 513). The obvious dysfunctionality of trust occurs in the first situation, which may be labeled as blind or naive trust; and it may occur either when one ignores any indications of trustworthiness and makes a pure "leap of faith," or when one discounts the negative evidence, or when one is misled by purposefully contrived fake trustworthiness. Blind or naive trust provides an opportunity for costly losses, and in the case of entrusting or evocative trust opens the door to abuse and exploitation. The partner will most likely use the extended freedom for action, received with the credit of trust, against the donor, abusing and breaching trust. "If the trustee is not trustworthy, the truster is worse off than if trust were not placed" (Coleman 1990: 98). Think of a woman who finds her husband lying, or an investor cheated out of his money by a con man, or a tourist purchasing a trip at a fake travel agency that becomes bankrupt next day, or a bank that has to write off a bad credit. Apart from current losses, blind and naive trust encourages untrustworthy conduct in the future; it shows that breaching of trust may pay. An interesting, and particularly vicious, case of this pathology of trust occurs in politics. It is a blind and naive trust in an autocratic ruler or charismatic hero (e.g., the so called "personality cult" in the case of Stalin, the *Fuehrer Prinzip* in the case of Hitler). Trust is manipulated here by indoctrination and propaganda, with extreme aggrandizement of the cues to trustworthiness. There is the glorification of reputation (heroic deeds, war victories, proofs of wisdom, performed miracles), fabricating credentials (medals, prizes, degrees), the exalting of performance (bringing peace to the country, keeping enemies at bay, providing prosperity), enhancing appearance (the "generalissimo" uniforms of Stalin or Mussolini, rows of medals on Brezhnev's suit), impressing with situational props (sumptuous palaces, high lecterns, huge offices, enormous desks, dozens of bodyguards, stretch limousines).

Distrust may be equally dysfunctional. This occurs in our second case of distrusting the trustworthy. This may be called obsessive, or paranoic, distrust. It may be manifested by complete disregard of available cues to trustworthiness (one distrusts "in principle"), or disbelief in the positive estimates (one "knows better"), or in the rare case when one takes seriously a playful pretense of untrustworthiness (e.g., one shoots at a friend disguised as a robber at a carnival). The main dysfunction of such obsessive distrust is forfeiting the potential opportunities of a relationship, or abandoning an existing beneficial relationship completely. On the side of the unjustifiably distrusted partner it creates strong resentments, frustrations, and alienation from the relationship. An interesting variation of obsessive distrust becomes institutionalized in distrusting roles: customs officers, ticket controllers, security guards, police. By the demands of their occupations, they are condemned to this notorious situation of distrusting at least the great numbers of trustworthy people (with spotting smugglers, or passengers without tickets, or catching thieves at supermarkets, only sporadically). The attitude of the public toward such occupations gives a good illustration of our earlier point. There is resentment and specific uneasiness in their presence. It stems from the offended dignity, an emotion of unjustified suspicion, and the dissonance with the strongly internalized rule "innocent until proven guilty."[2] Subjected to unjustified distrust, people usually manifest stronger self-control, emit cues of non-guilt, adopting an innocent appearance, to help reject the a priori assumption of guilt and prove themselves trustworthy (e.g., just look at the appeasing body language and reassuring smiles of the people who pass through customs at airports, or the standard jokes of those who pass through the magnetic gates before the flight).

It may be argued that under some circumstances extending trust a priori, without any grounds, as a pure "leap of faith," may be functional. "Inability to show trust limits the chances of winning trust" (Luhmann 1979: 40). And we may be in a situation when sufficient evidence of trustworthiness, or of untrustworthiness, is unavailable. Sometimes it may pay to take the risk of blind trust. In such a case "trust is predicated not on evidence but on the lack of contrary evidence" (Gambetta 1988b: 234). It may be functional, as it may elicit responsibility, the obligation to reciprocate and improve the trustworthiness of the partner. The balance of motivation may be tipped toward reciprocating by trust-worthy conduct. "The mere fact that someone has placed his trust in us makes us feel obligated, and this makes it harder to betray that trust" (Dasgupta 1988: 53). In this way, trusting may make the trusted trustworthy. Several precepts of Christian faith are based on this principle. "In its Christian religious form . . . this ideal is defined as the brotherhood of men in God; each man's trust in and for one another is transcended only by the trust of all in God as the omnipotent but all-caring fiduciary" (Barber 1983: 16). Also "Gandhi . . . in the spirit of 'satyagraha', taught that continued trust will ultimately elevate one's opponent to the point where he will respond in good faith, even if he does not reciprocate immediately" (Chong 1992: 699). But the risk of that is certainly high, as all dysfunctional effects will occur once the partner turns out to be too insensitive, or too excessively cynical, to succumb to that beneficial effect. On the other hand there are no arguments that would indicate the functionality of the opposite situation: the blind leap into distrust. Obsessive distrust seems always and unexceptionally to be dysfunctional.

Systems of trust

So far we have been describing the functionality or dysfunctionality of single relationships in which trust or distrust occurs. Now we have to move our discussion toward more complex "systems of trust" (Coleman 1990: 175) and inquire about the functions or dysfunctions of combined networks of such relationships. The need for trust and the importance of trust grow as such networks become more complex: "Without trust only very simple forms of human cooperation which can be transacted on the spot are possible . . . Trust is indispensable in order to increase a social system's potential for action beyond these elementary forms" (Luhmann 1979: 88).

The systems of trust may be schematically classified in four categories (even though normally, all kind of mixed types will occur). If the predominant case in the network is met – confirmed, returned, or reciprocated – trust, cooperation develops most smoothly, and acquires a self-enhancing capacity. Trust breeds trust. It leads toward the culture of trust, when the routine of trusting and meeting trust turns into a normative rule for both the trusters and the trustees. If the predominant case is blind, naive trust, it may temporarily produce a culture of trust, but it will be only one-sided (binding solely the trusters, and not the trustees), and will break down very soon with accumulating evidence of breaches of trust.

If the predominant case is justified distrust, in the face of prevailing untrustworthiness and constant breaches of trust, then the culture of distrust will inevitably emerge, and a self-enhancing vicious spiral of deepening cynicism and suspicion will start. Distrust breeds distrust. "Distrust has an inherent tendency to endorse and reinforce itself in social interaction" (Luhmann 1979: 74). The mechanism of this process is unraveled by Sissela Bok: "instances of deception can and will increase, bringing distrust and thus more deception, loss of personal standards on the part of liars and so yet more deception, imitation by those who witness deception and the rewards it can bring, and once again more deception" (Bok 1979: 110).

Finally, if the predominant case is obsessive distrust, it may temporarily acquire normative sanction as the unilateral rule of suspiciousness. It may also initiate a vicious spiral: "Once distrust has set in it soon becomes impossible to know if it was ever in fact justified, for it has the capacity to be self-fulfilling, to generate a reality consistent with itself" (Gambetta 1988b: 234). In general, distrust shows particularly strong resilience: "trust is easier to transform into distrust than is distrust into trust" (Luhmann 1979: 89). "If presented with a clear breach of trust by someone our faith in that person will be fatally undermined. However, if an untrustworthy person behaves well on one occasion, it is not nearly so likely that the converse inference will be made" (Good 1988: 43). But in the long run, confronted with consistent and repeated manifestations of trustworthy conduct, the vicious spiral may be reversed, unjustified distrust may be undermined, giving way to the slow rebuilding of the culture of trust.

Once trust or distrust becomes embedded in cultural, normative systems, they acquire functions and dysfunctions of their own. The culture of trust usually encourages cooperation and community. "Culture may be the limiting factor which determines the amount and character of organization" (Banfield 1967: 9). But it is functional only if the rules are two-sided, they prescribe – and therefore release – trust, but also strongly condemn – and therefore prevent – breaches of trust. The functional culture of trust must include strong norms with positive sanctions, motivating trustworthiness, and strong taboos with negative sanctions prohibiting breaches of trust. When the culture of trust is one-sided, focused exclusively on prescribing trust, but ignoring or condoning breaches of trust, it is in fact a culture of naiveness, and has highly dysfunctional consequences. It is dysfunctional when it is preserved by inertia in conditions of repeated breaches of trust, and prevailing untrustworthiness. Defensive precautions that could save costs and losses are forgone. The culture of trust is even more dysfunctional when it requires blind trust prohibiting criticism and scepticism, forbidding any monitoring or checking of the trustee. We find it in the case of autocratic rulers, mentioned earlier, but also in the so-called "group-think syndrome" described by Irving Janis, when the extreme cohesiveness of the group leads to complete conformity and prohibits any dissent (Janis 1982).

The culture of distrust is typically dysfunctional; it prevents cooperation and destroys community. "To the extent that trust is undermined, all co-operative undertakings, in which what one person can do or has reason to do is dependent on what others have done, are doing, or are going to do, must tend to break down" (Warnock 1971: ch. 6, quoted in Bok 1979: 307). The culture of distrust narrows down the pool of potential partners for interaction and discourages the initiation of interactions. In this way it implies a long string of lost opportunities for potentially beneficial actions (Hardin 1993: 519). One of its consequences is described in the classic study of the Italian South as "amoral familism": "the inability to concert activity beyond the immediate family" (Banfield 1967: 10). With respect to the external social world it leads to a climate of obsessive paranoic cynicism. Social life is pervaded with mingled worry, chronic diffuse fear, suspicion, conspiracy theories, anxiety and foreboding, paralyzing action on any wider scale (Banfield 1967: 106).

The culture of distrust becomes particularly dysfunctional when it loses any real grounds and is preserved only by inertia in the conditions of raised trustworthiness and growing readiness to meet (confirm, return, or reciprocate) trust, if only given. This is precisely what Banfield observed in the Italian context: "The present ethos will tend to perpetuate itself for a long time, even though many of the circumstances which give rise to it no longer operate in the old way. Long established ways of thinking and valuing have a life of their own independent of the particular conditions which gave rise to them" (Banfield 1967: 160). In more general terms, the same time lag and asynchrony in the dynamics of trust, as compared with other areas of social life, is noticed by Eisenstadt and Roniger: "The tempo and direction of change in some crucial aspects of social division of labour – as manifest above all in levels of technological and economic development – may differ from those that develop in the construction of trust and meaning" (Eisenstadt and Roniger 1984: 28).

Looking at the culture of distrust as basically dysfunctional, we must not forget that in some circumstances it may also play a positive role. Let me give just two illustrations of such exceptional cases. First, at the macro-historical level we must notice the importance of the pervasive culture of distrust as preceding all major revolutions. This is a limited distrust, though; it refers to political authorities, or class enemies, and is usually coupled with a strong culture of trust within the ranks of the revolutionaries.[3] In that sense the limited culture of distrust contributes to bringing about social change. A second illustration, from the micro-sociological level, has already been discussed earlier, in a slightly different context. It is the culture of distrust emerging within some occupational groups, indispensable for the proper execution of its duties. Customs officers, border guards, airport controllers, public prosecutors, police-officers, spies must cultivate suspiciousness as the orientation necessary for their roles. But again, this is limited distrust, directed at potential suspects, which is usually accompanied by a culture of trust, or esprit de corps among the members of the occupational group.

Moral qualities of trust

So far we have attempted to answer the question whether, and under which conditions, trust is functional or dysfunctional. But is it the same as saying that trust is good or bad? Judging the functionality or dysfunctionality of trust – and of trust cultures – we have taken objective traits of society as points of reference. One was the general level of activism, another intensiveness and wide scope of interactions, the next their innovativeness, openness, and spontaneity, still another cooperation and strong bonds of community. But is it always good for society if such traits are there? Look at some counterexamples: there is a high level of activism, a lot of cooperation and community, as well as intense interactions, in the Mafia. And there is a lot of trust, or trust culture, pervading the world of the mafiosi (Gambetta 1993). Or take another example: strong bonds of cooperation and trust certainly accompany the extreme chauvinism of some ethnic or national communities, as well as the radical fundamentalism of some religious groups. Can we be happy with this kind of trust? And if not, how do we distinguish it from the good kind of trust? This question causes us to leave the objective criteria of functionality and move the debate to another level, where we have to apply meta-judgments of the non-objective, moral sort. We have to ask: trust for what? and trust for whom? And here valuations will inevitably enter.

Trust is neither intrinsically good or bad, it depends. "There are immoral as well as moral trust relationships" (Baier 1986: 232). To determine which are which we have to refer to wider contexts in which the networks of trust relationships, or trust-pervaded communities, or trust cultures, appear. It is no longer a question of functionality for the partners, or for the groups to which they belong, but to the wider social system, the whole society. At such a meta-level this becomes the more extensive frame of reference for estimating functionality. But what traits of wider society do we consider as crucial for estimating functionality? There is no escape for ideological or moral choice here. No values are self-evident, or empirically provable. Hence various axiological options are available. But let us choose arbitrarily a very general option: the preference for societies that are peaceful, harmonious, and unified; rather than fighting, conflict-ridden, and divided. Without entering into a possible debate on the validity of such a choice, I propose to use it as a frame of reference for appraising the meta-functionality of trust, its merits and demerits relative to such a valued state of society.

There seem to be two possible cases. The first is when there is a coincidence between internal functionality of trust (for the partners and their immediate group), and the external functionality of trust (for the wider society, and specifically the preservation of its peaceful, harmonious, and unified condition). This may be called cosmopolitan, ecumenical trust, focused on inclusion. It is not hostile to others, but rather is open to others, embracing them, incorporating them into the network of trust. Examples are provided by the bonds of trust to be found in cooperative institutions, committees, work brigades, task forces, universities, and the like, where internal trust helps collective activities, useful for wider society: providing goods, information, services, leisure, and so forth. Reversing Banfield's term it may be called "moral familism," binding the internally cohesive – family-like – groups in cohesive, beneficial ties with wider society, appearing as a quasi-family on a grand scale. Famous examples come from Japan, when the kinship structures and occupational structures intermesh, guided by the common rules of inclusive trust. Encouraging this kind of trust, turning it into the normative culture of trust, is clearly functional for the wider social system (from the axiological perspective that we have assumed).

The opposite case occurs when the internal functionality of trust (for the partners and their immediate group) does not coincide with the external functionality of trust (for the wider society and its assumed beneficial condition), but rather appears dysfunctional from that perspective. Trust assumes a localized, particular, divisive character focused on exclusion. It raises a rigid border between "us" and "them," it separates from others, is suspicious of others, hostile to others. Sometimes it even refuses the others any moral rights, including the right to existence. This kind of "sectarian solidarity" (Misztal 1996: 217) is akin to Banfield's "amoral familism." As he describes it, there is the rule to "maximize the material short-run advantages of the nuclear family; assume that all others will do likewise . . . One who follows the rule is without morality only in relation to persons outside the family – in relation to family members, he applies standards of right and wrong" (Banfield 1967: 83). Mutatis mutandis, this description fits other examples that would include the Mafia, criminal gangs, juvenile street gangs, chauvinistic ethnic communities, nationalistic movements, religious sects, football fans, and many others. More dated illustrations may come from medieval society, with its emphasis on loyalty, honor, and strong condemnation of betrayal and treachery, where trust "bound together some factions, families, corporations, or patrons and their dependents, in struggles against others" (Silver 1985: 54). In all these cases internal moral bonds are used for externally amoral purposes. Groups are pervaded with strong, but exclusive trust, directed against others. There is a highly developed within-group trust, and even full-fledged cultures of trust, but at the same time there is strong across-group distrust. In such cases "social trust may be strictly a within-group affair – ethnocentric, factionalizing, conflict-producing" (Earle and Cvetkovich 1995: 7). Undermining such internal and exclusive culture of trust would be beneficial for the wider social system.[4]

Functional substitutes for trust

Our discussion of the functions of trust has shown that – with a number of exceptions, relativizations, and reservations, that were examined – it has generally beneficial consequences for the partners in social relationships, and the groups to which they belong, as well as for the peaceful, harmonious, and cohesive quality of wider social life. The logic of functionalist reasoning leads us to suspect that, when trust is missing, the resulting vacuum will be filled with some alternative arrangements providing similar functions and meeting universal cravings for certainty, predictability, order, and the like. These are the functional substitutes for trust.

Such substitutes appear in three guises. First as individual, personal practices devised to cope with the persistent uncertainty and risk involved continuously, in the absence of trust, in all dealings with other people. "Anyone who does not trust must . . . turn to functionally equivalent strategies for the reduction of complexity in order to be able to define a practically meaningful situation at all" (Luhmann 1979: 71). Second, such substitutive practices may turn into more patterned strategies, as they become typical, and spread widely in a society. Then they provide a pool of ready-made procedures helping to substitute for the trust that is lacking. People need not invent them anew, they just imitate what other people are typically doing. Third, the typical and widespread standardized ways of coping with deficiencies of trust may acquire a normative sanction, turn into cultural rules prescribing certain conduct, or even into complex institutions designed to deal with the lack of trust. The problem is that some of these practices, strategies, and institutions are clearly pathological. Appearing as functional substitutes to correct for the unfulfilled functions of trust, they themselves produce dysfunctional consequences for the wider society.

The first adaptive reaction is providentialism: the regression from the discourse of agency toward the discourse of fate, resorting to ancient "Fortuna" rather than effort. The supernatural or metaphysical forces – God, destiny, fate – are invoked as anchors of some spurious certainty. They are thought to take care of a situation about which nothing seemingly can be done.[5] For the Italians of Montegrano studied by Banfield, "only the intervention of God . . . will restrain the mad fury of events, establish a few moments of order and predictability, and so set up the conditions under which the successful effort becomes possible" (Banfield 1967: 108). But the common people can only "wait and see." This "vague and generalized sense of [quasi] trust in distant events over which one has no control" (Giddens 1990: 133) may bring some psychological consolation, repress "anxiety, angst and dread," but at the social level it produces disastrous effects – passivism and stagnation.

The second, quite perverse substitute for trust is corruption (Elster 1989: 266). Spreading in a society, it provides some misleading sense of orderliness and predictability, some feeling of control over a chaotic environment, some way to manipulate others into doing what we want them to do. Bribes provide a sense of control over decision makers, and the guarantee of favorable decisions. "Gifts" accepted by medical doctors, teachers, bosses, are intended to guarantee their favors or preferential treatment. "The amoral familist . . . will take bribes when he can get away with it . . . It will be assumed by the society of amoral

familists that he does . . . Bribery and favoritism are widespread"
(Banfield 1967: 92). The same tissue of social bonds is replaced by the net
of reciprocal favors, "connections," barter, sick "pseudo-Gemeinschaft"
(Merton 1968: 163) of bribe-givers and bribe-takers, the cynical world of
mutual manipulation and exploitation (Gambetta 1988c: 158–175; 1993).

The third mechanism is the overgrowth of vigilance, taking into
private hands the direct supervision and control of others, whose
competence or integrity is put into doubt, or whose accountability is seen
as weak, due to inefficiency or lax standards of the enforcing agencies.
The numbers of private security forces exceeding the public police,
walled communities with sentries, the proliferation of weapons in private
hands, the installation of protective devices in cars and apartments,
private agencies for the collection of debts and enforcement of other
business obligations, using brutal methods – all those and similar
developments are clear indicators that trust has collapsed.

The fourth mechanism is excessive litigiousness. If businesspeople do
not trust their partners, a handshake will no longer do. They will attempt
to safeguard all relationships formally: draw up meticulous contracts,
insist on collaterals and bank guarantees, employ witnesses and notaries
public, and resort to litigation in any, even the most minuscule, event of
breaching trust by their partners. What the contemporary social critics
call "the increased litigiousness," "the increasing use of binding arbitration," "the rise of an interventionist judiciary" (Wolfe 1991: 8) is another
indicator of depleted trust. As Fukuyama observes: "There is usually an
inverse relationship between rules and trust: the more people depend on
rules to regulate their interactions, the less they trust each other, and vice
versa" (Fukuyama 1995: 224).

The fifth mechanism may be called ghettoization, that is, closing in,
building impenetrable boundaries around a group in an alien and
threatening environment. The diffuse distrust in the wider society is
compensated by strong loyalty to tribal, ethnic, or familial groups,
matched with xenophobia and hostility toward foreigners. People close
themselves into ghettoes of limited and intimate relationships, isolated
and strictly separated from other groups, organizations, and institutions.
By cutting the external world off, they reduce some of its complexity and
uncertainty. For example Polish emigrant groups coming to the United
States in the first half of the twentieth century have never been able to
assimilate and still tend to live in closed communities, cultivating traditions, religious faith, native language, and customs. This may be explained by the culture of distrust arising in relatively uneducated, poverty
stricken groups coming from a pre-industrial setting and finding them-

selves in an entirely new and alien social environment (Thomas and Znaniecki 1918–20).

The sixth reaction may be called paternalization. When the "culture of distrust" develops, with existential "angst and dread" becoming unbearable, people start to dream about a father figure, a strong autocratic leader, a charismatic personality (Das Fuehrer or Il Duce), who would purge with an iron hand all untrustworthy ("suspicious" or "alien") persons, organizations, and institutions, and who would restore, if necessary by force, the semblance of order, predictability, and continuity in social life. "In a society of amoral familists the weak will favor a regime which will maintain order with a strong hand" (Banfield 1967: 93). When such a leader emerges he easily becomes a focus of blind, substitute trust. "The rise of a charismatic leader (such as Sabbatai Sevi, Peter the Hermit, or Adolf Hitler) is likely to occur in a period when trust or legitimacy has been extensively withdrawn from existing social institutions" (Coleman 1990: 196). A similar craving for abdication of responsibility is also satisfied by other institutions, spreading cults, sects, "voracious communities," demanding full loyalty, and total undivided commitment (Coser 1974). They become quasi-families, with a strong substitute father taking full care of the members.

The seventh reaction may be called externalization of trust. In the climate of distrust against local politicians, institutions, products, and so forth, people turn to foreign societies, and deposit their trust in their leaders, organizations, or goods. "The consequence seems to be, whatever the arena of life in which trust is withdrawn, that there is placement of trust elsewhere" (Coleman 1990: 196). By contrast with locally targeted distrust, such foreign targets of trust are often blindly idealized, which is even easier because of the distance, the selective bias of the media, and lack of direct contrary evidence. In this vein we believe in foreign economic aid, or military assistance, the help of IMF, membership in NATO or the European Union, as providing a panacea for all our troubles.

6

The culture of trust

There are two ways in which the culture of trust may be treated. One was taken in chapter 4. The trust culture was considered as one of the foundations on which people base their bets of trust. The other foundations were the reflected trustworthiness and the trusting impulse. But neither of those foundations of trust is in fact a given. Rather, each of them is built up through complex processes. We have traced the intricate calculations involved in estimating the trustworthiness of others, and pointed to several structural and situational arrangements that push those estimates in the direction of trusting. We have sketched the path through which the trusting impulse is born and establishes itself in the individual personality, emphasizing the role of some socializing situations and contexts for stimulating trustfulness (e.g., robust family life, intimacy, and care). In the case of trust culture we have remained most vague, indicating only that it is historically rooted, and depends on a sequence of collectively shared positive experiences with trust. Now we must take the next step, and try to determine the social conditions which make such collective, shared experiences more likely, and therefore which create a context conducive for the emergence of a lasting trust culture.

The social becoming of trust

The process of the emergence of a trust culture is just an instance of a more general process through which cultures, social structures, normative systems, institutions, organizations, and all other macro-societal entities come to be shaped and crystallized. In my earlier work I have proposed a theoretical model to deal with such processes, under the label of "social becoming" (Sztompka 1991a, 1993a). I will apply and elaborate this model to unravel the social determinants of trust culture. The becoming of the culture of trust will be treated just as an exemplification of wider processes of social becoming.

There are four assumptions of the model of social becoming that are central for our further discussion. First, the driving force of social processes is human agency, that is, individual and collective actions, decisions, and choices taken by specifically endowed actors, within the framework of opportunities provided by existing structures. Second, the ongoing events making up the social praxis are always complex products of some traits of actors combined with some traits of structures, or to put it otherwise they result from the exploration of existing structural opportunities by willing and competent actors. Third, the structural context itself and the opportunities it provides are shaped and reshaped by ongoing praxis; they are the accumulated, lasting outcomes, often unintended, of the multiplicity of earlier actions. Fourth, the structural effects of past praxis, crystallized as structural tradition, become the initial conditions for future praxis, and are explored as structural resources, and this cycle proceeds interminably making all processes contingent and open-ended.

Applying these assumptions to the building of trust culture, we must first emphasize the continuity of the process, which unfolds incessantly from the past through the present toward the future. Taking the perspective of the present, we shall notice that the relevant praxis consists of actions – individual and collective – in which people deploy trust, and make the bets of trust in all three forms: placing trust, entrusting something, and evoking trust. Looking backward, toward the past, we shall see that people act within some received tradition concerning trust, that is, the prevailing cultural climate of trust, or the reverse, the culture of distrust. That surrounding normative climate makes their bets of trust more easy, or more difficult, as the case may be. Looking forward, toward the future, we shall see that those bets of trust bring some results: predictive trust is confirmed, entrusted values are returned, evocative trust is reciprocated. It may also be the reverse: predictive trust is disappointed, entrusting is abused, evocative trust is ignored. Cumulative experiences of this sort, if widespread and shared, will turn into normal routines, and eventually into normative rules. Positive experiences of confirmed trust will generate the culture of trust; negative experiences of breached trust will generate the culture of distrust. In this way the normative climate for future bets of trust will be created, the tradition of trust or distrust passed on, and the process will continue interminably.

We may note the self-amplifying sequence from previous traditions of trust or distrust to current bets of trust, and toward future cultures of trust or distrust. There is the virtuous loop that starts from an already existing culture of trust, proceeds through granting trust that is confirmed, and results in an enhanced culture of trust. There is the vicious loop, which starts from an already existing culture of distrust, proceeds through withholding trust, and results in an enhanced culture of suspicion. Now, the central moment in these sequences comes when trust is confirmed or breached. If trust is usually met – predictive trust confirmed, entrusting repaid, and evocative trust reciprocated – the process moves toward building the culture of trust, and even the vicious spiral of self-amplifying distrust may be deflected toward recuperation of a trust culture. On the other hand if trust is usually breached – predictive trust disappointed, entrusting abused, and evocative trust ignored – then the process moves toward building the culture of distrust, and even the virtuous loop of self-amplifying trust may be deflected toward the rules of suspicion.

Both historical and contemporary evidence indicates that some societies develop robust cultures of trust, whereas others are pervaded with endemic distrust. There are also some societies that evolve from the culture of trust toward the malaise of diffuse, generalized distrust (e.g., the US in the last three decades, see Bok 1979; Stivers 1994; Putnam 1995b, 1995c, 1996), and there are others that slowly leave behind the pervasive culture of distrust, acquiring growing measures of diffuse, generalized trust (e.g., the postcommunist societies of East-Central Europe, see Rose 1994; Sztompka 1995, 1996a). The search for causal factors explaining those phenomena must proceed in a structural direction with due recognition of the historical dimension and personal endowment of the agents. We must attempt to specify the wider social contexts conducive to the culture of trust, or conversely the culture of distrust, and see how their impact accumulates in time, establishing lasting traditions of generalized trust or distrust.

Are there any macro-societal conditions providing the context of actions for large masses of people, which would raise the likelihood that trust will be met rather than breached? If there are, they would provide the structural opportunities for taking rewarding bets of trust, and in effect engendering the culture of trust. The actual readiness to take such bets would still depend, though, on some widespread traits of the actors: their awareness of, and willingness to explore those opportunities. If the structural opportunities and agential resources coincide, the culture of trust is apt to emerge.

And of course these questions may be reversed to deal with distrust. Are there other macro-societal conditions that would raise the chances of the breaches of trust? And are there such agential resources, whose absence would further enhance the constraining effect of such structures? If both structural and agential factors coincide, the culture of distrust is the likely result.

Structural conduciveness

I would postulate five macro-societal circumstances as conducive to the emergence of a trust culture, through rewarding experiences of met trust; and their opposites, pushing toward the culture of distrust, through frustrating experiences of breached trust. The first is normative coherence, and its opposite is normative chaos, or anomie in the Durkheimian sense. The norms – of law, morality, custom – provide the solid skeleton of social life, and their viable enforcement assures their binding nature. This makes social life more unproblematic, secure, orderly, predictable, as there are fixed scenarios indicating what people should do and will do. Such normative ordering of social life raises the likelihood that other people will meet our expectations. The feeling of existential security and certainty encourages the bets of predictive trust. But apart from that, there are enforceable norms more immediately relevant for trust, demanding honesty, loyalty, and reciprocity. Their presence raises the likelihood of such conduct, and assures us that our bets of entrusting, as well as evocative trust, will also be met; that partners will fulfill obligations, and give us mutual trust. It is dramatically different in the condition of anomie. Here various social rules regulating human conduct, as well as agencies enforcing obedience, are in disarray. Actions become haphazard, moved by whims, momentary emotions, egoistic interests. Nothing can be predicted, except the most egoistic, self-interested conduct. The feeling of insecurity and uncertainty suggests the withholding of predictive trust (perhaps with the exception of instrumental trust, based on expectations of sheer efficiency). And the special norms dealing with honesty, loyalty, and reciprocity, as well as their enforcement, are also suspended. People lose any clear idea of binding obligations, and nobody cares to enforce them. Hence the likelihood of repaid or reciprocated trust collapses. Knowing that, nobody dares to entrust anything to others, and nobody believes that trusting may evoke mutual trust. Anomie undermines the normative tissue of social life.

The second structural condition relevant for the probability of rewarded trust is the stability of the social order, and its opposite, radical change. If the network of groups, associations, institutions, organizations, and regimes is long-lasting, persistent, and continuous, it provides firm reference points for social life, a feeling of security, support, and comfort. Repeated routines that people follow make it posssible to predict their conduct. Similarly, meeting obligations and reciprocating trust becomes not so much a matter of duty, but rather an unproblematic, habitual response. People simply do not entertain the possibility that one could act otherwise. Trust may therefore be more easily offered, as the chances that it will be met, repaid, or mutually extended, are high. As Giddens observes: "Tradition provides an anchorage for that 'basic trust' so central to continuity of identity; and it was also the guiding mechanism of other trust relations" (Giddens in Beck et al. 1994: 81). It does not mean that only a completely stagnant society is conducive to trust. Social change is compatible with trust, but only if it proceeds gradually, regularly, predictably, in a slow rhythm and consistent direction. A completely opposite situation occurs in periods of rapid and radical social change, with revolutions as their prime examples. Instability undermines the existential fabric of social life. People are suddenly faced with a totally overhauled social order: reshaped groups, new associations, institutions, organizations, regimes. Old habits, routines, and accustomed patterns of action, are no longer adequate. Feelings of estrangement, insecurity, and uneasiness arise. Everyday conduct, as well as longer life perspectives, lose their fixity and rootedness. Everything suddenly looks possible, nothing is excluded, and hence nothing can be certainly predicted. The chances that our expectations about the actions of others will not be confirmed, and therefore that our predictive trust will be breached, become high. Similarly, the chances that others will unreflectively follow the accustomed responses to entrusting or evocative trust diminish. All this fosters suspiciousness and the tendency to withhold trust. No wonder permanently changing, "post-traditional" societies are so ripe with distrust.

The third contextual, macro-societal factor relevant for the propensity to trust is the transparency of the social organization, and its opposite, the organization's pervasive secrecy. The availability of information about the functioning, efficiency, levels of achievement, as well as failures and pathologies, of groups, associations, institutions, organizations, and regimes provide a feeling of security and predictability. If their architecture, raison d'être, principles of operation, competence, and results are highly visible – openly reported, accessible to inspection, easy to understand – people are apt to relate to them with trust. They are assured about what they may expect, and even if failures or the breakdown of social organization were deemed possible, at least it would not take anybody by surprise. On the other hand if the principles of operation are vague, hard to comprehend, hidden from view, surrounded by a veil of secrecy, there is a supposition that there must be something ominous to hide; rumors, gossip, and conspiracy theories abound, and people hesitate to grant trust.

The fourth factor is the familiarity, or its opposite, the strangeness, of the environment in which people undertake their actions. We mean by the environment the immediate "life-world," natural, technological, and civilizational, that surrounds people. It includes various components: landscapes and topography, architecture, interiors, designs, colors, tastes, smells, images, and so forth. The logic behind the influence that this condition exerts on trust is similar to the earlier case of stability, as it also has to do with accustomed routine, except that it refers to situations when people find themselves displaced, in the new environment, rather than staying in their old but changed surroundings. Then it matters very much whether the new environment is similar or not to the one they are accustomed to. The feeling of familiarity breeds trust. As Giddens stresses, "familiarity is the keynote to trust" (Giddens in Beck et al. 1994: 81). It provides one with the feeling of security, certainty, predictability, comfort. In effect, it produces a trust-generating atmosphere, where it is easier to believe that trusting predictions will be borne out, that entrusted values will be cared for and returned, and that others will reciprocate with mutual trust. Business travelers and tourists usually look for the same hotel or restaurant chains, the same food, the same shops that they normally encounter at home. The consumer industry obliges, with their Holiday Inns, McDonalds, and Pizza Huts, as well as Benetton or the Gap stores to be found in practically every city of the world. And the emphasis in the advertisements is precisely that the rooms, meals, or clothes will be exactly the same as those left behind at home. On the other hand, when the environment is completely different, strange and unfamiliar, a lot of uncertainty and anxiety may be raised. People feel threatened and react with suspicion and distrust. The fate of some communities of emigrants provides a good illustration. Large sections of a classical study of Polish emigrants in the United States, by Thomas and Znaniecki, describe personal and group pathologies – loss of identity, disruption of communities, deviance, and delinquency – due in some part to the shock of completely unfamiliar new urban and industrial surroundings and alien technological civilization, but also the different landscapes into which the peasants were transplanted from their mountainous villages in the south of Poland (Thomas and Znaniecki 1918).

The fifth condition is the accountability of other people and institutions, and its opposite – arbitrariness and irresponsibility. This crucial factor was discussed extensively earlier, as the important cue to derived trustworthiness. It returns, at this phase of our discussion, in a slightly different guise. If there is a rich, accessible, and properly functioning set of institutions, setting standards and providing checks and controls of conduct, the danger of abuse is diminished, and the regularity of procedures safeguarded. If people can resort to such institutions when their rights are not recognized, or the obligations of others toward them not respected, then they acquire a kind of insurance, or backup option and therefore feel more safe. Everybody is confident that standards will be observed, departures prevented, and that even if abuse occurs it will be corrected by recourse to litigation, arbitration, restitution, or similar. This stimulates a more trustful orientation toward others. On the other hand, the lack or inefficiency of such agencies of accountability opens the door to complete arbitrariness of actions. Nobody can be sure whether others will not chose to harm their interests and, if that happens, whether they will have recourse to any superior body. If the only guarantee of everybody's rights rests in their own hands – because dependable arbiters do not exist, or are inaccessible, or are notoriously partial and unfair – people feel helpless. Suspicion and distrust will become a natural response.

Personality syndromes and social moods

The five macro-societal conditions indicated above – normative coherence, stability, transparency, familiarity, and accountability – provide the opportunities conducive for making the bets of trust, because they raise the chances that those bets will be won. But ultimately the bets are made by the people, so their decisions and choices are decisive. And those decisions and choices hinge upon the personal characteristics they have. In line with the theory of social becoming, the actor's endowment joins structural opportunities in producing a specific praxis. There are two types of characteristics that seem to count most for the praxis of trust. There is first a certain personality syndrome correlated with trustfulness. It includes, as most directly relevant, the trusting impulse discussed earlier, plus probably such personality traits indirectly linked with readiness to trust as general activism rather than passivism, optimism rather than pessimism, future orientation rather than a presentist or traditionalist orientation,[1] high aspirations rather than low aspirations, success orientation rather than adaptive orientation, innovative drive rather than conformity-proneness. The opposite syndrome seems to contribute to the emergence of a culture of distrust. Together with

suspiciousness and distrustfulness, it would include passivism, pre-
sentism, low aspirations, adaptive orientation, conformism. It also
possesses a self-enhancing capacity.

For such personality syndromes to contribute to the emergence of the
culture of trust, they cannot be sporadic or idiosyncratic, but rather have
to be widespread, common, typical for a given society (or a community
or group). Once they spread, a self-amplifying process starts to operate:
The syndromes are enhanced by imitation and mutual confirmation.
Spreading in the population, such complex personality syndromes turn
into a phenomenon of a macro-societal order, which may be called social
moods. The etiology of such moods is too intricate, and too little known,
to be touched on here. For our purposes we have to stop our retro-
gressive explanations here, and take this phenomenon for granted.

There seems to be no doubt that societies differ significantly in this
respect, and that the same society may experience different social moods
in various moments of its history.[2] It also seems uncontestable that such
different social moods facilitate or hinder the emergence of the culture of
trust.

Personal and collective capital

The other personal factors making people more capable and willing to
use the opportunities provided by the structural environment conducive
to trust, refer not so much to what people are (their personality traits),
but rather to what they have (their personal capital). People differ
significantly in the pool of various assets or resources that they
command: money and good looks, power and health, prestige and
friends – just to mention the first that come to mind. Several authors
observe that the command of such resources raises the readiness to
extend trust.

In my own research, several correlations supported that view. At the
most general level, the belief that "most people can be trusted" was
accepted by 43.6 percent of the elites and only 31.0 percent of the
unemployed, 38 percent of the highly educated and 33 percent of the
uneducated. The levels of trust toward various specific targets were also
shown to vary positively with the levels of personal capital. Thus, for
example, trust toward the government, the courts, the Catholic Church,
teachers, managers, and foremen is significantly higher among the
educational and occupational elites of high socio-economic status, than
among the unemployed and workers in low-level, badly paid jobs.

As the causal link between the two, Luhmann suggests self-confidence, which is enhanced by rich resources and in turn makes one more prone to take the risks involved in trusting others (Luhmann 1979: 78). Giddens takes the self-concept to be the mediating link between resources and trust, arguing that as self-concept is increased by the possession of vast resources, one has a more open, optimistic, compassionate, relaxed attitude and that translates into more trust toward others (Giddens 1991: 79). In my own research I have discovered a third causal mechanism, quite similar to the one suggested by Giddens. When I asked about the feeling of being trusted by others, I found very significant correlation between high estimates of one's own trusted status, and such variables as income, level of education, and a prestigious job (only 19 percent of the poor but as much as 45.1 percent of the rich believe that others strongly trust them, for the uneducated versus educated the numbers are 20.7 percent and 35.4 percent, and for unemployed versus occupational elites, 17.5 percent and 36.6 percent). Now assuming, as we did before, that trust is reflective, that is, that being trusted encourages trustfulness toward others, we would expect those with high resources to be more trustful.

I would also suggest a fourth causal mechanism contributing to the same effect of personal resourcefulness. The assets we possess serve as a kind of insurance of our trust, because they lower our relative (subjective) vulnerability in case trust is breached. Having large resources we have backup reserves, the potential losses mean less to us, and thus our relative (subjective) risk is lowered. This predisposes us to more uninhibited bets of trust.[3] For example, for a multi-millionaire to risk a million or two in new investments is a relatively easy decision, because the possible loss is endurable. It is easier for a supermarket to expose goods to the customers at the risk of theft, than for a corner grocery. The opposite logic operates in case of poor resources. People devoid of backup resources tend to be distrustful (suspicious, susceptible to conspiracy theories, hesitant to extend trust). This is because for them a possible breach of trust could mean a relative disaster. Of course the individual "disaster thresholds" differ depending on the levels of poverty, but generally the fewer resources people command, the higher their readiness to withhold trust. Luhmann gives two relevant examples: "subsistence farmers are highly averse to risk because they are under constant threat of hunger, of losing their seed, of being unable to continue production," and similarly "entrepreneurs facing liquidity problems are less willing to take risks than those who are not plagued by this problem when the risk is of a given magnitude" (Luhmann 1994: 2–3).

There is also a fifth mechanism, again suggested by my own research. When the context of accountability was discussed above as an important factor explaining the readiness to trust and lowering the risk of trusting, I hinted that the access to such institutions of accountability, insuring people against the potential breaches of trust (courts, the Ombudsman, arbitration agencies, insurance companies, consumer protection associations, etc.), is unequally distributed. Some people have easier access than others, and make use of such institutions more often. And here personal capital enters as an important mediating variable. In my research, the elites, educated, and rich much more often indicated various backup institutions as those to whom they would resort in case of some personal loss or calamity (e.g., 76.1 percent of the rich would be ready to resort to litigation in court, while 53.2 percent of the poor would consider this option, for elites versus unemployed the percentages are 76.2 and 61.2, for highly educated versus uneducated – 72.3 and 58.2). This applies to losses incurred by breaches of trust, and suggests that the presence of the context of accountability will evoke stronger tendencies to be trustful among those who see better chances of actually using it, thanks to their higher personal capital.

For the emergence of the culture of trust, it is not the individual, idiosyncratic resourcefulness that matters, but rather the typical level of resourcefulness, shared by the members of a society. In other words it is not the personal capital of this or that member, but the collective capital:[4] an emergent aggregate of individual resources typically possessed by societal members.

There is a vast array of resources that may be included in this category. But for the emergence of the culture of trust, only some of them seem to be particularly relevant. Let me hypothetically list those which provide people with the strongest backup insurance of their bets of trust. We have already mentioned wealth. "Those low on the socioeconomic ladder are, not surprisingly, somewhat more likely than others to feel that people will not try to be helpful . . . Their class position has probably created situations in which distrust and pessimism were realistic" (Mansbridge 1983: 111). And the opposite effect is due to the high socioeconomic position.

Another factor of similar importance is a good, secure job. As work occupies such an important part of human life, a stable and reliable occupational position is crucially important as the base, from which one may project a more trustful orientation toward the world. Research consistently shows high levels of distrust among the unemployed. It seems a plausible hypothesis that it is the dramatic spread of unemployment in East Germany, reaching and in some regions exceeding 20 percent, that is partly responsible for the endemic culture of distrust. But it is not only the sheer fact of employment that counts, but also the stability of employment. It may be hypothetically suspected that the highly developed trust culture in Japan has something to do with the common practice of lifelong, assured employment.

A factor related to occupation is the plurality of social roles that individuals play, a richness of their position-set. The more roles one plays, the less one is dependent on each, particular role. Rose Laub-Coser argues that such a situation raises individual autonomy, because one is less bound by the role demands emitted from each single status (Laub-Coser 1975). There is a possible substitution of one role for the other, if for some reason one role is no longer attractive. One of such reasons may be breached trust. For example, if I give lectures at two universities, and one of them does not pay me in time, or refuses to pay my travel expenses, as I initially expected, it is easier for me to resign and overcome that breach of trust, if I have an alternative job.

The next important resource is power. This is for two reasons. First, because power is one of the most convertible types of capital, and therefore may hedge our bets of trust in various domains. And second, because sometimes it may be directly used to coerce others into trustworthy behavior, to enforce the meeting of obligations. It is particularly true in cases of entrusting some valuable goods to others. Creditors are more ready to extend trust if they have some power over the debtor, which may be used if necessary to recover the debt. For example, I am more willing to lend a precious book to my student than to my neighbor, because in the former case I have some means of pressure or coercion in my hands, while lacking those in the latter case.

Education is rather akin to power. This factor plays multiple roles in the generation and deployment of trust. It is crucial for making discerning and adequate estimates of trustworthiness. Therefore it makes one more confident of not falling into the trap of naive, blind trust, or obsessive distrust. With that assurance, extending trust comes easier. But also, like power education is a highly convertible resource. It may guarantee higher socio-economic status, it may be a springboard to power, it opens the variety of occupational options, and allows more flexibility in changing occupational choices if trust placed in some is not met.

Another important resource is social networks, or "connections."[5] My research shows that those are closely correlated with other forms of personal capital. When asked about "acquaintances that may help in solving problems one encounters in life," 35.4 percent of the rich, and only 11.7 percent of the poor declared that they have them. For highly educated people the percentage was 28.2 and for uneducated 15.4; for the occupational elites 36.6 percent and for the unemployed or those employed in menial jobs 16.5 percent. Tested business partners, professional colleagues, "invisible colleges" of scholars working in the same field, dependable friendship circles, "old boys" networks, help to develop trustfulness in two ways. First, the interactions within such networks are usually pervaded with trust, and often with met, returned, or reciprocated trust. Thus they provide a good breeding ground for the generalized propensity to trust, a good "school of trust." But they also influence trustfulness in a different way, namely by bolstering the feeling of rootedness, security, solidarity, and potential support in the case of various life calamities, some of which may derive from breaching of our trust. Thus their existence encourages easier expanding of trust to partners or social objects external to the networks themselves. For example, I am more ready to enter a foreign, unknown, and risky market if I am strongly attached to a viable business community in my own country. It was quite striking that asked about the secrets of their commercial successes, the leading industrialists in postcommunist Poland almost unanimously mentioned personal networks at the top of their lists. My research shows that among occupational elites and the rich, this factor locates high among the factors "most important for life success" (with about 50 percent of indications), but is outranked by education (with about 70 percent of indications), and diligence (with about 60 percent of choices). The proliferation of such networks in various domains of social life increases the chances for the emergence of a culture of trust.

The other social resource relevant for trust is a robust family. Of course, family life links with trust in many ways. One of these was discussed earlier, when the family was seen as central for the emergence of trusting impulse, or basic trustfulness. The family obviously serves as a ground for everyday testing of particularly intimate and intense trust. But here we have in mind the importance of a strong, extended family as a kind of springboard for the "leaps of trust" in various external domains of life, beside the family. Family support allows many young people to take quite risky and easily breached bets of trust about their future employment, by choosing certain courses of prolonged education. Similarly, family resources are crucial in making the bets of marriage and establishing new households. The tradition of pooling resources from the extended family, and delegating one member to start a commercial or industrial enterprise, typical at one time in Italy, has recently re-emerged in Poland, where a number of new capitalist ventures were possible only through tapping the savings of wide, extended families. In case of adversities, some of which may be due to breached trust, a healthy family always provides ultimate support. It seems plausible to suspect that one of the reasons why children from broken families or single parent families, or those who have completely severed ties with their families, manifest strong levels of distrust, is to be found precisely in the lack of that ultimate support or backup insurance that the family usually provides.

In my own research it seems that the family and close friendships provide a crucial substitute capital resource for those who lack higher socio-economic status. Among the unemployed, family and friends are indicated by 42.7 percent and 35 percent respectively as the potential source of support in case of losses or other calamities, and among the occupational elites, only by 28.7 and 27.7 percent. Similarly among the poor, the percentages are 37.7 and 31.2, and among the rich 28.0 and 28. In a more direct probe, the view that "in our times one may trust only the family" is supported by 23.4 percent of the poor, and only 14.6 percent of the rich, 27.2 percent among the unemployed and 13.9 percent among the elites, 22.1 percent among the uneducated and 16.4 percent among the highly educated. Even stronger differences appear when the particularly demanding and risky form of trust, namely entrusting something valuable, is considered. The view that "one can entrust an important secret only to a member of the closest family" is supported by 23.3 percent of the unemployed, and only 7.9 percent of the occupational elites, and the statement that "the care of the children can be entrusted only to the closest family" is fully accepted by 30 percent of the unemployed, and only 16.8 percent of the elites.

Similar reasons make religious belief another important factor in strengthening inclinations to trust. My research shows that the statement: "all people can be trusted" is supported by 38 percent of practicing Catholics, and only 27.6 percent of atheists. The feeling of support and security may have metaphysical sources in religious faith, the belief in the special care that God extends to his faithful. But apart from that, religious people may feel more secure and trustful for earthly, socio-logical reasons. They are similar to those relating to networks and families. In fact the metaphors of the family commonly apply to the domain of religion: the terms "Holy Father," "brothers and sisters in faith," "children of God," intuitively grasp this similarity. Namely, the integration into tight religious communities – churches, sects, and so forth, like membership in strong networks and robust families – gives people a feeling of rootedness, solidarity, mutual support. They are not left on their own, they feel they can rely on other members of the church, or priests, or the church hierarchy when in need. Apart from that, religious communities provide a quasi-familial context for intense and intimate interactions pervaded with trust. In this way they become a training ground, another "school of trust."

In this chapter we have drawn a hypothetical model describing the emergence of trust culture. The "social becoming of trust" starts from some inherited level of trust culture: the tradition of trust or distrust. Then the actual structural circumstances – normative coherence, stability, transparency, familiarity, accountability, or the lack thereof – raise or lower the likelihood of rewarding, positive experiences with trust, bets of trust being met or breached. These opened or closed structural opportunities for easier venturing of trust are taken or ignored, depending on the endowment of the actors. Social moods, emerging as the collective outcomes of trustful or suspicious personality syndromes typical for multiple societal members, may encourage or block the crystallization of a trust culture. Similarly, the collective capital, emerging as the aggregate of various resources possessed by societal members, provides the security of insurance and backup options, if sufficiently rich, or the insecurity and helplessness if sufficiently poor. Accordingly it stimulates or hampers the appearance of the culture of trust. This sequence is presented in diagram 4.

Once the culture of trust or distrust emerges, it becomes a background condition for the next cycle of the social becoming of trust. Thus the model incorporates four sets of variables in its processional, sequential interlinkages: the background variables (pre-existent traditions of trust or distrust), the independent variables (structural opportunities for positive or negative experiences with trust), the mediating variables (social moods and collective capital encouraging trustfulness or suspiciousness). The model provides a framework, within which the decisions to trust or distrust are taken, accumulate, and acquire normative sanction, turning into cultural rules of trust or distrust. Each of those decisions involves estimates of trustworthiness, taking into account all the manifold cues analyzed earlier in the book. Thus the substantial content, the real flesh of the formal framework provided by the model, is the incessant process of appraising "reflected trustworthiness" in each individual case, when granting or withdrawing trust is considered as an option. The culture of trust or distrust is an emergent, cumulative product of the myriads of such decisions. But once it emerges, it acquires independent force, pushing the decisions in the direction of trusting or distrusting, and in this sense supplementing and modifying the calculation of trust.

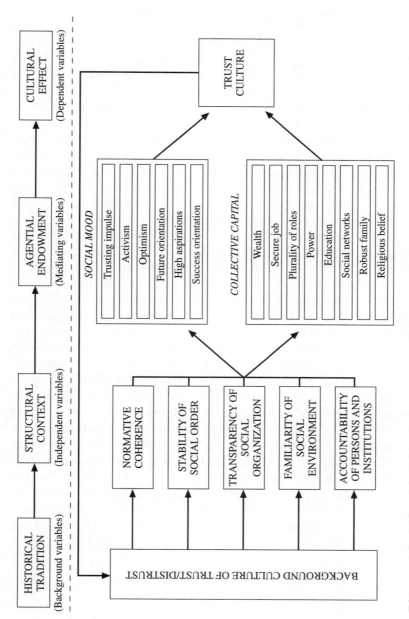

Diagram 4: Social becoming of trust culture

Tentative implications for policy

Every explanatory model has some practical implications. It indicates what are the crucial areas that should be targeted by the policy. Let us see what the model presented here tells us about the possible practical measures to produce or sustain the culture of trust.

The model, as was emphasized earlier, represents only one link in the continuous chain of social becoming. It operates under some given, received conditions and it produces the outcome, which turns into initial conditions for the next phase. For the sake of our discussion let us take as the starting point the situation of considerable collapse of trust, the pervasive distrust syndrome inherited from the earlier phases of the process. For example, such was the dominant condition of East-Central European societies immediately after the events of 1989, with their strong legacy of distrust inherited from the communist period. This example will be explored in detail in chapter 8, so if we take such a starting point in our considerations now, the analysis will be immediately applicable then.

If our purpose is to restore and rebuild the culture of trust, the focus of the policy should obviously rest on the variables considered as most causally effective for producing trust. The five categories of conditions that we listed under the heading of structural conduciveness, are potentially sensitive to practical intervention, and particularly to institution-building efforts. Through "learning pressure" (Offe and Preuss 1991: 145), the reshaped institutions are able to reshape the ways of life of the members of society into larger trustfulness and trustworthiness, more readiness for giving and meeting trust. Once the structural environment is reconstructed and social and political conditions conducive for trust are instituted, it will act as the first push toward continuous rebuilding of trust. The virtuous, self-fulfilling mechanism will be switched on, because trust, once implanted, breeds even more trust. Let us review the five independent variables of our model once again, with a view to practical means for exerting a trust-building influence. The more concrete recommendations are relevant for the illustrative case of postcommunist transition in East-Central Europe, but may be applicable – mutatis mutandis – to other areas.

Shaping institutions

To enhance normative coherence, the core instrument of political influence is legislation. There must be a consistent effort to make the system of law coherent and non-contradictory, simple and not overloaded, transparent and not secret, persistent and not transient. The law must become a solid foundation of consistency and stability of the whole social organization. Once law approaches this ideal, it exerts influence on other extra-legal forms of normative regulation, moral and customary. It provides a sort of pattern to which those other systems of rules adapt.

To strengthen the feeling of stability of the social order, consistency and irreversibility of policies must be safeguarded. The constitution and the solid framework of immutable laws, which are not subjected to ad hoc, opportunistic changes or adjustments, provide the main guarantee of that. In the case of postcommunist societies it means guaranteeing the persistent pursuit of democratic and market-directed reforms. They must be followed according to a clear pattern, blueprint, or logic. They must document the unwavering, reform oriented will of the authorities, by means of creating fait accomplis and pre-commitments. Hesitation, ad hoc reversals, slow downs on the democratic course, must be avoided. People must feel that the authorities know what they are doing and where they are going, that they have a clear program and can execute it with strong political will. The atmosphere of tentativeness, of trial and error, of another grand "political experiment" must be eliminated, even if that provides the politicians with easy excuse for their failures. Jon Elster makes an excellent point: "The very notion of 'experimenting with reform' borders on incoherence, since the agents' knowledge that they are taking part in an experiment induces them to adopt a short time horizon that makes it less likely that the experiment will succeed" (Elster 1989: 176).

To raise the transparency of a social organization, governmental actions must be made as open and visible as possible. An efficient media policy aiming at that must be worked out and implemented. Pluralistic independent media and autonomous institutions for gathering statistical data, census offices, and reform-monitoring centers must be developed. Politicians must be made more familiar by disclosing some aspects of their private lives. Continuous polling, monitoring, and reporting of the public mood must become the rule. Survey results feed back to the public and eliminate the unawareness of the opinions of others, the pattern of "pluralistic ignorance," so detrimental for trust.

To give a flavor of the familiarity and intimacy of the surrounding life-world, perhaps the crucial factor is the behavior of those who represent institutions in daily contact with the citizens, those who work at the "gates" of huge, impersonal structures of contemporary society: administrative officers, clerks, police officers, bank tellers, nurses and doctors, customs officers, sales persons, tax collectors, teachers and professors, priests, and the like. Their attitude toward clients or customers should be kind, helpful, understanding, cooperative. All of them operate at "access points" to the systems (Giddens 1990a: 90). Their demeanor may exude trustfulness – when they show professionalism, seriousness, competence, truthfulness, concern with others, readiness to help. On the other hand, any bad experiences at "access points," any frustrating contacts – even when vicarious, through the media, and not personal – are immediately generalized to the whole system, according to our hypothesis of "bottom to top" contagion of distrust. "Attitudes of trust, or lack of trust, toward specific abstract systems are liable to be strongly influenced by experiences at access points . . . Bad experiences at access points may lead either to a sort of resigned cynicism or, where this is possible, to disengagement from the system altogether" (Giddens 1990a: 90–91). The extensive training, meticulous screening, highly selective recruitment to all positions of high social visibility – including first of all the political offices – is a prerequisite for generalized, institutional, and positional trust.

For enhancing accountability, the most important task is to consolidate democratic institutions. As will be argued in detail in chapter 7, there is an intimate link between democracy and accountability. From the very top of the political system, democratic governments are accountable through elections, the division of powers, and mutual checks and balances, as well as the constitutionalism and rule of law, binding them equally as citizens. The crucial role is played by judicial reviews of legislation, independent courts, as well as the efficiency of enforcement agencies of all kinds. This structural framework must be filled with appropriate actions. And thus in legislation and application there must be no place for voluntarism, arbitrariness, or ad hoc, opportunistic stretching or modifying of laws. The immutable principles of the constitution must precisely define the foundations of a social and political organization, and include provisions preventing easy amendments; they must have the aura of being infinite. The laws must be applied equally for all citizens irrespective of their status. Enforcement of laws and citizens' obligations must be rigorous and must not allow for exceptions. Strong measures must be taken against crime. But on the other hand, the fundamental rights of citizens have to be assured. In the condition of postcommunist societies, perhaps most important is the right to private property. Consistent privatization and constitutional affirmation of private property are necessary. Clear and precise financial laws, banking statutes, and trading codes must safeguard the security of investments and economic transactions. Strict and consistent currency policies must restore the faith in local money.

Educating for trust

So far we have discussed factors having to do with the structural, institutional environment of actions. But our model suggests that equal attention should be given to the actors operating in these environments. The most important institutional measures intended to shape their personal endowment relevant for being trustful and trustworthy, fall under the aegis of education. Educating for trust includes a number of aspects.

First, there is education in a general sense: raising public enlightenment (factual knowledge), as well as moral sensitiveness. To build trust, "an educated and discerning public is needed" (Giddens 1991: 173). "Indeed, cognitive competence is essential for effective citizenship, in close inter-action with moral sensitivity and imaginative insight" (Bellah et al. 1991: 178). It is a prerequisite for "paying attention" and formulating informed judgments that are "fact-regarding, future-regarding, and other-regarding" (Offe and Preuss 1991: 155). Only a considerable level of education makes it possible to avoid the pitfalls of naive, blind trust and obsessive, paranoic distrust. Education must be treated as the core aspect of "cultural citizenship" (Lash in Beck et al. 1993: 123).

Second, there is the implicit teaching of trust in healthy, close, and intimate family life. "The psychological development of a propensity to trust involves extensive investment, especially by others, such as parents" (Hardin 1993: 515). Intimate family life is a crucial early force in shaping trust (Eisenstadt and Roniger 1984: 31). All political measures at-tempting to improve the condition of the family are therefore indirectly helpful in building trust.

Third, there must be a direct emphasis on trust at schools. It is crucial to build and sustain trust in the relationships of teachers and pupils, as well as among the school kids themselves. There is also a space in the school curriculum, particularly in the study of history and literature, to emphasize exemplars of trust.

Fourth, to raise the importance of trust in people's perception, one of the possible measures is evoking tradition, emphasizing continuity of life-ways, rules, customs. "In traditional societies there is more ontological security and trust. Where tradition rules, the future is at least in part predictable, it will follow traditional ways" (Giddens 1991: 48). While traditional society cannot – and perhaps should not – be regained, it may be imaginatively recreated in vicarious experiences – art, literature, media – with the emphasis on trust, honor, loyalty, and other traditional virtues.

Fifth, an attempt must be made to link trust in people's imagination with other available moral resources. For example, much can be gained by the recourse to religion, and borrowing from it the emphasis on metaphysical trust, as well as on the more earthly virtue of trusting others. Religion may also provide a pool of persuasive exemplars and arguments for trust, to be found in the conduct of the martyrs, saints, prophets, and heroes. "If we are lucky enough to live in a society which holds some moral and religious beliefs – a side effect of which is to motivate cooperation for its inherent virtues – we can make good use of them" (Gambetta 1988b: 224). "Trust may emerge as a by-product of moral and religious values which prescribe honesty and mutual love" (Gambetta 1988b: 230).

Sixth, the public debate, both directly and through the media, must be open to the issues of trust and distrust, and their current illustrations. What Bok calls "public discourse about moral choice," is "needed in classes, in professional organizations, in government" (Bok 1979: 103). "Basically it is through the exercise of such appeals and the debates that they engender that a more finely tuned moral sense will develop" (Bok 1979: 98).

Seventh, there must be the education for trust not only by precept, but through everyday experience. Trust must be shown to pay, by being rewarded, and breaches of trust must prove to be costly, by being punished. "Throughout society . . . all would benefit if the incentive structure associated with deceit were changed: if the gains from deception were lowered, and honesty made more worthwhile in the short run" (Bok 1979: 260). An instrumental value of trust, as an ultimately profitable way of conduct, must be demonstrated. Trust must be linked with self-interest. For example to raise the trust in the regime or government it would be advisable to "encourage citizens to participate on the instrumental ground of furthering their interests and checking that their interests have indeed been furthered" (Parry 1976: 142). And conversely, the agencies of social control – formal and informal – must ensure that breaches of trust are condemned and simply do not pay.

7

Trust in democracy and autocracy

In this chapter we are going to explore the place of trust in two opposite forms of political system: democracy and autocracy. The relationship is believed to be intimate and mutual. The political system is viewed as embedded in culture, including the culture of trust. This embeddedness manifests itself in two ways. On the one hand, trust is considered as the prerequisite for political order. "A system – economic, legal, or political – requires trust as an input condition. Without trust it cannot stimulate supportive activities in situations of uncertainty or risk" (Luhmann 1988: 103). "Trust is a necessary condition for both civil society and democracy" (Rose 1994: 18). "Democracy requires a degree of trust that we often take for granted" (Bellah et al. 1991: 3). On the other hand, trust is considered as a product of a political order of a particular type. Usually democracy is seen as the regime most conducive to the emergence of trust. To summarize current belief: trust is produced by democracy, and helps to sustain democracy. Let us look at both sides of the equation, starting from the generation of trust by a democratic regime.

Democracy begets trust

I shall claim that all other things being equal, the culture of trust is more likely to appear in a democracy than in any other type of political system. Let us trace the mechanism through which this effect is produced. It seems that a democratic regime bases its trustworthiness primarily on two of the criteria discussed in chapter 4: accountability and pre-commitment. First, democracy provides a rich context of accountability. "Rulers are best trusted when the rule of law can be relied upon to force them to abide by their trust . . . It is still permissible to trust one's rulers, but only as a consequence of one's confidence in political mechanisms"

(Parry 1976: 139). In a democracy we rely not on the elite's "ethic of responsibility" but rather on a political, constitutional "machinery of accountability" (Parry 1976: 141). "Democracy is only a safeguard against the abuse of power, not a guarantee that it will be used wisely" (Benn and Peters 1977: 351). "When I trust a political official who may be held at least somewhat accountable for failing to fulfill my interests, we are related in our intentions, though we may never meet" (Hardin 1991: 191). Second, democracy through the emphasis on binding and stable constitution, creates the context of pre-commitment. Constitutionalism is the guarantee of continuity and persistence of the political system, as it preempts or limits the possibilities of its change (Przeworski et al. 1995: 50). "Merely institutionalizing government and the implementation of policies should lead to greater stability of expectations, and hence to greater trust" (Hardin 1991: 204).

The first paradox of democracy

There is a paradox involved here. The emphasis on accountability and pre-commitment means that trust in a democratic regime is due precisely to the institutionalization of distrust in the architecture of democracy. "A democratic polity requires legitimate criticism based on democratic allegiance; some distrust, in this sense, is essential for a viable democratic order" (Barber 1983: 81). Most of the principles constitutive of democratic order assume the institutionalization of distrust, which provides a kind of backup or insurance for those who would be ready to risk trust, a disincentive for those who would contemplate breaches of trust, as well as a corrective of actual violations of trust, if they occur. In effect the spontaneous, generalized, culture of trust is likely to emerge. In brief: the more there is institutionalized distrust, the more there will be spontaneous trust.[1] I refer to this as the first paradox of democracy.

Principles of democracy: institutionalizing distrust

Let us now examine more closely some of the fundamental principles of democracy, and see how they imply institutionalized distrust. Perhaps the most important is the principle of legitimacy. The fundamental premise of democracy is the suspicion of all authority. Democracy requires justification of all power, which *per se* is seen as suspect (Holmes 1993: 24). It is only when the authority is shown to emanate from the popular will, through elections, and when the elected representatives of the majority realize the interests of the people, that the government is recognized as legitimate.[2] But even here, "institutionalized doubt" persists. The majority itself is shifting, it is an "unstable aggregate, whose members, motives and interests will vary from day to day, and whose concern for the interests of any given individual may be no greater than the autocrat's" (Benn and Peters 1977: 323). And the representatives of the majorities may not fulfill their mandate. Therefore the democratic system allows institutions of civil disobedience,[3] or revocation of representatives, which assume the possibility of breaches of trust, and provides corrective mechanism, for such contingencies. "Both legislative and executive may be held to account by the community if they act in breach of trust" (Parry 1976: 131).

Second is the principle of periodical elections and terms of office. This shows distrust in the willingness of the rulers to surrender their power voluntarily and to subject their performance to periodical scrutiny. It is assumed that they will incline to the temptation to preserve their privilege, and this tendency is institutionally prevented by the mechanism of the turnover of power. "Rationally grounded trust in officials . . . requires that the officials be responsive to popular needs and desires. To have incentive to be responsive, they must be somehow accountable, most plausibly, perhaps, through competitive elections" (Hardin 1991: 204). It is also the existence of an opposition contesting for power that guarantees permanent critical monitoring, checking, and prevention of abuses by those in power (Benn and Peters 1977: 281).

Then there is the third principle, the principle of division of powers, checks, and balances, and limited competence of institutions. This clearly implies the suspicion that institutions will tend to expand, monopolize decisions, abuse their powers. The mechanism of mutual controls is explicitly constructed and sanctioned, among different institutions, branches of government, and so forth.

Fourth, there is the principle of the rule of law and independent courts. Legislators are subject to the same laws that they themselves institute. This implies distrust in the spontaneous good will of citizens and institutions alike. To prevent arbitrariness, abuses, and deviant acts, both must be subjected to the common, universally binding framework of law. "Legal norms of procedural fairness that structure state and some civil institutions, limit favoritism and protect merit are the sine qua non for society-wide 'generalized trust,' at least in a modern social structure" (Cohen and Arato 1992: 27). Law is situated above the individuals and institutions, including governmental agencies. They are all equally bound by law, and equally responsible before the law. "We should not ask about a politician whether we would buy a second-hand car from him but whether we would be adequately protected by a Sale of Goods Act if he sold us a bad one" (Parry 1976: 142). Various safeguards of the autonomy of courts are intended to guarantee that laws will be impartially enforced (Holmes 1993: 47). All these measures contribute to the emergence of system-wide trust: "The law may protect civil rights, freedom, and property even in the face of political opportunity. Thereby, it may create a confidence in the legal system and in positions of security which then makes it easier to place trust in other relations" (Luhmann 1988: 194).

The fifth is the principle of constitutionalism and judicial review. It implies distrust in the integrity of legislating bodies, which may be tempted to bend the laws to their particularistic interests, or to change the laws opportunistically. Hence the need for the "basic law" above all specific regulations, preempting the easy possibility of its change and making a sort of pre-commitment for the future (Przeworski et al. 1995: 50). The institutions protecting and supporting the constitution, by interpreting and enforcing its precepts, are usually supreme or constitutional courts or tribunals.

The sixth is the principle of due process. Some measure of distrust extends even to the law enforcing and arbitrating institutions themselves. Even the courts are not beyond suspicion of partiality or negligence. Hence the need for the institution of appeal, and sometimes several grades of appeal, before the rulings become valid and binding.

The seventh is the principle of civic rights. This implies the distrust in the spontaneous good will of authorities in satisfying the needs and interests of the citizens. It also implies that citizens may be subjected to abuse by the authorities. Such possibilities require a mechanism through which the people must have measures to demand such satisfaction, and protect themselves against abuse. Safeguarding the civic rights in the constitution, opening the possibility of suits against public institutions, establishing the office of the Ombudsman, or in some countries even allowing a direct "constitutional suit" against the state, are meant to meet this need.

The eighth is the principle of law enforcement. This implies distrust in the spontaneous following of laws by citizens. At least some of them may be suspected of non-compliance or disobedience. Hence there must be mechanisms for checking whether the citizens' duties are fulfilled, and of enforcing them if necessary. Those who choose not to meet their obligations toward the state and toward fellow citizens must be made to do so. The establishment of such institutions as the police, public prosecutors, tax collectors, and the like, serves this purpose.

The ninth is the principle of open communication. Neither all people nor all institutions can be trusted to be truthful, open to argumentation, recognizing the views of others. There is the need to counter the temptation toward censorship, indoctrination, limiting free expression of opinions, dogmatism, or outright deception that may occur both with authorities and citizens. The defense of tolerance, open debate, pluralistic and independent media is necessary to safeguard the fundamental operational principle of democracy, which is the search for truth, compromise, or consensus. The very existence of the "fourth estate" of the media, and protection of its autonomy, provides a powerful check against abuses of power, biases, and prejudices.

The tenth is the principle of community politics. Democracy opens opportunities for mass involvement and activism of citizens through voluntary associations, civic organizations, and local power. This is taken as an antidote against bureaucracy and self-serving state and administrative apparatuses. Civic groups take the duty of controlling, monitoring, and exerting pressure on public authorities. All this assumes distrust of the state and the administration. Other groups that flourish in a democracy are consumer protective associations, trade unions, sectional associations, interest groups, and lobbies. Again they assume distrust, this time in the ability of the government and public authorities to care sufficiently for sectional, particular interests (Benn and Peters 1977: 281). There are two additional mechanisms that enhance general trust: first, the support in a rich network of associations adds to "personal capital," and gives each member the feeling of more security and therefore raises readiness to be trustful; and second, delegated local powers signify some measure of trust of the government toward the citizens. Like all credits of trust, it may produce the obligation to reciprocate and raise trust in government. Trusted citizens extend trust more readily.[4]

These constitutive principles of democracy obviously relate to the structural, contextual conditions conducive for the culture of trust, which have been analyzed in chapter 6. They help to establish normative certainty, transparency of social organization, stability of the social order, accountability of power, enactment of rights and obligations, enforcement of duties and responsibilities, and the personal dignity, integrity, and autonomy of the people, as well as their feeling of empowerment. To put it briefly: people are more prepared to trust institutions and other people if the social organization in which they operate insures them against potential breaches of trust. Democratic organization provides this kind of insurance.

Democracy in action

So far our discussion has been carried out at the ideal-typical level. We have reconstructed the normative model of democracy, and it was shown to be a potentially powerful factor in generating the culture of trust. But the actual emergence or decay of trust is contingent on the manner in which democratic principles are implemented, the way in which they operate in social and political life. It seems that in order to evoke a strong culture of trust, two operational conditions must be met. On the one hand, democratic principles must be dependable, that is, applied consistently, invariably, and universally. But on the other hand, the checks and controls they involve must be applied sparingly, as a kind of last resort or backup option.

For the undermining of trust and spreading of cynicism, probably nothing is more dangerous than the violations and abuses of democratic principles. When people live in a democracy, they develop a kind of meta-trust, trust in democracy itself as the ultimate insurance of other kinds of trust they may venture. Once this meta-trust is breached, and the insurance defaults, they feel cheated. This is immediately reflected in all other relationships where they invested trust; the culture of trust is shattered (Offe 1996: 34). It may perhaps be argued that the failure of democracy is more destructive for the culture of trust than an outright autocratic regime. In the latter case, people at least know what to expect, they have no illusions, whereas in the former case their hopes are disappointed and their expectations violated, producing even stronger disenchantment.

The typical failures of "democracy in action" (as opposed to "democracy in codes") may be listed in the order of ten fundamental principles of a democratic system and their possible violations. First, the legitimacy of the authorities may be fragile. One typical case occurs when low electoral participation and proportional electoral laws produce the effect that large segments of society feel unrepresented and the authorities are in fact elected only by a minority of the population. Another case is the deficiency of the procedures leading to the revocation of representatives and public officials, when in spite of their manifest failures in office they are not deposed. Second, the turnover of power may be impeded. One way is by manipulation of electoral law in a way that raises the chances for re-election for ruling groups. Another example is the prolongation of the term of office (e.g., the president for life), even if it is done in a formally correct fashion, through a former change of laws. Third, some branches of power (e.g., the executive, the military, the secret police) may acquire preponderance over others, undermining the mechanism of mutual checks and balances. Fourth, equality before the law may be violated by the use of double standards, depending on the political clout of the villain, leading to the immunity of bureaucracy, unpunished breaches of law by public officials, and so forth. Fifth, the constitution may be interpreted or even changed in an arbitrary manner, retroactive legislation practiced, the verdicts of the constitutional tribunal overruled by the legislature. Sixth, opportunities for appeal may be limited, the period of custody prolonged, the conditions of serving prison terms may be inhumane, and parole unattainable. Seventh, civic rights may be purely declarative, due to the lack of resources for their implementation, or the means of effective claiming. Eighth, law enforcement may be lax, the enforcing agencies inefficient or corrupt, with a permissive atmosphere emerging. Ninth, the pressure on the media may lead to more or less masked forms of censorship, selective bias, curbs on critical messages. Tenth, the prerogatives of local power may be curbed, and the influence of citizens' voluntary groups limited. Centralization or even oligarchization of rule may lead to the decay of civil society.

The impact of these and similar abuses of democracy on the culture of trust depends on their scale: whether they are sporadic or permanent, incidental or common. It also depends on their visibility: the awareness of the abuses by large segments of the population. Usually the existence of vigilant opposition as well as pluralistic and autonomous media provide for such visibility. If the failure of democracy is widely perceived, generalized trust is replaced by pervasive distrust. On the other hand, if the abuses of democracy are hidden from view, and the people keep faith in a democratic facade, their trust is blind or naive. It is also very fragile, as the shock of disclosure is sooner or later inevitable, and then it has a devastating effect on trust.

The second paradox of democracy

For a generalized culture of trust to develop and persist, democratic principles need not only be implemented consistently, but also applied sparingly. Democratic principles institutionalize distrust because they assume that trust can potentially be breached and provide correctives for such a contingency. The fact that the principles are put to use, that the corrective mechanisms are activated, controls actually applied, indicates that trust had in fact been breached. As long as this happens sporadically, exceptionally, as a last resort, the culture of trust is not undermined, but rather enhanced by the confirmation of effective accountability. But there is some threshold where this may backfire and the trend reverses itself. Hyperactivity of correctives and controls indicates that there is perhaps too much to correct. For example, if citizens constantly resort to litigation and the courts are flooded with suits, if the Ombudsman is overloaded with claims, if the police are overworked and prisons overcrowded, if the media constantly detect and censure political corruption, and citizens denounce or revoke their compromised representatives, then obviously something is wrong with the system, and the culture of trust may easily break down. "When regulation and litigation become ways of life, distrust comes to dominate social interaction" (Earle and Cvetkovich 1995: 66). This becomes a signal for the citizens of prevailing untrustworthiness. To be pervasive and lasting, trust cannot be due merely to efficient controls. Rather, it must see in the potentiality of controls only the ultimate defense against unlikely and rare abuses of trust. Institutionalized distrust breeds spontaneous trust most effectively as long as it remains latent, at the level of normative institutionalization, and does not turn into actual, routine practice. This I would label as the second paradox of democracy: the extensive potential availability of democratic checks and controls must be matched by their very limited actualization. Institutionalized distrust must remain in the shadows, as a distant protective framework for spontaneous trustful actions.

Depending on the ways in which democratic corrective mechanisms are actually implemented, two alternative loops of self-amplifying causality may be initiated – the vicious or the virtuous one. When the culture of distrust prevails, the apparatus of enforcement, enactment, and control is mobilized. Its hyperactive operation seems to signal to the people that their distrust was warranted, that breaches of trust are pervasive, and such perceptions only enhance and deepen the culture of distrust. This is the vicious circle. On the other hand, when the culture of trust prevails, the apparatus of enforcement, enactment, and control is resorted to only occasionally. Its subdued operation suggests to the people that their initial trust was warranted, that breaches of trust are rare, and such perceptions obviously enhance and deepen the culture of trust. This is the virtuous circle.

Trust as a prerequisite for democracy

Let us look now at the other side of the equation. It is not only that democracy engenders trust, but also, once in place, the culture of trust helps to sustain democracy. There are some fundamental practices of democracy that cannot and will not be followed without some elementary measure of trust (Cladis 1992: 213). Lucien Pye distinguishes two types of political cultures: "those built upon the fundamental faith that it is possible to trust and work with fellow men" and those built upon "the expectation that most people are to be distrusted and that strangers in particular are likely to be dangerous" (Pye and Verba 1965: 22). It is the former one that he associates with democracy. What are those democratic practices requiring a measure of trust?

First, democracy requires communication among the citizens: the exchange of opinions, the formulation of political choices, the articulation of political support, and so forth.[5] By encouraging interactions, making them more uninhibited and spontaneous, trust facilitates communication. "Mutual communication required in a polyarchy best occurs where men trust one another" (Parry 1976: 129). Trust also allows us to assume that partners are truthful, serious, and authentic in the opinions they formulate. To put it briefly, trust helps us to speak, but also to listen.

Second, democracy requires tolerance: acknowledgment of differences, recognition of plurality of opinions, lifestyles, ways of life, tastes, and preferences. As we have argued before, trust provides people with more security and certainty, and so makes it possible to embrace differences as opportunities rather than threats.

Third, democracy replaces conflict and struggle by compromise and consensus, as the main mechanisms of formulating policies, and taking decisions. Every compromise and consensus is possible only if partners accept some commonly binding rules of the game, some common platform on which they may build mutually acceptable solutions. The minimum of trust they must have refers to the mutual willingness to obey such meta-rules (e.g., the rule of freely presenting their standpoints, of deciding by majority vote). Trust also allows us to assume the integrity and good will of others.

Fourth, democracy demands some level of civility of public disputes: focusing on the subject, avoiding ad hominem attacks, recognizing the dignity of the opponent, and so forth. Mutual trust seems indispensable for that. "A feeling of trust prevents political disputes from turning into severe enmity" (Parry 1976: 129).

Fifth, democracy requires participation: it needs active citizens, ready to get engaged in the democratic institutions, as well as the associations and organizations, of civil society. Citizen participation – electoral, self-governmental, associational, and so forth – requires some measure of trust in the political regime, fairness of the rules, the potential effectiveness of their efforts. It also requires at least a minimum of trust in their fellow citizens. "Men need to trust one another if they are to associate together in the achievement of those objectives which they cannot gain by their own individual action" (Parry 1976: 129).

Sixth, democracy requires educated citizens. Effective democratic participation, even in the basic form of elections, demands a considerable amount of information, knowledge, evaluative and discerning capabilities. To acquire civic competence, people have to trust the sources of political information and knowledge: to believe in the truthfulness and authenticity of public messages, the credibility of the media, accuracy of statistical data, adequacy of personal information about candidates for offices, and so forth.

Trust in autocracy

Trust operates entirely differently in autocratic regimes: despotic, dictatorial, totalitarian systems. Whereas, as we have shown, democracy institutionalizes distrust, and only as a paradoxical consequence, through the establishment of accountability and pre-commitment, begets trust, autocracy attempts directly to institutionalize trust, and turn it into a strongly sanctioned formal demand. There are two types of objects for such demanded trust. One is the monarch, dictator, leader, charismatic ruler. Trust takes here the paternalistic form, is highly personalized, and unquestionable. It is often blind, ignoring any relevant evidence about the deeds or misdeeds of the ruler. In fact it may even be improper to make any estimates or evaluations, not to speak of any critique. One trusts the ruler unconditionally, not because of what he does, but because of who he is, just as one trusts one's father, a priori and without any proofs of trustworthiness really being needed. Another object of institutionalized trust is the whole system of authority: feudal monarchy, or national socialism, or dictatorship of the proletariat, or socialist "democracy," and so forth. Its principles are not questionable, they are rooted in dogmatic ideologies and treated as final truths. What is in effect demanded is total and unconditional support for the rulers and the system of rule.

The institutionalization of trust, in those two forms, proceeds through a double mechanism: first, through political socialization, indoctrination, censorship of the media, closing the flow of information from the outside; second, through rigid political control, harshly punishing all breaches of trust, like dissidence, contestation, and opposition, and even milder doubt and criticism.

If the institutionalization is successful, and the unreflective trust installed, there seems to be no need either for accountability, nor for pre-commitment. Just the reverse, arbitrariness becomes the principle of power. The architecture of the polity is constructed in directly opposite ways than in the case of democracy. And thus, first, the legitimacy of the regime is based on ideological indoctrination and coercion. The people are considered as the trustees of the rulers, rather than the rulers being the representatives of the people. Second, power does not know temporal limitations, like terms of office, and tends to perpetuate itself. Third, there is no division of power, and all branches if at all distinguishable are fully subjected to the executive. Fourth, the laws, if at all articulated in more permanent form, are only applied to the citizens, and even that on particularistic, and not universalistic grounds. They certainly do not embrace the rulers. Fifth, the will of the ruler substitutes for the constitution, and of course it cannot be subjected to any judicial review or other controls. The existence of a legal opposition is inconceivable. Sixth, the procedures carried out by the rulers and touching the citizens are arbitrary. There is no due process. Seventh, citizens have no rights, and hence no claims, to the spontaneous and whimsical benevolence of the ruler. Eighth, law enforcement is equally arbitrary, and citizens cannot depend on state protection in case their interests are endangered by other citizens. Ninth, the flow of communication is mostly one-directional, from the top downwards, and fully controlled by the rulers. Tenth, any forms of community politics – local government, civic groups, social movements – are actively discouraged or entirely forbidden.

There are two main reasons why institutionalized trust is highly fragile, and easily collapses. One is the immediate result of the arbitrari-ness, distance, opaqueness, unaccountability, uncertainty, implied by autocratic politics. According to the same logic that we proposed with respect to the trust-generating features of democracy, but operating with the opposite "vector," the autocratic regime breeds pervasive distrust. The second reason has to do with the mechanism of reciprocity. Even if institutionalized, trust is unilateral, directed upward toward the rulers and the regime, it is not coupled with reciprocal trust of the rulers toward the citizens. The citizens are treated with suspicion, a permanent pre-sumption of disloyalty, disobedience, and guilt.[6] Therefore they are under constant surveillance and control. As we have argued on numerous occasions earlier, just as trust breeds trust, distrust produces mutual distrust. Too much surveillance, control, and coercion by the rulers has a boomerang effect: the perception of suspicion, manipulation, and deception produces resentment and cynicism, and undermines trust in authority. Widespread distrust in political authority, which the political scientists label as the withdrawal of legitimacy, is found to accompany most autocratic regimes. This is the paradox of autocracy: institutionalized trust produces pervasive distrust. Quite often this is of course not enough to undermine autocratic regimes. Sheer coercive power may suffice to keep them going for a long time as fully oppressive governments, without any pretensions to the continuing support of citizens.

When spontaneous trust becomes depleted and institutional trust collapses, substitute functional adaptations are apt to emerge. Three of them are most common. First, providentialism with its recourse to fate, and passive, resigned acceptance of the existing conditions. Second, corruption (bribery, favoritism, nepotism), which replaces all normal channels of power and influence by the pleasing of authority and purchase of favors. Third, ghettoization, when people escape from the public domain to the only remaining enclaves of closeness, familiarity, and security, namely families and friendships.

8

Trust and rapid social change: a case study

In this chapter we shall attempt to illustrate and corroborate some of the theoretical analyses of trust by selected historical and empirical evidence. It seems a sound assumption that most social phenomena and processes are most open to scrutiny in conditions of deep and rapid social change. When the tempo of social becoming accelerates, and its scope broadens, the causal mechanisms of social life are more salient, the variables take more extreme forms, the dynamics are easier to grasp. This must undoubtedly refer to the vicissitudes of that "fragile resource" of trust: its emergence or decay.[1] Accepting such a rationale, I have selected as a "strategic research site" for this empirical glance at trust, the current transformations in East-Central Europe following the collapse of communism.[2] I shall trace the fluctuations of trust and distrust in the period preceding the revolutionary events of 1989, during those events, and particularly in the present phase of the construction and consolidation of democratic and market regimes of the Western type. Do the concepts and models developed in this volume help to explain the complex trajectories of trust and distrust in the postcommunist world? The account will refer specifically to Poland but, with necessary corrections for local historical contingencies, it may also have relevance for other societies of the region. Thus, I propose to present a sketch of history with a key. The historical events will only provide a necessary background, and the focus will rest on the intangible "climates" of trust or distrust. This will be a bird's eye view of the recent history of Poland seen from a "soft" culturalist perspective.

From communist rule to anti-communist revolution

The historical flow is continuous; it knows neither beginnings nor ends. But in order to write about history, one must cut into that flow at a certain moment and choose a conventional starting point for the narrative.

The background for the story I wish to tell is provided by the experience of a communist regime which, in Poland, was imposed after World War II, as the result the Yalta and Potsdam agreements between the winning powers. In the theory of social becoming that I have proposed in my earlier work (Sztompka 1993a, 1995), trust, like all other cultural and structural ingredients, is treated as a product of accumulated historical experiences. The traces of earlier events are sedimented in institutions, rules, symbols, beliefs (e.g., law, morality, custom, doctrines, ideologies, religious creeds), as well as in the minds of social actors (e.g., their typical mentalities, knowledge, orientations, preferences). Common experiences produce common structural, cultural, and mental patterns. And these in turn provide the encountered (constraining or facilitating) conditions for future actions. The bridge between the influences of the past and the evolving future is provided by generations: congeries of people who – in their formative years – happen to be exposed to similar, significant social forces, and experience the same important social events. There is a "generation effect, when a particular age cohort responds to a set of stimuli . . . and then carries the impact of that response through the life cycle" (Almond and Verba 1980: 400). This explains how the influences of some former, and already replaced, structures may still be felt in the present.

Bloc culture

Several generations coming of age during the period of communist rule have been exposed to a unique culture-generating setting of a vast scope: the communist bloc (perhaps the closest historical analogy would be the cultural complexes of huge ancient empires). Imposing Soviet institutional and organizational forms, similar life-ways and ideologies on a number of nation-states of Eastern and Central Europe, and enforcing them for several generations, the communist regime succeeded in creating a common cultural framework, over and above distinct national cultures, and relatively insulated from the wider global culture: the unique syndrome of values, rules, norms, codes, and standards typical for the bloc as a whole. Even though there were obvious national varieties in the rigidity and style in which those cultural precepts were implemented (DDR was not the same as Hungary, Poland was not the same as Czechoslovakia, etc.), there were also fundamental, underlying commonalities. Life under so-called "real-socialism" has produced the unique legacy of a peculiar cultural-civilizational syndrome. "Russians are not only Russian, nor Poles Polish, Germans German, nor the lot of them simply human. They are residents of societies which all underwent between 40 and 70 odd years (very odd years) of communist rule. This was something special that they had in common, and that other societies did not have" (Krygier 1995: 7). This may be labeled as the characteristic "bloc culture." The more dominant the bloc culture was over indigenous, national traditions (through coercive indoctrination), and the more it was insulated from global cultural flows (through imposed isolation), the more powerful and devastating that syndrome became. Its grip on thoughts and actions outlives the system that brought it about and weighs on current democratic reforms: "The basic problem which the reformers must recognize has to do with the fact that everyday actions of individuals will be modelled by habits developed in the course of social experiences radically different from those which should fill out new institutions" (Marody 1990: 167).

One of the components and consequences of bloc culture was the widespread erosion of trust. How has this result been produced? Among many aspects of bloc culture, which I analyze elsewhere (Sztompka 1991a, 1993a), some seem to be immediately responsible for the decay of trust.

The most fundamental and lasting cultural code organizing thought and action in the conditions of real-socialism was the opposition of two spheres of life: private (personal) and public (official). As Stefan Nowak puts it: "The life of the average Pole is lived in the two, overlapping worlds: the domain of private contacts and the institutional-official sphere" (Nowak 1987: 30). This opposition appears in a number of guises: "society versus authorities," "nation versus state," "the people versus the rulers," "us versus them." To put it in more theoretical language, we may use Talcott Parsons' terminology, recently applied for similar purposes by Jeffrey Alexander, and define the common core of all these phrasings as the dichotomy of "particularism versus universalism" (Alexander 1990). Following Alexander's hunches a step further we may also notice that the opposition has an unambiguous evaluative, moral flavor (Alexander 1991, 1992; Alexander and Smith 1993). The private (particularistic) sphere is the domain of the good – of virtue, dignity, pride; whereas the public (universalistic) sphere is the domain of the bad – of vice, disdain, shame. Activities carried out in the private sphere are elevating, while any contact with the public sphere is – to use another of Alexander's terms – "polluting." There is a clear "cultural bias" (Thompson et al.

1990) toward the private world, and away from the public world. Perhaps Durkheim would accept treating the former as the domain of the "sacred," and the latter as the domain of the "profane." This polar, binary opposition is the central organizing principle, the core cultural premise on which the whole discourse of real-socialist society is founded. If one agrees with Alexander that the affirmation of universalism is the distinguishing trait of democratic discourse (Alexander 1990), then the discourse of real-socialist society is shown, not surprisingly, to be basically anti-democratic. No wonder that we shall find it standing in the way of democratic reforms, even when the institutional surface of the autocratic regime has been crushed.

Two manifestations of the dichotomy of "public and private" seem most consequential for the decay of trust. First, in the area of beliefs, the most vicious was the double standard of truth: official and private. It was manifested in the obvious discrepancy between official statistics and everyday observations, the messages of the media and common knowledge ("TV lies!" was the common wisdom), official scientific claims and censored truth (typical in the case of biased historiography, ideological social sciences, dogmatic philosophy), and even – especially in the Stalinist period – between accepted art styles (so called "socialist realism") and the spontaneous creativeness of artists. In effect there was a generalized distrust in everything that was linked to the state and its institutions, and by contrast a naive faith in all information coming either from private sources, or from external media (e.g., Radio Free Europe, Voice of America, Deutsche Welle). An often noted vulnerability to all sorts of rumors and gossip – even the most far-fetched – testifies to this condition of cognitive chaos.

Second, in the area of action, devastating effects were produced by autocratic rule (in the brief period up to the middle fifties coming close to the totalitarian model, but later, after the death of Stalin and a wave of pro-democratic movements in 1956, much more liberalized). The despotic or paternalistic style of politics meant that citizens were subjected to voluntaristic and arbitrary policies, the criteria of political or administrative decisions were secret and entirely opaque, procedures and rules were inconsistent, and bound to expediency as defined by the rulers. This produced widespread apathy and passivism, coupled with anxiety, uncertainty, and suspiciousness. Authorities – both central and local – were perceived as alien and hostile; the government was seen as the arena of conspiracy, deceit, cynicism, or at least stupidity and inefficiency. Trust in the whole social order, its continuity and predictability, was undermined.

Fluctuations of trust

Against this background of the communist past, I choose to begin the account in the second half of the seventies. It will be taken to be phase one in our short history of trust. The relative prosperity and liberalization under the rule of Edward Gierek was accompanied by the growing optimism and aspirations of the population. In the nationwide survey carried out in 1975, 92 percent of the respondents perceived economic and social developments to be more rapid than before, 16 percent believed that their life conditions would improve radically during the next five years, and 65 percent that they would improve slightly (Sufin 1981: 6). This mood suddenly changed in 1976 when economic recession set in and the government raised food prices. That year 72 percent of the nationwide sample perceived difficulties in the further development of the country (Sufin 1981: 166). A wave of strikes and popular protests broke out and the striking workers of the cities of Ursus and Radom were harshly repressed. This was the moment when organized democratic opposition was finally crystallized in Poland, in a coalition between groups of intellectuals and some sections of the working class. Its main pillars were KOR (Committee for the Defense of the Workers), and KPN (Confederation of Sovereign Poland) (for a detailed account see Ekiert 1996: 230–236). Polish sociologists describe the popular mood as one of widespread alienation, deep frustration, or the pervasive feeling of deprivation relative to earlier rising expectations. The theoretical accounts of the situation attain a deeply critical edge. Leszek Nowak (1991) formulated the theory of "triple power," which claims that the communist party is a unique ruling center monopolizing political rule, economic command, and ideological control at the same time. Jan Lutyński analyzed the varieties of "fake actions" (Lutyński 1977). This concept signifies puzzling ritualistic activities devoid of any intrinsic meaning or purpose at all. Their meaninglessness is clearly recognized by the actors, but also – paradoxically – by the authorities who expect or demand them. A classic case is that of the reports on the realization of production plans, almost unexceptionally exaggerated and skewed. Stefan Nowak advanced the idea of a "sociological vacuum," understood as the missing sphere of civil society between state institutions and the families (Nowak 1979).

A profound distrust syndrome emerged and became rooted in the culture. There was a deep decay of trust in the public sphere (the communist party, the regime, the ruling elite), with a complete shift of trust to the private domain (the primary groups – family, friends, neighbors). An escape into the private domain was a typical reaction to the situation. The opposition of "us," the people, and "them," the rulers – deeply rooted in Poland's unfortunate past full of foreign domination and oppression – attained its strongest form. There was a complete separation between public authorities and private citizens. With the atrophy of an intermediate sphere of "civil society,"[3] loyalties and commitments were withheld from public institutions and turned exclusively toward families and private networks. The normative, and not just factual, aspect of this condition is seen in the fact that trusting the state or the ruling party was considered as naiveness or stupidity, and actively supporting the regime was seen as treason. On the other hand, opposing the state, "beating the system," or at least outwitting the authorities – even by illegal, or illicit means, evasions of laws, and so forth – became a widely recognized virtue. Sociologists have given this a name: "parasitic innovativeness" (Marody 1991: 238). This may be a euphemism for downright cheating or fraud. But it may also take more subtle forms. One is the search for loopholes in legal regulations; a rather easy job considering the legislative chaos, antinomies, inconsistencies, and excessively casuistic, detailed character of "socialist law." Another mechanism produces widespread "institutionalized evasions of rules"; and those are partly due to intentionally loose or otherwise inefficient enforcement. Finally there is a constant vigilance against expected irrational changes in terms of trade – higher prices, taxes, duties – with the attempt to beat them by hoarding food, or gasoline, or rushing to import or export goods, or opening businesses oriented for quick profit rather than long-term investment. The prevalence of such "grab-and-run" attitudes shows that most people try to attain their private goals "in spite of the system" rather than "through the system." It is interesting to note that such actions are often treated as virtuous, and those who are successful inspire wide esteem, tinged with envy. The underlying, more or less conscious justification is based on the belief that it is a sort of equitable retribution against the system, which is cheating the citizens, and a way to obtain some vindication of benefits unjustly lost.

There are striking similarities between this orientation and what Banfield diagnosed, in a completely different context, as "amoral familism." Among his peasants of Montegrano – just as among the Poles in the seventies – he observed "a pathological distrust of the state and all authority" (Banfield 1967: 36): "it will be assumed that whatever group is in power is self-serving and corrupt" (Banfield 1967: 99). Therefore, "for a private citizen to take a serious interest in a public problem will be regarded as abnormal and even improper" (Banfield 1967: 85), and "the claim of any person or institution to be inspired by zeal for public rather than private advantage, will be regarded as fraud" (Banfield 1967: 95). One has to agree with Rose that "distrust is a pervasive legacy of communist rule" (Rose 1994: 18). In Poland it reached its peak at the end of the seventies.

Phase two demonstrates the significance of contingent events. The election of the Polish cardinal Karol Wojtyla as Pope John Paul II, and his subsequent pilgrimage to Poland in 1979, led to a dramatic change in popular spirit.[4] Two rich traditional resources of communal bonds, that had been partly dormant, were masterfully reawakened and linked by the Pope: nationalism and Catholicism. There was a tremendous outburst of national pride, religious emotion, and interpersonal solidarity. The quality of trust found so far only within the close networks of family and friends extended to wide segments of the population. A family-like solidarity was rediscovered on a much wider social scale, private trust was raised to the level of national-religious community. To paraphrase Banfield, one may say that "amoral familism" of the exclusive, defensive, negative kind turned into "moral familism" of a much more inclusive, positive sort.

Less than a year later, in August 1980 "Solidarity" (Solidarność in Polish) was born, the greatest political movement of modern history, embracing at its peak almost ten million enlisted members. With its working class core, it extended to all other classes and became a truly nation-wide force. It also attempted to become an international "family," with a manifesto inviting membership from other neighboring countries. As its name indicates, the movement was based on strong interpersonal bonds, a consensus on basic values, and pervasive mutual trust among the members. Wlodzimierz Wesołowski describes the "Solidarity ethos" in this way:

It focused on certain fundamental values in social thinking. These included national independence, human dignity, societal solidarity and fair industrial relations . . . It was determined to avoid the distinction between leaders and led. Accordingly, workers reached decisions in their factories by means of direct democracy. Further, it was assumed that everyone viewed the situation in the same way and had the same goals. Personal contacts mattered a great deal . . . All these were strong communal elements.   (Wesołowski 1995: 113)

To the nationalist and religious, the third powerful bond was added: the class solidarity of state employees directed against the monopolistic employer.[5] On all three counts the state became the object of deepest distrust. It was seen as a foreign imposed power oppressing the nation, as an atheist conspiracy suppressing religion, and as a greedy employer exploiting the workforce. Thus the clear-cut polarization of two cultures appears: the culture of trust pervading the popular movement, and the culture of distrust toward the regime. This is an aspect of a wider phenomenon that Charles Tilly identified at the roots of every revolution, namely the "duality of power," "a break of the polity into at least two blocs" marked by: "(1) the appearance of contenders, or coalitions of contenders, advancing exclusive competing claims to control of the state, or some segment of it; (2) commitment to those claims by a significant segment of the citizenry; (3) incapacity or unwillingness of rulers to suppress the alternative coalition and/or commitment to its claims" (Tilly 1993: 10–11).

Phase three was the last-ditch attempt of the regime to defend itself through the imposition of martial law in December 1981 (for a detailed account see Ekiert 1996: 256–282). In spite of the relatively low level of repression and its highly selective application, distrust toward the regime had reached its peak. The battle front between "us" and "them" was defined in even more unambiguous ways. People were made to define their ideological and political options. Many of those who so far supported or passively accepted the regime were pushed toward the opposition; the communist party itself was decimated. As a reaction to the birth of Solidarity and particularly to martial law, in the period between 1980 and 1986, 1,160,000 members left the communist party (Ekiert 1996: 276). The forced demobilization of the democratic movement revived narrow, exclusive forms of "familism." The process of "internal exile" led to complete detachment from public life, and closing behind the confines of family or friendship circles.[6] Only the core of committed activists persisted in oppositional struggle. In conditions of conspiracy and combat, the logic of polarization prevails, the world is seen in black-and-white terms, neatly divided into friends and enemies, "us" and "them." "Who is not with us, is against us" is the main principle of demarcation. In such a world, trust is generally inadvisable. Suspension of trust, caution, and suspiciousness is the most rational policy, because naive trust may be highly dangerous. This initiates another self-fulfilling mechanism of mutual distrust; as the hostile parties become more cautious, secretive, and distrustful, it provides evidence for the opposite party that they have something to hide, some wrong intentions, or vicious schemes. And the distrust is strengthened.

Phase four was the slow regrouping and revival of the movement as repressions were lifted, and the economic crisis heightened by martial law provoked repeated strikes and demonstrations by the working class. "The post-martial-law state failed to deliver on its promise to stabilize the economic situation and to revert the progressing collapse of the Polish economy" (Ekiert 1996: 265). The anti-regime mood became widespread. In 1988 93.9 percent of respondents blamed economic and social problems on the mistaken decisions taken by "wrong people at the wrong places," 88 percent on "bribery, corruption and abuse of power for private benefits," and 95.3 percent on "overgrowth of bureaucracy" (Koralewicz and Ziolkowski 1990: 62). A new phenomenon was the crisis of morale and undermining of the mutual trust within the ruling groups. This was partly due to the change of the geo-political environment brought about by the "Gorbachev phenomenon" and the loss of external legitimacy due to his revocation of the "Brezhnev Doctrine." It was also partly due to the obvious failure to control society internally, and to suppress the re-emerging democratic opposition, even by the strongest measures of martial law. "The civil society that became conscious of itself after August 1980 could not just be bottled up to die" (Ost 1990: 155). The split between the hard-liners and reform-oriented, liberal-democratic wing within the communist party became obvious, with the latter's ranks growing fast. This led to the fateful decision to enter "round-table" talks with the opposition in February 1989. Any ideological pretensions were abandoned, and the communist rhetoric was fully replaced by nationalist and pragmatic discourse. The negotiated pact opened the door to semi-free elections, with the participation of oppositional groups including the relegalized Solidarity, but guaranteeing one third of the mandates in the lower house to the communists.

Phase five was marked by the sweeping electoral triumph of Solidarity in June 1989. The morally broken communist party, left only with its non-democratically guaranteed pool of mandates, accepted the first non-communist government and dismantled itself in January 1990. The collapse of the communist regime was a time of an unprecedented eruption of the national and religious community. "We are finally in our own house" became the slogan of the day. "Today, the communism has died" declared a famous actress on public TV. This was the time of revolutionary enthusiasm, elation, excitement, exhilaration, and effervescence (it may be called the "five E syndrome"). "We," the people, had won against all odds, and contrary to most expectations. The victors could afford to be magnanimous, and to open the ranks of "us" even to their former enemies. National solidarity reached its peak, and with the policy of the "thick line" cutting off the past, declared by the first democratic Prime Minister Tadeusz Mazowiecki, it embraced even the earlier rulers and their supporters. Another pilgrimage of the Polish Pope provided an opportunity for a symbolic demonstration of national and religious unity. The intense trust for the first time assumed both forms: horizontal, among the people, cutting across all social divisions, and vertical, toward our own, democratically elected representatives and the government led by Solidarity. The immediate postrevolutionary regime commands trust by contrast, whatever its actual performance, due to the sheer fact that it replaces the old and distrusted regime. In other words, the trust put in the first Solidarity dominated government of Tadeusz Mazowiecki in post-1989 Poland was determined more by the fact that it was postautocratic, than that it was pro-democratic. With time the strength of this negative asset diminishes, the old regime as the comparative negative framework fades away, and people look for positive achievements. Apart from personal failures or mistaken policies, the immediate postrevolutionary situation is not conducive to any perceivable improvements in life standards. Just the reverse, there soon appeared a "sharp decline in real incomes, the rapid growth of unemployment, new social inequalities and rising insecurity" (Ekiert and Kubik 1997: 1). This was to some extent due to the necessary radical, market-oriented economic changes introduced with the so-called "Balcerowicz plan" (known also as the "big-bang approach" or "shock therapy"). The new politically active generations were no longer comparing the present with the past, but looking toward the future for betterment. As it seemed to come too slowly, trust was eroded and distrust started to grow.[7]

The pains of transformation and the collapse of trust

The enthusiasm and celebratory atmosphere that accompany a revolution never last for long. The radical transformation of the economy, polity, and culture toward democratic and capitalist forms requires time. And it does not proceed smoothly, without frictions, blockages, backlashes, and huge social costs. Phase six of our story covers the early nineties. The "post-revolutionary malaise" or "the morning after syndrome" (Sztompka 1992), set in, and with that a profound collapse of trust. "The integration of Polish society which resulted from the rejection of the Party-and-State system, and the elation following its abolition, gives way to social disintegration and the diversification of interests" (Kolarska-Bobińska 1994: 12).[8]

The diagnosis

Evidence for that can be sought in three directions. First we may examine inferential indicators. If our theoretical assumptions about the functional substitutes for trust are correct, the decay of trust will be marked by the spreading of such phenomena as providentialism, corruption, vigilantism, paternalism, and the externalization of trust. Second, we may look at some behavioral indicators: what people actually do, or seem ready to do, or more precisely, typical modes of actual or intended conduct, which would signify the lack of trust. Third, we may examine verbal indicators: straightforward declarations or evaluations of various aspects of social life, elicited by surveys and opinion polls, in which various types of distrust find more direct articulation. Thus, we can see how the postcommunist populations adapted to the new conditions, what they did and thought in the period immediately following the change of regime, and in this evidence unravel what might be the signs of deep distrust.

Several functional substitutes can be observed, indicating the deficiency of trust. First, the retreat from the discourse of agency (reaching its peak in 1989) back toward the discourse of fate is perceivable in survey results. In 1994, 68.3 percent of respondents from the city of Warsaw believed that "the planning of the future is impossible because too much depends on chance," 74.2 percent agreed that "most people do not realize how their lives are guided by chance," and 62.8 percent claimed that "most of us are victims of forces which we can neither understand nor control" (Marody 1996: 216). The behavioral symptom of these beliefs was an eruption of gambling. The popularity of games of chance (Lotto and others), the emergence of casino chains and bingo establishments, as well as TV programs providing a virtual experience of winning (e.g., by watching the "Wheel of Fortune" or many similar entertainments), may be indicative. In 1990 one fourth of the nationwide sample (26 percent) declared that they had purchased some sort of lottery ticket (CBOS Bulletin No. 8/1998: 8).

Second, people were clearly aware of spreading corruption, nepotism, and favoritism. In the nationwide poll carried out in 1992, 86 percent of respondents defined corruption as a very grave social problem, and 54 percent claimed that giving bribes was the only effective way to deal with the administration, even in simple and uncontroversial cases (CBOS Bulletin, April 1992: 40–42). As the domains of life where corruption is most pervasive, the respondents indicated the public and governmental sphere: administration and public institutions (44 percent), courts and judiciary (41 percent), police (39 percent) (CBOS Bulletin No. 5/1994: 113). Third, distrust in the social order and public safety was visible in the spread of all sorts of self-defensive and protective measures. Vigilance developed as a functional substitute for trust. The sales of guns, gas sprays, and personal alarms the installation of reinforced doors, specia-lized locks, and other anti-theft devices in homes and cars; the training of guard dogs; building walled and heavily guarded residences and con-dominiums, have grown into a flourishing business. There has been a real eruption of private institutions and organizations, making up for the undependable operation of state agencies: private security guards, detective agencies, debt collectors, and so forth.[9] There has also been an increase in voluntary associations aimed at the defense of citizens against abuse: consumer groups, tenants' associations, creditor groups, tax-payers' defense organizations, and the like.

Fourth, the externalization of trust is visible in expectations of foreign help from governments and international agencies, dependence on foreign investments, and high support for joining NATO or the Eur-opean Union. More than 49 percent of people were aware of European integration treaties, and 48 percent declared a positive view of the European Union and its policies. As many as 80 percent would like Poland to join the European Union, and 43 percent opted for doing it immediately (Central and Eastern Eurobarometer, No. 3, Feb. 1993). The support for joining NATO was even stronger, as the result of pervasive external distrust toward Russia and other post-Soviet repub-lics. But this substitution of external for internal trust was also mani-fested in consumer behavior. People consistently preferred foreign over local products, even of comparable quality, and even if local prices were lower. This refers equally to agricultural products, food, clothing, and technical equipment, all the way to automobiles. The positive stereotypes of foreign nations and firms as producers of the best goods are common and uncritically accepted: German precision, Japanese innovativeness, French comfort, Italian style; and more specifically Mercedes as a synonym for the best car, IBM of the best computers, Sony of the best audio-visual equipment, and so forth. Another sign of externalized trust is to be found in investment decisions. Among those who saved, foreign currency was still considered more dependable by a large segment of the population, in spite of much lower interest rates compared to local currency. Approximately 36 percent of all savings were put into foreign currency, most of that in US dollars and Deutsche Marks (*GW*, April 3, 1994), and 25 percent of Poles believed that saving in dollars is the best defense against inflation (CBOS Bulletin, January 1994).

Fifth, the craving for paternalistic care, strong rulers, and simple solutions of economic problems opens the doors for all kind of populists and demagogs. There is still a persistent expectation, typical of the old regime, "that the state is responsible for all aspects of economic and social life and, therefore, should solve all problems" (Ekiert and Kubik 1997: 26). This attitude explains perhaps why assuming that the wages were equal, 65 percent of people said they would choose to work in a state-owned enterprise, and only 15 percent a private one (CBOS Bulletin No. 4/1995: 98). The case of Stanislaw Tyminski, the businessman from Canada who was able to draw almost one fifth of the electorate in the presidential elections by empty promises of immediate prosperity, seems a telling indicator of that populist claimant orientation.

Let us turn now to behavioral indicators: the typical forms of conduct manifested by members of society. Perhaps the strongest sign of generalized distrust in the viability of one's own society is the decision to emigrate. This is the clearest form of the "exit option" (Hirschman 1970), which people take when life conditions become unbearable and no improvement is in sight. The stream of refugees fleeing East Germany in 1989 via Budapest; "boat people" escaping Haiti, Cambodia, Vietnam, or Cuba; or Mexicans slipping through the American border, are strong indications that the people had lost any "internal trust" in the political or economic system of their own society. At the same time, the functional substitute of "external trust" develops: either in the vague, diffuse notion of the "free world," "the West," and so forth, or in the more specific idea of a targeted, most attractive country of immigration. Now look at the Polish case. Long after 1989, when the previous political motivations were no longer present, a considerable stream of emigrants was still flowing out of Poland, coming especially from the higher educated groups and professionals (doctors of medicine, engineers, artists, musicians, sport players, etc.). The ranking of the preferred direction of emigration was as follows: US, Germany, France, Switzerland, Canada, Italy, Australia, Austria, Sweden, Greece (Slany 1997: 94). In the years 1991–1995 112,716 emigrants left Poland permanently (*Rocznik Demograficzny* [Demographic Yearbook] 1997: 312). In the American "visa lottery," Poles consistently had the largest quotas, which indicates that the number of applicants was also the largest. A very telling special case is provided by the "resettlement" to Germany of Polish citizens claiming German origins. According to the estimates of the German Red Cross, in 1980 there were at most 100,000 ethnic Germans living in Poland. And yet, between that date and 1991, 790,000 "resettlers" came to Germany (Okólski 1996: 33). This shows the scale of the "exit" drive and the aspiration to abandon Polish citizenship by pretending, and sometimes faking, foreign origins. This is supported by survey data that show that 29 percent of citizens, or approximately one in three, seriously consider emigrating (Central and Eastern Eurobarometer, March 1993). Around 59 percent of the people declare readiness to go abroad temporarily, for work (CBOS Bulletin No. 8/1992: 46). And in fact, in 1995 more than 900,000 Poles traveled abroad, a considerable percentage of those in a search for temporary employment (Rocznik Statystyczny [Statistical Yearabook] 1997: 112).

A phenomenon akin to emigration, just another variant of the "exit" option, is the withdrawal from participation in public life (an internal exile). In spite of the new democratic regime, "the 'us-versus-them' conceptualization of politics, in which the 'state' is seen as the main antagonist of the 'society,' was regaining its popularity after a short decline in 1989" (Ekiert and Kubik 1997: 26). Let us mention just two symptoms of this. One is electoral abstentions. In the first democratic presidential elections in Poland, almost 50 percent of citizens chose to abstain, and in later municipal elections overall participation was around 34 percent, falling to 20 percent in the cities. In the parliamentary elections of 1991 only 43 percent participated, and 57 percent abstained (Miszalska 1996: 172–188). Another aspect of the same phenomenon is the continuing reluctance to support the state in the economic domain. In a relatively poor country, it is quite amazing how enormous amounts of money can be raised in philanthropic actions, as long as they are defined as spontaneous and private, and not run by the government. The same people who donate huge sums for the "Great Orchestra of Festive Help" (a nationwide telethon to raise money for disabled children) will strain all their wits to evade taxes.

Pervasive distrust may alternatively be manifested by the "voice" option rather than the "exit" option. Those who do not want to emigrate or to choose passiveness take to collective protest. The amount of "protest events" is a good indicator of public distrust. Of course, this must be accompanied by some level of trust in the contesting groups or movements and their potential efficacy. Distrust in official politics is substituted with trust in "alternative politics" from below. The life of postcommunist society is quite rich in protest events. In the case of Poland, there have been repeated waves of strikes, street demonstrations, protest rallies, marches, road blockades, prolonged fasts, expressing generalized distrust in government or more specific distrust in particular policies. As Ekiert and Kubik claim, on the basis of thorough analysis, "Poland of the early 1990s would rank among the most contentious nations in the world" (Ekiert and Kubik 1997: 17). Their count of "protest events" shows 306 for the year 1990, 292 for 1991, 314 for 1992, and 250 for 1993 (p. 19). The numbers of workers on strike doubled between 1990 and 1991, from 115,687, to 221,547 (p. 21). During the year from 1992 to 1993 the number of those who believed that nothing could be attained without strikes, rose from 20 to 40 percent (CBOS Bulletin No. 5/1993: 115).

Distrust may be observed when we examine forms of behavior directed toward more distant future, in which some image of the future must be present. If that image is unclear or negative, we shall observe a presentist orientation: concern with the immediate moment, to the neglect of any deeper temporal horizon. In this respect, some authors refer to contemporary Poland as a "waiting society," showing "reluctance to plan and think of the future in a long time perspective" (Tarkowska 1994: 64–66). Generalized distrust in the future is reflected in many ways. One example is found in educational decisions, which in many cases are not correlated with tendencies in the labor market, nor motivated by long-range life plans, but rather seem aimed at prolonging unproblematic youth by spending many years in an enjoyable academic milieu, and postponing serious occupational decisions for as long as possible. How else could one explain the huge popularity of such university departments as archeology (and particularly Mediterranean archeology), history of art, religious studies, philosophy, and psychology (source: recruitment statistics for Jagiellonian University at Krakow for 1992, 1993, and 1994). Other evidence of similar attitudes is found when we turn to some prevailing types of economic behavior. One of them is conspicuous spending on consumer goods, to the neglect of investing or saving. Fifty-nine percent of people declared that saving is entirely unreasonable (*GW*, October 18, 1994). Most people were still reluctant to invest in private business; only 14 percent considered it seriously, and only 7 percent are ready to invest in stocks (*GW*, April 30, 1994). But even among those who decided to invest, a characteristic pattern appears. It is striking that most investments still went into trade, services, and financial operations, rather than production or construction (Poland: International Economic Report 1993/1994: 125). This reflects the uncertainty about legal regulations, terms of trade, and consistency of economic policies. An attempt to make immediate profits, instead of waiting for larger but deferred profits, is the rational response to such anxieties. Similarly it is characteristic that the institution of life insurance is still in its early phase, and attracts only a marginal group of clients.

Institutional distrust in the economic area may be indicated by the typical behavior of investors at the stock exchange, a new institution in the Polish economy. Most of the investors completely disregard "fundamental analysis" based on objective indicators of performance reported by the firms, using at most the "technical analysis" of price curves, according to some fashionable magical recipes ("Elliott Waves" are particularly in vogue). Investors seem to rely on the wildest rumors, and exhibit pervasive suspicion of all official pronouncements, statistical data, or economic prognoses. They are pushed and pulled by blind imitation of others and herding instinct, which results in alternating waves of enthusiasm and despair.

In the area of services, the distrust in public institutions is glaring. If the choice was available, people most often elected private over public services. When socialized, state-run medicine lost its monopoly, a large portion of patients switched immediately to private doctors and their clinics, in spite of high expenses. More and more private schools at elementary and secondary level drained students from public education, in spite of excessive tuition. This slowly extended up to the level of higher education, where even highly prestigious state universities have been abandoned by some students in favor of new private establishments. The assumption seems to reign that the only dependable guarantee of good services is money.

Let us move now to direct opinions, evaluations, and projections, in which people verbally exhibit some measure of distrust (verbal indicators). At the most general level, the best indicator of trust is the appraisal of systemic reforms, their success up to now, and their future prospects. In 1991 only 13.6 percent of respondents in the working-class center of Lodz considered the direction of changes as right and proper (Miszalska 1996: 50). In 1993 only 29 percent of the nationwide sample unconditionally approved reforms, while 56 percent declared distrust (Central and Eastern Eurobarometer, February 1993). In another poll 58 percent of respondents appraised the current political and economic situation as deteriorating (*GW*, February 22, 1994). In yet another, 69 percent judged that nobody was currently controlling the development of events in the country (CBOS Bulletin No. 1/1992: 8). When asked about more specific dimensions of reforms, only 32 percent said that democracy is a good thing, while 55 percent were dissatisfied with democratic institutions (Central and Eastern Eurobarometer, February 1993). When relating it more specifically to the Polish democracy, people were even more critical: In 1993, 39 percent still described the political system as non-democratic, with only 22 percent seeing it as close to true democracy (CBOS Bulletin No. 5/1993: 18). Two years later 43 percent believed that democracy was

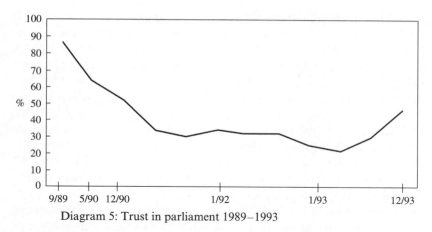

Diagram 5: Trust in parliament 1989–1993

functioning badly, and only 1 percent said that it operated well (CBOS Bulletin No.1/1995: 62). Trust in parliament was visibly falling down.

Similarly, only 29 percent believed that privatization brings "changes for the better" (*GW*, April 17, 1994). And asked about who benefits through privatization, in 1992 46 percent indicated wealthy people, 55 percent the conmen and tricksters, 20 percent the old communist "nomenklatura," and only 4 percent the common people (CBOS Bulletin No. 9/1996: 102). Asked "who loses?" 66 percent responded: "the common people" (p. 103). In 1991, 59 percent predicted the deterioration of their personal economic situation (CBOS Bulletin No. 1/1992: 9). In July 1993 the negative evaluation of the national economic situation reached its peak with 70 percent of the nationwide sample perceiving it as bad, and only 5 percent as good (CBOS Bulletin No. 2/1994: 6). For the whole of the year 1993 the standard of life of the Polish people was estimated as bad by 71–82 percent of respondents (CBOS Bulletin No. 2/ 1994: 7). When pressed about concrete changes, which after all did take place, the respondents show a strikingly negativistic bias, perceiving mostly the dark side of the reforms. As crucial changes, 93 percent indicated the growth of crime, 89 percent – the appearance of economic rackets, 87 percent – socio-economic disparities and the growing polarization into rich and poor, 57 percent – reduced social security and care for the needy, 62 percent – weakened mutual sympathy and helping attitudes among the people (*GW*, June 17, 1994).

Another indicator of generalized distrust is the comparison of the present socio-economic situation with the past. Asked about their own, personal condition, 53 percent felt that they were living worse than before (*GW*, June 17, 1994). In the industrial city of Lodz the percentage was even higher – 75 percent (Miszalska 1996: 68). During the whole year 1993, only around 12–13 percent defined their living conditions as good (CBOS Bulletin No. 1/1994: 7). Appraising the situation of others, around half of the respondents believed that people were generally more satisfied under real-socialism. This surprising result is confirmed by three independent polls, estimating the percentages at 52, 48, and 54 percent (*GW*, June 28, 1994). When thinking about their society in the future, people were even more pessimistic. Only 20 percent thought that the situation would improve, 32 percent expected the turn for the worse, and 36 percent hoped that it would at least remain unchanged (*GW*, April 17, 1994). Another poll shows as many as 64 percent of pessimists, against just 20 percent of optimists (CBOS Bulletin No. 1/1994: 5). More specifically, referring to the overall economic situation, 62 percent believed that it would not improve (Central and Eastern Eurobarometer, February 1993), and 55 percent expected costs of living to rise (CBOS Bulletin, January 1994). A confirmation of distrust in the future is found in the list of problems that people worry about: 73 percent indicated lack of prospects for their children as something that worries them most (CBOS Bulletin, January 1993).

More specific institutional and positional distrust takes many forms. Trust in governmental institutions consistently fell. Even the Catholic Church, traditionally one of the most trusted institutions (with declared trust of 82.7 percent of a nationwide sample in 1990. See Marody 1996: 252), seemed to be affected by the climate of distrust, especially when it usurps a more political role; 54 percent disapproved of such extension of the Church's functions, and 70 percent would like the Church to limit its activities to the religious area (*GW*, May 10, 1994).

The mass media, even though much more independent and not linked directly to the state, do not fare much better. Apparently they have not yet regained trust, devastated by their instrumental role under real-socialism. Forty-eight percent of people still did not believe the TV, and 40 percent distrusted the newspapers (Central and Eastern Eurobarometer, February 1993). The institutions of public accountability do not fare any better. The tax collecting offices were believed to be helpless against tax fraud by 62 percent of the respondents, and only 14 percent considered them effective in tax collection (CBOS Bulletin No. 8/93: 26); 72 percent disapproved of the operations of the police, and 52 percent of the courts (CBOS Bulletin No. 7/94: 72). The only exception was the army, which keeps its relatively high level of trustworthiness (with 75–80 percent expressing consistent approval).[10]

But it is the politicians that are treated with the greatest suspicion; 87

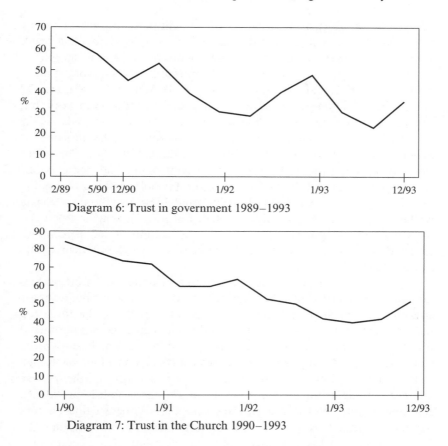

Diagram 6: Trust in government 1989–1993

Diagram 7: Trust in the Church 1990–1993

percent of a nationwide sample claimed that they take care only of their own interests and careers, and neglect the public good (*GW*, July, 11, 1994); 77 percent believed that they use their offices for private profit (CBOS Bulletin, October 1995: 1), and 87 percent that they take care exclusively of their careers (*GW*, No. 159/1994). If anything goes wrong in society, 93 percent of the people declared: "the politicians and bureaucrats are guilty" (Koralewicz and Ziolkowski 1990: 62); 48 percent see public administration as pervaded by corruption, and only 8 percent perceive corruption in private businesses (*GW*, March 19, 1994). The veracity of high office was also doubted: 49 percent did not believe information given by ministers (*GW*, March 25, 1994); 60 percent were convinced that data on levels of inflation, or GNP growth, released by the state statistical office, are false (CBOS Bulletin, January 1994). Not much trust was attached to the fiduciary responsibility of government or administration: 70 percent believed that public bureaucracy is entirely insensitive towards human suffering and grievances (Giza-Poleszczuk 1991: 76). Fairness and justice were found to be absent in public institutions: 71 percent said that in state enterprises "good work is not a method of enrichment" (Koralewicz and Ziolkowski 1990: 55), and 72 percent believed that people advance, not because of success in work, but due to "connections" (Giza-Poleszczuk 1991: 86). This extends to the courts of law: 79 percent claimed that verdicts would not be the same for people of different social status (Giza-Poleszczuk 1991: 88). The police were considered with traditional lack of confidence, and hence public security was evaluated very low: 56 percent of people tried to avoid going out after dark (*Polityka*,[11] May 14, 1994), and 36 percent did not feel safe in the streets at all, day or night (CBOS Bulletin, November 1993). To the question: "Is Poland an internally safe country?" 67 percent responded in the negative, and only 26 percent claimed to feel secure (*GW*, March 21, 1994).

Any contact with politics seems polluting. Taking public office does not add to popularity, just the reverse. The distrust of active politicians is striking. In a prestige ranking of most popular persons, the three top places were taken by persons visible on the political stage, but not linked directly to any political office: an oppositional intellectual Jacek Kuron, Cardinal Joseph Glemp, and the famous heart surgeon Zbigniew Religa (*GW*, June 18, 1994). When the question was asked in the reverse manner: "Who brought shame on Poland?" three Polish presidents, Boleslaw Bierut, Wojciech Jaruzelski, and Lech Walesa came on top, together indicated by 49.7 percent of respondents (*Polityka*, June 25, 1994). The case of Lech Walesa is particularly telling, as we observe the dramatic fall of his popularity once he took presidential office: 24 percent of people declared that he brought shame on Poland by the way he handled the presidential job, as opposed to his earlier status of charismatic and heroic leader (*Polityka*, June 25, 1994).

Finally, if we look at interpersonal trust in everyday life, people also perceived its decay. In one of the surveys 56 percent estimated that mutual sympathy and help had markedly deteriorated (OBOP Bulletin No. 10/1996: 2). According to the Polish General Social Survey the tendency of falling interpersonal trust persisted up to 1994. The belief that "most people can be trusted" was expressed by 10.1 percent of a nationwide sample in 1992, 8.9 percent in 1993, and 8.3 percent in 1994. And the opposite view that "one can never be careful enough in dealing with other people" was supported by 87.8 percent in 1992, 89.5 percent in 1993, and 90.3 percent in 1994 (Marody 1996: 224).

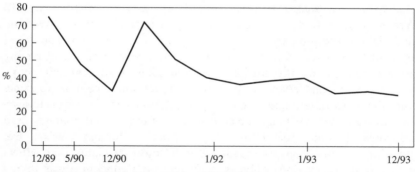

Diagram 8: Trust in president 1989–1993

Structural variation

So far, our diagnosis is one-dimensional, and makes it appear as if trust spreads uniformly across the entire society. In reality, this never happens; trust is unevenly distributed among various segments of society, which exhibit the "distrust culture" in various degrees. Similarly, trust un-equally affects various levels of society – social order as such, institutions, expert systems, roles, positions, persons – which are subjected to distrust in various measures. Both the trusting agents and trusted objects differ along many dimensions.

Hypothetically, it would appear that the varieties of scope and intensiveness of distrust pervading different groups in the postcommu-nist period will depend on two major sets of factors. The first set refers to historical experiences, and in particular the vulnerability to the negative impact of the communist system, or conversely the relative insulation from the system. Groups markedly differed in this respect. We may expect that those groups, or social categories, which were most prone to fall under the impact of alternative cultural pressures – whether national or global – will be most insulated from the grip of communist culture and its syndrome of cynicism. There were groups relatively insulated from the impact because of apolitical occupations (e.g., scientists), relative autonomy of self-employment (e.g., farmers or artists), participation in the private sector (e.g., shopkeepers or artisans), security of professional expertise (e.g., medical doctors or lawyers), and by the same token more exposed to alternative culture-generating influences. Some were sensitized to indigenous traditions (e.g., Catholi-cism, nationalism, aspirations to sovereignty, opposition to foreign rule), resulting in cultural localism, provincialism, ethnocentrism, and xenophobia. In Poland, some segments of the peasantry were typically the carriers of such traditions. Some others were oriented toward Western culture (e.g., the work ethic, secularization, personal freedom, civil rights), resulting in cultural cosmopolitism, liberalism, and tolerance. In Poland such a cultural syndrome was most often found among professional groups, the intelligentsia, and some private entrepreneurs, who had skills and resources (cultural and economic capital) to penetrate the gates raised against cultural flows; they had the requisite level of education, foreign language competence, international contacts, and a surplus of money for cultural consumption or foreign tourism. But most importantly, a group that is naturally more insulated than others is the young generation, whose socialization and education was taking place at a time when the communist system was already weaker, much less oppressive, and obviously decaying. The "educational effect" of the communist system was markedly lower in their case (Miszalska 1996: 81).

The second set includes factors that relate to contemporary conditions, and in particular the experience of relative deprivation, or conversely the relative success under the new regime. Anita Miszalska advances a hypothesis about the split of the society into "populist and claimant Poland" and "business and pro-capitalist Poland" (Miszalska 1996: 32). For example, at present, the most distrustful will probably be found in the groups that lost most – in absolute and relative terms – due to the democratic transition. Look at the predicament of the working class. Large segments face unemployment, in absolute terms their wages have not been significantly raised, but comparative standards of success have been set much higher, with the conspicuous affluence of new entrepreneurial groups, and stores full of attractive but expensive goods. This is also the group that was constantly made to believe in its special, privileged position in a society of real socialism, and then as the group that had been the true force behind the anti-communist revolution. Now it is blocked from enjoying the fruits of victory. The experience of deprivation and consequent distrust is especially painful. Or take the peasants, who have lost their monopolistic position on the food market and are facing more efficient, and cheaper competitors from abroad. Or the state-employed white collar workers, as well as some groups of artists and intellectuals, who are drastically underpaid compared to those employed in the new private sector.

On the other hand, considerably more trust can be expected from those groups who have reaped the benefits of current reforms. It includes the political elites active in governmental and administrative apparatus, as well as new entrepreneurial elites active in economic ventures of various sorts. Similarly it includes some groups of professionals, such as medical doctors, lawyers, and notaries, able to start lucrative private practices. There is also a special group of the "new nomenklatura," which was able to convert the political capital derived from the old regime, by means of personal connections, considerable skills, and organizational competence, into real capital of personal riches and high economic positions under the new regime as well. The satisfied also include those who have been successful in partly illegal or even outright criminal economic endeavors: the inhabitants of the "gray" or "black" sphere of the economy. They have no reason for distrusting the reforms, which open so many legal loopholes and other opportunities for their operations. For the intelligentsia and professional groups, even if they are not advanced materially, the intangibles of democracy like freedom of speech and association, lack of censorship, openness to foreign countries, and the like, matter sufficiently to evoke more trust in ongoing reforms. Finally, for some groups, deeply embedded traditional values of honor, "noblesse oblige," and so forth will also imply some measure of continuing trust, independent of other circumstances. Perhaps proportions of trust and distrust will also differ with gender, age, the level of education, urban or rural dwelling, and religious belief.

If we turn to the targets of trust, they also present considerable variety, and several permutations are possible. Specialized distrust may appear, due to some publicized events, for example, against the police or banking system, when corruption or abuse are discovered. Or more diffuse distrust may engulf various objects. There may also be incongruencies: for example, trust may be vested in some persons in power, but distrust touch the whole institution of government; or the reverse, trust in the principles of democracy may be accompanied by strong distrust in current parliamentarians. Institutions themselves may present a whole gradation of trust and distrust. In the Polish case it is striking how high a degree of trust – for various historical reasons – is vested in the army or the Church, and how much distrust targets on the police, bureaucracy, or the government. In 1991 the Poles ranked the trustworthy institutions in the following order: the army, the Church, the Ombudsman, TV, the parliament (lower house), the police, the senate, the trade unions, the government (CBOS Bulletin No. 1/1991: 52). Similarly, roles and positions may command extremely varied measures of trust, from university professors, medical doctors, and teachers at the top, to police officers, public officials, and politicians at the bottom.

Even with the corrections introduced above, the diagnosis of the postcommunist situation is certainly incomplete; many aspects of social

life were ignored for lack of data. But the picture, even if tentative, is
strikingly consistent. Trust appears to be the most rare of social
resources. The "culture of distrust" seems to be deeply embedded. And
once the decay of trust reaches this cultural level, distrust becomes
contagious and self-enhancing. From now on it is a "normal," accepted
reaction to be distrustful, and all displays of trust are considered as signs
of credulity, naivety, and simple-mindedness, and meet with ridicule,
mockery, and other negative sanctions. Sadly and paradoxically, cynicism has been raised to a virtue.

A tentative explanation

We must ask now why the syndrome of distrust develops in the aftermath
of a victorious revolution. There are two time perspectives that we may
take: the short and the long. In the immediate aftermath of the
revolution, a kind of "postrevolutionary malaise" appears, which –
paradoxically – helps to revive the pre-revolutionary legacy of distrust,
blocking the emergence of grounded trust. The malaise is due to several
circumstances. First is the widespread anomie or postrevolutionary
axiological chaos, a common disorientation as to the binding norms and
values, valid rules, and right ways of life. Old patterns have fallen down,
new ones have not yet been legitimized. Thrown into uncertainty and
devoid of moral guidance, people feel isolated and lonely, and turn their
resentments against others. Interpersonal suspicion, distrust, and hostility destroy whatever social bonds have been left intact by totalitarian
rule. Second, the emergence of new life chances, and opportunities to
raise social status, by freshly opened access to wealth, power, and
prestige, generates brutal competition, in which stakes are high but the
rules of the game remain undeveloped. Civility, fair play, cooperative
attitudes, and mutual trust do not find conducive soil in which to put
down roots. Third, rigid social controls, both external and internal, are
suddenly released. The police force and the judiciary get disorganized
and lose any legitimacy they might still possess. The law is undermined
by claims that its totalitarian origins make it illegitimate and not binding.
And law enforcement agencies are visibly inefficient. The demise of
dependable social controls breeds anxiety, disorientation, and uncertainty, fertile ground for the expansion of the distrust syndrome.

Fourth, new political elites often do not stand up to their freshly
acquired responsibilities. Power corrupts, and this applies even to
heroically attained democratic power. The opposition politicians, once in
power, quite often start to resemble the old guard. Some of the same
arrogance of power is manifested. Factionalism, the greed for office, and

lack of concern for the public good become obvious. Asked in the survey in 1992 whose interests the parliamentarians primarily represent, 40 percent answered "their party or faction," 27 percent "their own private interests," and only 6 percent "the interest of the whole society" (CBOS Bulletin 9/96: 45). Clearly, the politicians have been evicted from the "us" category and are again perceived as "them." The public is disenchanted with the picture of constant personal fights, ugly accusations, open hostilities at the very top of political hierarchies. The salaries and fringe benefits of politicians are viewed as overblown and unjustified. Favoritism and nepotism is observed with disgust. There are equally obvious cases of ignorance, ineptness, and incompetence: mistaken information and unfounded and hastily revoked decisions of the highest authorities. There is visible inconsistency between political proclamations and election promises, and actual policies. Some laws are passed and remain unenforced. The decisions of the central government are sometimes ignored by local authorities, and vice versa, decisions of the center are imposed against the will of local government. There are difficulties in informing public opinion and openly dealing with the media. Pretensions of secrecy, and even repeated attempts to pass legislation sanctioning secrecy, by limiting the access of the media to state operations, increase the alienation of politicians from the wider public. There are also constant efforts to influence the content of the media, to control TV, to impose quasi-censorship.

Finally, there is arbitrariness of decisions, sometimes stretching the law, but sometimes clearly violating the law, and in occasional cases breaching the fundamental principles of legal order itself (e.g., the Roman rule of *lex retro non agit*, or the fundamental principle of democracy that all citizens – including the highest officials – are equal before the law). All those abuses of power, demoralization, and sometimes even criminal acts committed by politicians, are highly visible, even more than before, due to the democratic transparency provided by independent media.

Now we have to take a longer perspective and to ask why, several years after the revolutionary events and deep into the construction of an open, democratic, market society of the Western type, the syndrome of distrust is still so prominent. The legacy of the past, plus "postrevolutionary malaise," provide only part of the answer. The other part must be sought in new conditions appearing in postcommunist societies, which enhance or engender distrust.

In accordance with our theoretical model, the most important is the condition of uncertainty, insecurity, ambiguity, and opaqueness in the "life-world" of postcommunist people. Trust, as we remember, is based on anticipations of the future. "Such anticipations in turn imply certain ideas about the future social structure, its scope and mechanisms of social mobility, and about gains and losses resulting from the transformation process." But "the shape of the future system remains obscure" (Kolarska-Bobińska 1994: 8). Hence "under such circumstances, preferences and interests are strongly influenced by stereotypes, prejudices, hopes and anxieties" (Kolarska-Bobińska 1994: 8). The uncertainties are manifested in many ways. First, there is a greatly expanded "environment of risk that collectively affects large masses of individuals" (Giddens 1990a: 35). The most acute is the risk of unemployment, in the early nineties a fact of life for 15.7 percent of the Polish labor force (Poland: An International Economic Report 1993/1994: 77), and the subject of grave concern for 69–70 percent of the population, who put it at the top of the list of problems facing the country (CBOS Bulletin No. 2/1995: 71).[12] In another survey, as many as 58 percent of the respondents expressed concern about possible loss of job (due to bankruptcy, or liquidation of the enterprise employing them). (CBOS Bulletin No. 4/1995: 77). Unemployment and its threat obviously breed anxiety, insecurity, frustration, and generalized distrust in the system and its future. Almost equally threatening is the risk of inflation and financial instability. The rate of inflation went down from its peak, but in that period was still high, in the range of 35–40 percent per year (Poland: International Economic Report 1993/1994: 22). It clearly undermines trust in money, the meaningfulness of savings, and stability of terms of trade. No wonder that 64 percent of the people name inflation among their most serious daily worries (CBOS Bulletin, January 1994). In 1993 66 percent of respondents declared that they were afraid of poverty (CBOS Bulletin No. 12/93: 83), and only 3 percent judged their standard of living as high (CBOS Bulletin No. 6/93: 77). A highly detrimental effect is produced by an unstable taxation policy, with repeatedly added tax burdens. It prevents any certainty about future income, and provides easy justification for cheating, law evasions, and even crime: "When people feel that they are being taken advantage of, why should they not rip off the system in return" (Elster 1989: 180). An additional factor breeding distrust in the financial system is the collapse of several, newly established private banks, and the occasional crashes at the stock exchange, after a period of unprecedented boom.

The third aspect of risk appears in free competition and market transactions. It is felt by producers and consumers alike. The early phase of capital accumulation produced brutal, aggressive, untamed business conduct. Raising prices, lowering quality, taking false credits, forging documents, and negative advertising became common practices. Newspapers report that as much as 75 percent of the cases scrutinized by a consumer protection agency have shown evidence of cheating. The fourth factor of risk is the tremendous escalation of crime and delinquency, resulting in a mood of instability, permanent threat, and danger. From 547,589 crimes recorded in 1989, there was a jump to 883,346 just a year later (Frieske 1996: 118). No wonder that 56 percent of people are afraid to go out after dark (*Polityka*, May 14, 1994). But common crime is not the only reason for anxiety. Growing organized crime and penetration of foreign mafias is another. And perhaps most destructive for generalized trust are repeatedly revealed cases of misconduct, abuse of office, and "white collar crime" among the political and administrative elites. When parliament repeatedly has to waive the criminal immunity of some of its members; when ministers, or mayors, or bank presidents, have to be dismissed and prosecuted, it produces devastating effects for public trust. "The normalization of deviancy" (Stivers 1994: 2) is highly demoralizing. "One such social effect [of growing crime] is the damage it does both to interpersonal trust and to trust in institutions which violate the law and those which are responsible for law enforcement" (Short 1984: 714).

The general feeling of uncertainty is also due to normative disorganization or anomie. The legal system is a fragmented mosaic of partial regulations, old and new, often inconsistent, repeatedly changed, and arbitrarily interpreted. The overload of rules, regulations, administrative codes, and conflicting interpretations of laws makes them incomprehensible. The new constitution is still missing, as twenty-seven projects are vigorously debated by a divided parliament, and the old one is a patchwork of ad hoc amendments. The rule of law is compromised by extra-legal decisions of the highest authorities, including, the presidential office, and by the retroactive legislation occasionally passed by the parliament. Trust in the continuity, stability, and orderliness of social life is effectively undermined. The condition of anomie extends to the political domain. Among wide groups of the population, there reigns a complete disorientation in the mechanisms of excessively pluralistic and democratic politics. The staggering number of political parties, clubs, and factions operating on the public stage, plus permanent personal feuds of leading political personalities, plus an atmosphere of secrecy engulfing the decision-making processes, add to "the sense many of us have of being caught up in a universe of events we do not fully understand and which seems in large part outside of our control" (Giddens 1990: 2–3). This description, given in another context by the British theorist, fits perfectly the mood of Polish society at that time.

The new phenomenon of immigration (32,504 official immigrants in the years 1991–1995. [Rocznik Statystyczny 1997: 111]), opens up contacts with people from other countries, foreign entrepreneurs but also beggars, refugees, those employed in the "black economy," and mafias. The appearance of "strangers" adds to the climate of precariousness and uncertainty. There is also a pervasive feeling of external insecurity (particularly the threat from revived Russian imperialism, as well as the historically rooted resentments toward neighboring post-Soviet republics).

The second general factor relevant for the demise of trust, is the perceived inefficiency or laxity of control agencies, supposed to guard the order, stability, and continuity of social life. Law enforcement agencies, from police, through public prosecutors' offices, to courts, are often seen as incapable, or even worse, as biased or corrupted. The inability of the police to curb the wave of street crime, burglaries, car theft, and the operation of the mafias, is glaring. Cases of outright corruption in some regional police forces have been revealed, and have led to the dismissal of high police officers including a police chief (in the city of Poznan). Inconsistent prosecution of "white collar crimes," especially those compromising political activists, is widely reported. Some court verdicts seem to violate the common sense of justice, conferring disproportionately low penalties or even acquittal (the trial of Generals Ciaston and Platek was a recent example). Tax and duties enforcement is also perceived as negligent, in view of massive smuggling and tax evasions estimated at 10 trillion Polish zloty (Poland: International Economic Report 1993/94: 130). All this erodes faith in due process of law, enforcement of standards, fairness, and justice.

The third factor is the depletion of some forms of personal capital touching considerable segments of the population. The most important is actual pauperization. In 1991 the number of Poles falling below the poverty line (with income lower than the "social minimum" enabling the satisfaction of basic needs) was estimated as 35 percent, whereas at the end of the seventies it did not exceed 8 percent (Miszalska 1996: 68). The estimates of the World Bank show around 5.5 million people suffering acute poverty in 1993 (Gucwa-Leśny 1996: 109). Some deterioration of health standards, as well as shortening of life expectations, is also observable. In 1990 the average life expectation for both sexes was only 71 years, compared to around 80 in most developed countries of the world (Okólski 1996: 24).

The final factor, aggravating the effects of all those mentioned earlier, is the relatively high level of expectations and aspirations borne by the "glorious year 1989." Experience of trust and distrust is always relative to the standards with which we evaluate social objects (Barber 1983: 83). Obviously, if the standards of trustworthiness are set low, the likelihood of trust being met is higher than when the standards are set high. Generally, the more realistic the expectations, the better the chances for successful trusting, and therefore for the emergence of a trust culture. And the less realistic the expectations, the more chances for breaches of trust and consequent distrust culture.

In the euphoria of victory over communism (the "five E syndrome"), the standards of expectations were set very high: The transition will be smooth and rapid, standards of living will rise soon, the democratically elected power elite will consist of intellectually and morally impeccable people, the state will act only in the name of the public good, entirely for the benefit of citizens. It is interesting to note how the legacy of real-socialism still enhanced those expectations. All that socialism promised, but never delivered, was to be realized now, in a free, democratic order. The paternalistic model of the "welfare state," taking care of citizens and providing them with basic goods, is accepted by 40 percent of the people (Mikolejko 1991: 62). In more concrete terms, 55 percent believe that the government should take care of those who need help, and only 13 percent put this responsibility on the family (CBOS Bulletin: January 1994). And in a different survey as many as 90 percent claimed that the state should provide jobs, apartments, education, medical services, and even facilities for leisure (Koralewicz and Ziolkowski 1990: 100). The realities of the transition departed radically from those dreams. The gap between the level of aspirations and the level of realizations is always frustrating and painful (Gurr 1970). In effect, deep and pervasive distrust, already instilled by earlier conditions of real-socialism, continued unabated. It is more rational to be distrustful in an environment devoid of trust. Those who manifest trust will not only lose in the game, but will be censured for stupidity, naivety, credulity, and simple-mindedness. Cynicism, cheating, egoism, evasion of laws, outwitting the system, turn into virtues. And that cannot but lead to even deeper corrosion of trust.

Democratic consolidation and the revival of trust

The crisis of trust as described above seemed at the time to activate a vicious, self-amplifying loop of growing cynicism, passivism, and alienation. Appraising the situation at the beginning of the nineties I had arrived at a pessimistic prognosis, believing that the recuperation of trust would be a very long and arduous process (Sztompka 1995, 1996a, 1996b). And then in the middle of the nineties something happened that turned the direction of the trend and initiated a revival of trust: one more of those notorious surprises that we have encountered in the process of transformation (Lepenies 1992), but this time optimistic and hopeful. Looking at the indicators of trust in the second half of the nineties, we see a completely changed picture.

Evidence of change

The change is particularly clear when we look at the declarative level of verbal indicators. My own research carried out in 1997 shows that 55.6 percent of the people believed that their life was better than before 1989, and only 26.5 percent declared that their standard of living had fallen. In nationwide surveys in 1991–1993 only around 20 percent of the respondents evaluated the past year as good for themselves, whereas in 1997 the number was 45. And in a parallel way, in 1991–1993 41 percent considered the past year as bad, whereas in 1997 it was only 18 percent (CBOS Bulletin No. 8/1998: 2). Looking forward, 50.1 percent thought of the future with hope, and only 21.6 percent were worried (data from my research). This is congruent with the nationwide surveys, which show that in 1993 only 18 percent predicted the next year to be good for themselves, but in 1997 the number had grown to 30 percent. (CBOS Bulletin No. 8/1998: 11). Of course such evaluations are strongly varied among socio-economic strata. Both backward-looking and forward-looking optimism are manifested much more by those who have succeeded themselves, or see a chance of success for themselves in the postcommunist transformation. Thus comparing life conditions with the past, 79.4 percent of the elite see them as better, while among the lowest occupations and the unemployed it is only 26.2 percent.[13] Similarly, 76.4 percent of the highly educated declare that they live better, while the same is true only of 36.1 percent of the uneducated. Looking toward the future, 60.4 percent of the economic elites declared hopefulness, while only 30.1 percent of the unemployed and those with low-paid jobs shared this hope. Of the highly educated, 58.5 percent expect an improvement of their situation, while for the uneducated it was 42.8 percent.

There is a particularly consistent trend of growing trust toward democracy. If we remind ourselves that in 1993 the support for democracy was expressed by only 32 percent of the respondents (Central and Eastern Eurobarometer, February 1993), the change is dramatic. Asked if democracy is a better regime compared to all the alternatives, in 1995 71 percent of respondents in the nationwide sample answered affirmatively, and only 12 percent were opposed (CBOS Bulletin No. 152/1997: 1). In 1998 the support for democracy had grown to 72 percent with 11 percent opposed (*GW*, July 2, 1998). Trust toward the parliament, the most obvious symbol of democracy, had risen.

There is also a tendency of growing trust toward public institutions. Just in the one year 1997 support for the government grew from 40 to 48 percent, for the parliament (*Sejm*) from 40 to 45 percent, for the Central Bank from 68 to 77 percent.

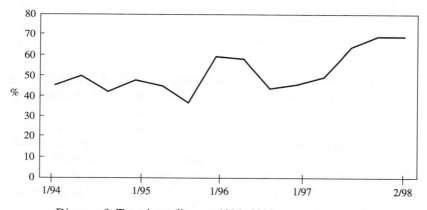

Diagram 9: Trust in parliament 1994–1998

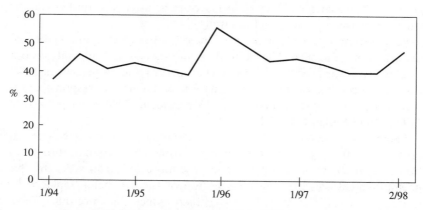

Diagram 10: Trust in government 1994–1998

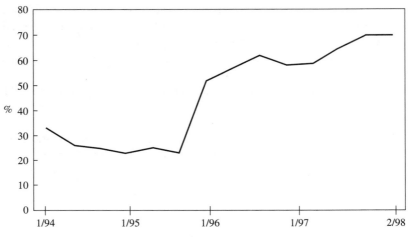

Diagram 11: Trust in President 1994–1998

The public media have also noted the growth of trust: TV from 68 to 77 percent, and Polish Radio to as high as 87 percent. (*GW*, February 28, 1998).[14]

Even though there is still considerable – and unfortunately often grounded – suspiciousness toward political elites, some of the politicians seem to fare better than before in the rankings of trust. The most striking is the consistent growth of trust for the President, reaching 68 percent in 1996 (*GW*, February 21, 1996: 5) and 73 percent in 1998 (CBOS Bulletin No. 5/1998).

The newly appointed Prime Minister is supported by around 50 percent of the citizens. The Catholic church, after a period of falling trust, has slowly started to gain as well.

People seem to have grown out of the discourse of fate, and embraced the discourse of agency. The claim that "life success depends only on our own efforts" was accepted by 68 percent in 1994 and 76 percent in 1996, and the percentage of those indicating fate as exclusively responsible for success or failure has dropped from 13 percent in 1994 to 11 percent in 1996 (CBOS Bulletin No. 7/1996: 98).

There is an interesting shift in the hierarchy of declared worries. It seems that the emphasis has changed from the external threats of transformation, to personal dangers of a more universal sort. In 1998 unemployment was no longer at the top of the list, being replaced by health problems (indicated by 66%), then comes the lowering of economic standards of living linked to inflation (58%), growing crime (53%),

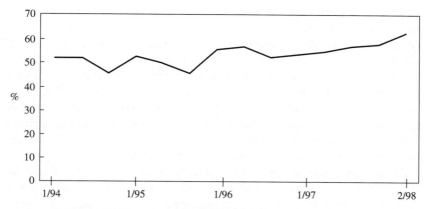

Diagram 12: Trust in the Church 1994–1998

war (50%), and only at the end, the loss of work (43%) (CBOS Bulletin No.41/1998: 1). The external threat from foreign powers, worrying 44 percent of people in 1991, was significant for only 27 percent in 1997 (*GW*, August 27, 1997: 2).[15] The perception of threats and dangers is clearly correlated with the level of personal capital, and particularly the economic status, of the respondents. The affluent are less concerned than the poor.

Some of the behavioral indicators reflect the changed social mood well. The numbers of emigrants are slowly falling. From an average of 28,000 per year in the years 1991–1995, it fell to 26,344 in 1995 and 21,297 in 1996 (Rocznik Statystyczny 1997: 111), and less than 20,000 in 1997 (*Polityka*, February 14, 1998: 6). There is a growing wave of returning emigrants, often purchasing homes and establishing private businesses, as well as considerable numbers of foreigners wishing to settle down in Poland. In 1997 their number reached 8,300 (*Polityka*, February 14, 1998: 6). Electoral participation has grown slightly, but is still quite low: from 43 percent in the parliamentary elections of 1991 to 48 percent in 1997.

Much more unambiguous evidence for growing trust is to be found in the steep decline of protest events. From 6,351 strikes in 1992 and 7,443 in 1993, engaging 752,472 workers, in 1996 there were only 21 strikes, engaging 44,250 workers (Rocznik Statystyczny 1997: 137). Attitudes toward strikes as a legitimate weapon for the defense of interests have changed as well. Asked about the strikes of the anesthetists in Polish hospitals, 76 percent perceived them as harmful, and 35 percent strongly condemned them (CBOS Bulletin No. 12/1997: 1).

Very significant signs of growing trust have appeared in the area of education. First, there has been an unprecedented push toward higher education, a true educational boom, in the sense of dramatically growing numbers of students, more than doubling from 403,824 in 1990 to 927,480 in 1997, which was accompanied by similar doubling of schools providing higher education, from 112 in 1990 to 213 in 1997 (Rocznik Statystyczny 1997: 240). Apart from state-run schools, where education is in principle free, there is also a new phenomenon of emerging private institutions of higher education, which in spite of high tuition draw great numbers of students. There were 18 such schools in 1992, and 114 in 1997 (Rocznik Statystyczny 1997: 244). Equally significant is the strikingly changing profile of educational choices, which have become clearly oriented toward future occupational opportunities. Hence, the most popular departments at the universities are: law, business administration, management and finances, medicine, computer sciences, sociology, political sciences, and European studies. Among private schools the most successful are those offering practice-oriented instruction in management, economics, and public policy. All those fields are obviously related to the emerging employment opportunities in a market-based economy and democratic political system.

Gambling seems to be less widespread than before. The number of those who have purchased some sort of lottery ticket fell from 26 percent in 1990 to 16 percent in 1996 (CBOS Bulletin No. 81/1998: 8). People save more than before. Bank deposits grew from 29,851 million in 1993 to 87,955 million in 1996 (Rocznik Statystyczny 1997: 464). People have turned from foreign currency to Polish zloty, and currency deposits fell from 36 percent of all savings in 1991 to less than 6 percent in 1997 (CBOS Bulletin No. 145/1997: 4). The institution of individual, voluntary life insurance, which did not exist before, has become quite popular since its inception: 13 percent of the respondents in the survey carried out in 1997 said that they put their savings in life insurance (CBOS Bulletin No. 145/1997: 4). A good sign of growing trust in the government guarantees is the rapidly increasing popularity of government bonds, and especially long-term ones. Just during the two months of May and June 1998, Polish citizens purchased seven million three-year bonds (*GW*, July 10, 1998: 2). A very characteristic recent phenomenon is the consumer credit boom. In 1997 one in every four households used some form of consumer credit, and the inquiry into the motivation indicates a belief in the future ability for repayment, related to the general mood of economic optimism (CBOS Bulletin No. 150/1997: 6). We can also observe some changes in spending behavior. More people obtain credit or use their savings for building houses. The amount of money invested in private housing almost doubled from 1993 to 1996 (Rocznik Statystyczny 1997: 404–405).[16] In a survey inquiring about the use that would be made of a hypothetical high lottery prize, 68 percent of the respondents indicated building a house. There are also other trends that we may take as indicative of growing trust. Many more people would spend such extra money for education (from 24 percent in 1996 to 32 percent in 1997), and health care (from 25 percent in 1996 to 36 percent in 1997), fewer for buying a car (from 43 percent in 1996 to 30 percent in 1997). One fourth of the respondents would start a private business of some sort (CBOS Bulletin No. 159/1997: 1).

Why the reversal of the trend?

Now we have to face the most difficult question: Why that reversal of the trend occurred and why it continues? Was it any single event that was responsible for the breaking of the vicious loop of distrust and turning it around to initiate a virtuous loop of growing trust? Or rather was it a fortunate combination of multiple factors? Or perhaps both? With the benefit of hindsight one may venture the following hypotheses.

It seems that the most important factor is the widespread perception of the continuity and success of democratic and market reforms. From the moment when the communist system collapsed in Poland and radical reforms were started, the obsessive question on many people's minds was: Is it for real? After all, Polish history after World War II was marked by repeated episodes of popular defiance and a sad sequence of failed reforms. The proverbial "Polish calendar" has become almost completely filled with memorable dates, the symbols of resistance against the communist regime and short-lived liberalizations: there was October 1956, March 1968, December 1970, September 1976, August 1980, June 1989. So many of those dates evoke sorrowful and sometimes tragic memories. This has led to a trained incapacity to believe that 1989 would be different.

The slow eradication of that fundamental distrust has resulted from the combined pressure of six sets of factors. The first, and most important, set encompasses all those circumstances that contribute to the awareness that transition has been continuous, persistent, and has acquired momentum which makes it truly irreversible. I venture a guess that there were two events, which for many people – quite paradoxically in fact – provided the final proof of such an irreversible quality of democratization and marketization. The first was the election of a former communist activist, Aleksander Kwasniewski, to the office of the president and his victory over the legendary leader of Solidarity, Lech Walesa. The second was the victory of the leftist parties of communist antecedents in the elections to the parliament, and the establishment of a government led by the former communists. Both electoral successes were partly due to the syndrome of distrust and seeking for the alleviation of the pains of transition. But paradoxically, they have resulted in the rebuilding of trust. How come? The mechanism of the paradox seemed to work in the following way. Due to the principles of proportional electoral law, as well as the diversification and disunity of the rightist and centrist parties, the communists were actually elected by the minority of the electorate. Large segments of the population who did not vote for them were manifesting deep anxiety that the reforms would be blocked, democratization and marketization halted, and perhaps even some elements of the communist regime restored. Nothing of the sort happened. The president has consistently and effectively acted in support of democratic and market reforms, and has shown a strong pro-Western orientation, playing an important role in negotiating Poland's access to NATO and the European Union. The government has continued with all the systemic transformations, given a legal stamp to them by presiding over the enactment of the new constitution, and achieved remarkable economic growth.[17] For the opponents and earlier prophets of doom, it has provided an irrefutable proof that even the communists cannot "spoil the game" and reverse the momentum of change. For the communist constituency it has shown that even "our people" are not willing to change the course of transformation. In both cases it has strengthened the feeling of inevitability, certainty, and predictability concerning the future. And this, as we know, is the fundamental prerequisite for trust.

The second factor confirming the success of transition was the vigorous take-off of economic growth. The delayed results of early "shock therapy" applied in 1990, according to the "Balcerowicz plan," plus a period of reasonable and professional management of reforms by the former communists in power from 1993–1997, finally started to assert themselves. Poland came to the fore of other postcommunist societies. GDP growth reached 6.1 percent in 1996, 6.0 percent in 1997, and an expected 5.2 percent in 1998.[18] At the same time inflation fell from 20.1 percent in 1996 to 16 percent in 1997 and an expected 12 percent in 1998. Foreign investors reacted (and partly contributed) to those facts, and Poland got ahead of all the countries of the region in cumulative foreign direct investment. It had reached 20.3 billion US dollars as of December 1997 (*International Herald Tribune*, June 24, 1998: 12). The costs of reforms began to be outweighed by benefits. Large sections of the population started to experience rising wages, growing prosperity, comfort, and sometimes true wealth.[19] The mood of optimism and buoyancy has been enhanced by the preceding periods of gloom. The economic success is cherished even more, as it came quite unexpectedly. As Parry observed: "Improving the regime's performance may be the most effectual way of building up confidence in it" (Parry 1976: 142).

The third factor affecting everybody's image of transition is the new quality of everyday life: an easier, more attractive, and "colorful" life-world. After the drabness and grayness of socialist city landscapes, the misery of the "queuing society," the deprivations of the economy of shortage, and the tyranny of the producer's market, most people enjoy the opportunities of the consumer society to a much greater extent than their blasé Western counterparts. Shopping, dining out, driving fast cars, foreign trips, plentiful entertainment, and leisure are the newly discovered pleasures that raise the general mood of satisfaction and optimism. And this provides a fertile ground for trust.

The second set of factors has to do with the consolidation of political democracy and constitutionalism. Building new political institutions was the earliest focus of reforms starting immediately after the revolution of 1989. The "hour of the lawyer" – as Dahrendorf puts it – came first (Dahrendorf 1990). But it took time before the formal, legal facade turned into an effective, operating framework of political life. "Creating a civil society is like cultivating a garden . . . It is a process that can be brought to fruition only by the patient cultivation of institutions on soil that communism for generations sowed with distrust" (Rose 1994: 29). But once the new institutions start to operate and become rooted in the civil society, they exert a strong educative pressure on trust. We have argued earlier how institutional democracy – through the paradoxical mechanism of "preventive distrust" – elicits the culture of trust. In the Polish case, three developments have marked the considerable progress in the consolidation of democracy. One, and crucially important, was the enactment of a new constitution, patterned on classical solutions of Western constitutionalism. Second was the successful multiple turnover of power through elections, proving that the fundamental mechanism of parliamentary democracy actually operates. Third was the practical verification of new democratic institutions: the Constitutional Tribunal, involved several times in correcting faulty legislation;[20] the Ombudsman office, highly active in defending citizen's rights;[21] the free independent media, providing visibility of political life and revealing abuses and pathologies of power. A functioning democracy enhances the feelings of stability, security, accountability, and transparency – all fundamentally important for producing trust.

The third set of factors relate to the consolidation of the capitalist market and private property. The enactment of the constitution, and a series of specific laws dealing with the economic sphere, have built a legal foundation under the new capitalist economy. The principle of private ownership has been reaffirmed, and the progressing privatization of state-owned enterprises, as well as the consistent reinstating of property confiscated during the communist period, prove that the policy is stable and irreversible. At the same time a new capitalist infrastructure has rapidly emerged: banks, stock exchange, brokers, insurance companies, credit associations, mutual funds, and so forth. All this provides a conducive framework for a true explosion of entrepreneurship, which over some years has evolved from street peddling and illicit financial speculations to large-scale industrial ventures. Stability and certainty of the terms of trade, as well as a conducive and secure business environment contribute in important measure to the climate of trust.

The fourth set of factors has to do with the realistic perspective of inclusion into Western military, political, and economic alliances. With the formal invitation to NATO, and acceptance of NATO expansion by numerous Western parliaments, including the American Senate, the perspective of lasting military security and the guarantee of political sovereignty seem to be open. This is not a trifling matter in a country so badly treated by history: invaded innumerable times from the East, South, North, and West,[22] partitioned among imperial European powers for the whole of the nineteenth century up to World War I, suffering Nazi occupation and Soviet domination for the greater part of the twentieth century. No wonder that the bid for NATO is a matter on which Poles come closer to unanimity than on any other political issue. It is supported by around 80 percent of the citizens, with 10 percent against it, and 10 percent undecided (CBOS Bulletin No. 90/1997: 1). And the motivations for support indicated by the respondents mention most often national security (68%) and full sovereignty (56%) (CBOS Bulletin No. 27/1997: 6–8). The beginning of negotiations with the European Union has a rather different significance. In spite of some doubts and anxieties that it raises in some sections of the population that are more vulnerable to foreign competition (e.g., among the farmers, 75 percent of whom express worries, and only 16 percent hopes [CBOS Bulletin No. 66/1998: 2]), there is one widely understood asset: the unification of the legal system – and hence the political and economic regime – with the well-established market democracies of the West, provides a strong, external guarantee that new institutions will be lasting and firm. With the incorporation into the EU there would be a kind of new accountability: of the whole polity, economy, and legal system before the authorities of the Union. The reversal of reforms seems even less probable. Thus, external security and external accountability, allow for more predictability and trust. This seems to be recognized by 71 percent of the Poles who in 1998 supported the access to the EU (CBOS Bulletin No. 66/1998: 4).

The fifth set of factors conducive for the rebuilding of trust has to do with the expansion of personal and social capital, and the growth of resourcefulness, at least of some considerable sections of the population. We have argued before that the pool of resources provides a backup insurance for extending trust. In this respect we observe crucial changes over the last years. A sizable, relatively affluent middle class has emerged in Poland, feeling more secure and rooted (Mokrzycki 1995b). With the powerful rush for higher education, the level of educational achievement has been significantly raised, and with that the overall competence to estimate trustworthiness and arrive at grounded trust. With the growing availability of proliferating voluntary associations, clubs, organizations, and the like, spontaneous social participation has risen and personal networks expanded. Again this gives people a feeling of security, roots, and support.

Apart from those new forms of personal and social capital, there are old, traditional resources that are being successfully tapped under the new conditions. There are strong personal networks of friendships, acquaintanceships, and partnerships inherited from the communist period, when internal exile, privatization of life, and "amoral familism" were typical adaptive measures. When asked about the secret of their business successes, top Polish entrepreneurs almost unanimously indicated the rich personal networks, even before actual capital assets. In the Polish General Social Survey 60.43 percent have indicated "good connections" as a decisive or very important factor of life chances (Marody 1996: 63). Another traditional resource available in Polish conditions is strong and extended families. They provide insurance in case of life calamities, support in raising children and therefore allowing the pursuit of educational aspirations or professional careers for the parents, but also are helpful in pooling capital to start business enterprises. It has been quite typical under the new conditions that the family "delegates" one of its members to start a business, mobilizing common resources for this purpose, including savings, or the labor power of other family members. The third, less tangible, but perhaps also important, resource is belonging to a religious community. In the conditions of one of the most religious countries in Europe, with more than 90 percent Catholics, and some 60 percent churchgoers, this kind of support and security provided by the Church may play an important role in increasing readiness to trust.[23]

The final, sixth factor, which supplements the earlier five in initiating the revival of trust, is the universal and inevitable process of generational turnover. As we have argued, distrust cultures are deeply rooted in history, produced as sediments of frustrated experiences with trust and sometimes additionally petrified by inertia. The carriers of such traditions of distrust are generations. This means that the powerful legacies of distrust derived from earlier history, and internalized by the generations whose life was spent within the cultures of distrust, may lose their grip as new generations emerge, raised under different conditions, more conducive to trust. And this is precisely what is happening in postcommunist societies. The young people graduating from universities and starting occupational careers today have been practically insulated from the destructive impact of the communist system on their capacity to trust. For them it is history long past. They have been raised when the system was already falling apart, and educated in a free, democratic society. Thus they have not fallen prey to all those "trained incapacities," "civilizational incompetences," "cultures of cynicism," and "deficiencies of trust" haunting their parents' generation. They have also been saved the anxieties and uncertainties of oppositional combat, the elation of revolution, and the early disappointments of transition. Their world is relatively stable, established, secure, and predictable. It may be taken for granted, and hence trusted.

Due to all those six categories of factors, it seems that the vicious loop of deepening distrust in Poland has been overcome, and the virtuous self-amplifying loop of growing trust culture has finally been started on its way. A trust culture has entered into a mutually beneficial interaction with the slowly crystallizing democratic and market institutions, providing support for their viable operation, and being facilitated itself by the conducive context of democracy and the market. If I am correct that this mechanism is already in place, then we may look into Poland's future with a considerable dose of optimism.

Notes

Preface

1 This is similar to the directive that Max Weber called the "principle of objective possibility and adequate causation" in constructing the ideal types (Weber 1949: 164–188).
2 I remember how ridiculous it looked to the young believer in rigid scientific methods, when one of my teachers, the Nestor of Polish sociology, Kazimierz Dobrowolski, was telling us of his conversations with taxi drivers, on which he based sociological conclusions. Now I know better how right he was in his approach.
3 The empirical research was sponsored by a grant from the Committee of Scientific Research (KBN), and carried out with the help of a number of colleagues from Jagiellonian University, among whom Jan Jerschina, Ewa Rylko, and Pawel Bienka deserve special acknowledgment.
4 As my main goal was to seek the mechanisms of the functioning of trust in social life, rather than determining the levels or degrees of the phenomenon in concrete society, the issue of the representativeness of the sample was not crucial. The categories of respondents, as well as the cities where the research was carried out, were selected according to theoretical, preconceived hypotheses, and the random drawing of the sample was performed only within those categories.
5 This feeling, so common for scientific writers, perhaps deserves a name, "Scott effect," to eponymously commemorate the plight of Robert Scott beaten to the South Pole by Roald Amundsen.

1 The turn toward soft variables in sociological theory

1 By means of illustration, three concepts may be indicated as expressing in their own, specific ways the core idea of the field image: "figurations" (Elias 1978), "structuration" (Giddens 1984), and "social becoming" (Sztompka 1991a, 1993a).

2 The personal pronoun "we" is perhaps the most important word for a sociologist.

3 Of course this relatively narrow and specific definition of loyalty is not universally accepted. For example, Barbalet proposes a much more general and comprehensive concept: "Loyalty . . . is a feeling of the viability of the arrangement of elements in which cooperation takes place: loyalty is the emotion of confidence in organization" (Barbalet 1996: 80). I find this usage rather unfruitful, as it merges too closely with other concepts, like "existential security," "system confidence," etc.

2 The idea of trust

1 Notice that we are speaking here of unconditional predictions, or what Karl Popper called "prophecies" that something will indeed happen (Popper 1964). In the case of conditional predictions based on well-grounded, verified laws, we can of course be sure that if certain initial conditions of type "a" occur, then an event "b" will be the case. But still the uncertainty remains about whether initial conditions "a" will or will not occur.

2 It is like trying to predict where the leaf carried by the wind will fall, or on which flower the butterfly will sit, famous examples from natural science, pointing to the indeterminacy of events due to the complexity of interacting causal forces.

3 This is a paraphrase of a famous argument by Karl R. Popper who claimed that "prophecies" of future social events are impossible on purely logical grounds, because saying that we can know future knowledge is a contradiction in terms (Popper 1964).

4 This is the reason for the humorous effect of the cartoon depicting a man with a dog on a leash. The dog barks and pulls violently. "Stop that, or I will lose trust in you" the man says.

5 The story of a Polish priest, Maksymilian Kolbe, voluntarily giving his life in exchange for the life of a fellow prisoner at Auschwitz illustrates well this ultimate human freedom.

6 A similar idea of confidence, with the emphasis on passive contemplation is to be found in Luhmann (1988: 97).

7 A different account of confidence, as basically distinct from trust, is given by Seligman (1997). In his account it is not the passive contemplation that distinguishes confidence, but rather the firmness of expectations on which action (or abstaining from action) is based. Confidence is to be found when the structure of roles is precisely and unambiguously articulated, the role demands binding, and therefore one can be assured (also by the possibility of sanctions) that the partner will play by the rules. On the other hand, trust is taken to appear only when "there is role negotiability, in what may be termed the 'open spaces' of roles and role expectations," when "whole arenas of human interaction can no longer be encompassed by externally attributable patterns of

behavior (i.e. by role expectations)" (Seligman 1997: 24, 54). I would argue against this view that the difference between confidence and trust so conceived is only of degree and not of kind. There is never a complete determinacy or certainty as to how role incumbents will actually behave, even if the rigid role systems makes conformity plausible. Role theory has always emphasized the discrepancies between role demands and role performance. Similarly, even in the "interstices of system, or at system limit, when for one reason or another systematically defined role expectations are no longer viable" (Seligman 1997: 25), full indeterminacy need not reign, as an actor may have a number of other cues as to the probable conduct of the partner. Thus for me, both are cases of trust, differing only in the strength of grounding, or justification. Hence I would insist on reserving the term confidence for passive contemplation of the possibly beneficial actions of others.

8 After forming this definition I have discovered that the metaphor of the bet has also occurred to James Coleman, even though he did not explore it further. "The elements confronting the potential truster are nothing more or less than the considerations a rational actor applies in deciding whether to place a bet" (Coleman 1990: 99).

9 Discounted sales items are usually non-returnable. The store pays for the stronger commitment of the customer by lowering the price.

10 It is in recognition of that stronger commitment that such institutions usually reward clients with higher interest.

11 In the case of a medical practitioner, the very fact that I come as a patient may be an implicit indicator of trust and elicit an obligation. But only if there is a wide and available choice. In the condition of monopoly this presumption does not operate. The anonymous practitioners in the state-run health service in communist Poland, who were the only available physicians in their villages, had no reason to suspect special trust of their patients vested in them. They knew they were there by necessity, and not through choice based on trust. Perhaps this is the reason why they were not obliged to give thorough treatment, and perhaps a part of the reason why privatized, competitive medical services are usually better.

12 Which could possibly be mitigated, at least among male faculty members, if only they knew that the girl was particularly good-looking.

13 The biographers relate that this was what actually occurred to Robert K. Merton some two decades ago. He took the risk and is still alive and well.

14 There are some hypotheses about a physiological basis for that, linked to the dynamics of adrenaline flow. The sociological explanation could refer to the association of risk-taking with courage, and the raising of prestige that courage brings as a widely recognized virtue.

15 Sports, and particularly dangerous sports, is one of the typical areas satisfying such cravings. Another is gambling.

16 Charles H. Cooley's "looking-glass-self mechanism" seems to be at work here (Cooley 1909).

17 As we shall argue later, it may also trigger the self-fulfilling dynamics raising the chances of a divorce.

18 I should have been aware of the strange general attitude toward returning borrowed books. Perfectly honest people sometimes act as if books were a communal property, and neglect to return them. Perhaps it has something to do with the belief that the ideas included in books, once published, become a public good.

3 Varieties of trust

1 As has been indicated, even if we sometimes say that "we trust ourselves," or that "we cannot trust ourselves," there is the implication that we take an objective perspective, step out of ourselves, so to say, and look at ourselves from a detached, distanced position. Self-trust or self-distrust implies that we look at ourselves, in imagination, as if we were the "other," of whose actions we cannot be certain.

2 During the communist period, Polish people used to joke that in the media only the obituaries are true.

3 I have had a memorable experience of staying in New York on the day of the famous "blackout" of 1978, when electric power broke down for almost twenty-four hours. The life of the city was largely paralyzed, and episodes of total chaos were in abundance. Similar experiences accompany any transportation strike, or the walkout of the sanitation services and trash collectors in our big cities.

4 In this case there is seemingly a slight departure from our definition of trust as a bet on the future actions of others. We seem to trust the past actions of the designers, constructors, producers, but in fact the expectations that we make when vesting trust in some products rather than others are to be fulfilled in the future: the future faultless performance of a car, the future usefulness of a detergent, the future lasting quality of shoes, the future enjoyment of a book. Thus in a sense we trust the past actions of producers, but embodied in the future performance of products.

5 Some authors believe truthfulness to be the central moral virtue in granting trust. This emphasis is to be found in a number of ancient theologians and philosophers, but also in contemporary writers: "If there is no confidence in the truthfulness of others, is there any way to assess their fairness, their intentions to help or to harm? How, then, can they be trusted?" (Bok 1979: 33). Cheating, if discovered, means particularly severe disappointment of trust, and may lead to withdrawal of trust of other sorts (there is a sort of "halo-effect" of cheating). "Veracity . . . is the cornerstone of relationships among human beings; to the degree that it erodes, to that degree is the confidence in the benefits, protection of harm, and fairness one has to count upon made haphazard, undermined" (Bok 1979: 81). A special case of veracity is keeping promises, taking one's word seriously (Silver 1985: 56).

6 "The essence of help . . . is acting on a spontaneous impulse, without expectation or calculation of ultimate reward" (Merton et al. 1983: 14).

7 Or A trusts B in matter Y.

8 In the election year Kuron had the top place in the rankings of trust, with 82 percent of indications, and yet received only around 10 percent of the vote. In spite of electoral defeat he was still leading in the hierarchy of trust in 1997, with 74 percent of indications (*Gazeta Wyborcza*, December 23, 1997; *Gazeta Wyborcza* [henceforth *GW*] is a popular daily newspaper).

9 In the Polish case, just preceding my research in 1997 there was a highly visible involvement of the army in fighting disastrous floods.

10 Known in the legal profession as "attorney–client privilege."

4 Foundations of trust

1 The complete, purposeful construction of reputation, with care for even the smallest details, is known among spies as "building cover." It may take years to give it full credibility, before it is used for deceit.

2 Special cases, when supplementary trust coincides with main trust, are obviously CVs or résumés, as well as autobiographies. Similarly personal Internet pages are usually constructed by the interested individuals themselves. We have to believe in the truthfulness of the very same person whose reputation we want to determine. This is why most often we do not rely exclusively on such documents, looking for independent referees or other corroborating evidence.

3 A recent example is Victor Chernomyrdin, the former Prime Minister of Russia, and previously the head of the huge industrial agglomerate, "Gazprom."

4 As recently Michele Platini, a famous football player, was given managerial responsibility for the immense enterprise of the World Cup 1998.

5 But interestingly, to some extent we also care for reputations in the eyes of complete strangers, clearly "insignificant others." Chong explains it by "embarrassment aversion . . . discomfort of walking out of the restaurant under the watchful eyes of its employees without leaving a sufficient tip" (Chong 1992: 703). It may also be due to being ashamed before our companion, or just the strongly internalized social custom, producing a guilt feeling if disobeyed.

6 With reference to the famous New York department store.

7 With reference to the famous Italian designer.

8 Every scholar knows how hard it is to write the next book, if the earlier one was successful, because one feels that it should be at least equally good, if not better. As Merton puts it: "the reward system based on recognition for work accomplished tends to induce continued effort . . . Such social pressures do not often permit those who have climbed the rugged mountains of scientific achievement to remain content" (Merton 1973: 442).

9 Steffi Graf had to struggle in eliminations for major tournaments when, due to health problems, she fell down from her No. 1 spot in the rankings.

10 We read of luxurious limousines being driven for days through rocky deserts. We read of Tag Heuer watches being exposed to extreme temperatures and tremendous pressures in special chambers. One sometimes wonders why and what for, and yet it normally raises trust, and consequently sales.

11 With common sense supporting the wisdom of a joke: there are three degrees of lies: lies, damn lies, and statistics.

12 The only occasion when my students at UCLA wear white shirts and ties on the campus is when representatives of corporations come to interview for jobs. This is the simplest trick for looking respectable, and winning the trust of prospective employers.

13 Even this facilitating condition for trust may be faked. Robert Merton describes a pattern he calls "pseudo-Gemeinschaft": "subtle methods of salesmanship in which there is the feigning of personal concern with the client in order to manipulate him the better" (Merton 1968: 163). Well-trained salespeople take an informal, almost intimate approach toward their clients. They pretend friendliness, care for our interests, call us by our first name – all in order to win our trust and sell their product. "What the salesman does is attempt to introduce personal factors into the exchange. By operating on a first-name basis and speaking in a familiar tone to the customer, he makes it more difficult for the customer to distrust him openly" (Chong 1992: 703).

14 Perhaps this is the causal link that connects trust and a rich network of associations, in the concept of social capital as advanced by Robert Putnam (Putnam 1995b, 1995c). He never spells out the nature of this link, but seems to take it for granted.

15 The famous cartoon in the *New Yorker* shows two dogs sitting in front of a monitor and reading sex messages through e-mail. "You see, on the Internet she even doesn't know I am a dog" says one to the other.

16 Rational shopping becomes quite a complex job, a bit akin to comparative research. Therefore many people follow the easier way and resort to gut-feelings, intuition, imitation, whims, snobbishness, commercials, to the delight of dishonest producers and sellers.

17 Perhaps it is the anonymity of modern urban settings, with their huge apartment blocks, which is an additional reason explaining the pervasive syndrome of distrust and untrustworthiness in our time.

18 I wonder if the recent recall of a small Mercedes A-model, or a new Volkswagen "Beetle," are not ingenious marketing devices intended to increase even more the visibility and demand for those new products.

19 This obvious measure to raise feelings of security and enhance trust is based on the commonly experienced feeling of anxiety at night, and raised confidence during the daytime.

5 The functions of trust

1 It is always only a chance, as trustworthiness is always only a probability grounded in our knowledge of the reputation (credentials), performance, appearance, accountability, and situational facilitations. Were it not a probability, but a certainty, no trust would be needed.
2 The controllers as one of their role demands have to assume the opposite principle: "guilty until proven innocent."
3 Political scientists refer to that as the pre-revolutionary "withdrawal of legitimacy from the regime."
4 This seems to be the main secret of the successes of Italian police in their struggle with the Mafia. The unassailable fortress started to crumble once a certain number of *pentiti* broke the bonds of loyalty and trust, testifying against their partners. The virus of distrust started to spread, destroying the internal solidarity of the crime organization.
5 This reaction is typical for situations of extreme uncertainty and indeterminacy of the future. I remember listening to the interviews with passengers boarding other planes at Kennedy Airport immediately after the fatal crash of TWA 800 over Long Island. The constantly repeated phrases were: "It is all fate," "what must happen shall happen anyway," "if my destiny is to die, I will be run over by a car if I don't board this plane," etc.

6 The culture of trust

1 As Giddens observes, the more future-oriented a person becomes, the greater is the relevance of trust in that person's actions (Giddens 1991: 87).
2 Just compare Poland with East Germany at the end of the nineties, or Poland at the end of the seventies with the Poland of today.
3 Let us notice that whereas the structural conditions – stability, transparency, familiarity, and so forth – produce lower likelihood of breaches of trust, and hence invite trust, in the case of personal resources the probability of breaches of trust is not smaller, but the relative (subjective) acceptability of such breaches and the losses they imply is higher, and hence the readiness to extend trust is apt to grow.
4 To avoid using the term "social capital," in one more, new sense of this highly fashionable concept.
5 Or "social capital," this time in the strict sense of the term, as introduced by Putnam (Putnam 1995b, 1995c, 1996). It is not accidental it seems, that Putnam links trust and networks by definition, in the connotation of his concept of "social capital." The intuition is right, but in my interpretation the link is not definitional, but empirical, causal, operating through that mechanism of providing backup insurance for trust.

7 Trust in democracy and autocracy

1 That is why we feel more secure – and more trustful of others – when visiting democratic countries, and feel insecure and threatened when visiting autocracies. In the latter we feel at the mercy of the arbitrary will of local authorities, protected only at a distance by our own trusted country and its passport in our pocket. In the former we feel that we have rights, and can resort for help and support to various institutions if our rights are endangered or abused.

2 As the classical political philosophers put it, the government is a trustee of the people, and is held accountable to fulfill this role (Silver 1985: 53).

3 "The rights of resistance" in John Locke's phrase.

4 This applies in fact not only to the delegating of power, but also to the everyday functioning of public institutions, and their style of operation. If citizens are treated with dignity, as partners and not as subjects or even suspects, they are more apt to extend trust. The style of policy is an important variable generating trust or distrust (Przeworski et al. 1995: 76). The more citizens perceive themselves to be distrusted by the government, the less they trust the government.

5 Some authors consider free, uninhibited communication to be central for democracy. See Jurgen Habermas' idea of public space, or communicative action (Habermas 1984, 1987), or John Dryzek's conception of "discursive democracy" (Dryzek 1990).

6 A famous cartoon in a Polish journal showed a communist party leader giving a speech to the Politburo. He was saying: "In view of problems, instead of changing the government we have just decided to exchange the society for a more obedient one."

8 Trust and rapid social change: a case study

1 This assumption is also made by Misztal, who emphasizes the importance of "unsettled, transitional periods" for the understanding of trust dynamics (Misztal 1996: 63), as well as Ekiert and Kubik, who observe that "regime transitions offer a unique opportunity to study the institutionalization of relationships among various domains in the society in statu nascendi" (Ekiert and Kubik 1997: 30).

2 The radical changes of the whole social system in the postcommunist world fit well as one of the cases that Merton describes introducing the term "strategic research site": "The history of sociology has its own complement of cases in which long-dormant problems were brought to life and developed by investigating them in situations that strategically exhibit the nature of the problem" (Merton 1982: 33).

3 Understood by Nowak by the concept of the "sociological vacuum."

4 The significance of this event is emphasized by many observers (See Garton Ash 1990a, 1990b; Ekiert 1996: 218).

5 This triple bond was clearly seen in the symbolism employed during industrial strikes or street demonstrations: the Polish flag, the cross, and the workers' helmets.

6 An interesting salient symptom of this in the life-world was the flourishing of social life at private homes, with the cinemas, theaters, concerts halls, restaurants, and cafés remaining empty.

7 A similar cycle is visible after each change of government. At the beginning, the novelty elicits trust. But then comes the time of delivery, and as over-ambitious election promises are rarely met, trust decays and distrust sets in.

8 This phenomenon is typical for the whole postcommunist world: "When Russians were asked whether they trusted or distrusted key institutions of civil society, the average respondent expressed distrust of seven out of ten. A similar level of distrust was expressed by people in the Czech Republic, Slovakia, Hungary, and Poland. In all these countries, levels of public trust in institutions are significantly lower than the level that researchers typically find in both Western Europe and the United States" (Rose 1994: 25).

9 The number of private security guards is estimated by the police to be 100,000–150,000.

10 This is a fascinating case of the pervasiveness of traditional attachments and trust, by means of inertia. In Polish history, the army has always been one of the strongest symbols of sovereignty and national causes, as well as the depository of memories of heroic struggles during the World Wars. The high ideologization and politicization of the army during the communist period, its role during the martial law of 1981, the cases of demoralization in the ranks and abuse of young recruits, and the low defense potential and internal disorganization – have not shaken this legacy of trust.

11 *Polityka* is an upmarket weekly journal covering political, economic, and cultural issues.

12 The dynamics of this phenomenon are unprecedented: from 568,000 in 1990 to 2,600,000 in 1992. See Kozek 1996: 94.

13 If you wonder how the unemployed may claim any improvement at all, just think about the vast "black economy" opened by the period of transition, as well as outright illegitimate opportunities, including organized crime.

14 These levels of trust are already quite considerable if we compare them to Russian figures, where only 10 percent declare that they trust the parliament (Duma), 11 percent express trust for the president, and 12 percent for the government (*Economist*, August 2, 1997: 18).

15 Of course the lower concern with crime is only relative, compared to other worries. Generally, there is still a widespread feeling of insecurity due to criminal acts. In 1997 only 34 percent declared that they felt secure, and 61 percent declared that they experienced insecurity due to the growing crime

rates (*Rzeczpospolita*, August 16, 1997). But even those high levels are lower than the peak of anxieties in 1995.

16 Even with correction for inflation and rising building costs, it indicates actual growth.

17 Retrospectively, evaluating all seven prime ministers heading Polish governments since 1989, 28 percent indicated the leftist Wlodzimierz Cimoszewicz as the best, with Tadeusz Mazowiecki receiving only 14 percent of indications (CBOS Bulletin No. 147/1997: 2).

18 But in fact in the middle of the year, at the time of writing, it already runs over 6 percent.

19 Just to mention one spectacular indicator: in the year 1997 the number of new cars purchased in Poland reached 470,000, the second largest in Europe after Italy, and in just one month of March 1998, this number exceeded 50,000 (*GW*, May 7, 1998).

20 The Tribunal quite early reached high rates of approval, with 59 percent of the nationwide sample judging its actions as good (CBOS Bulletin No. 2/1995: 101).

21 It was approved by 53 percent of the people (CBOS Bulletin No. 1/1991: 50).

22 As if it were really that "God's playground" that Norman Davies puts into the witty title of his monumental history of Poland (Davies 1981).

23 The importance of such traditional communal and familial resources is confirmed by the national auto-stereotypes of the Poles: 84 percent of respondents indicated patriotism, 93 percent religious attachments, and 80 percent orientation toward the family as most typical traits of the Polish people (CBOS Bulletin No. 9/1996: 16).

Bibliography

Alexander, J. C. (ed.) 1988, *Durkheimian Sociology: Cultural Studies*, Cambridge, England: Cambridge University Press.

Alexander, J. C. 1990, "Bringing democracy back in: universalistic solidarity and the civil sphere," Los Angeles: UCLA (mimeo).

Alexander, J. C. 1991, "Democracy and civil society," Los Angeles: UCLA (mimeo).

Alexander, J. C. 1992, "Citizen and enemy as symbolic classification: On the polarizing discourse of civil society," in: M. Lamont and M. Fournier (eds.), *Cultivating Differences*, Chicago: University of Chicago Press.

Alexander, J. C. 1998, "Civil society I, II, III: Constructing an empirical concept from normative controversies and historical transformations," in: J. C. Alexander (ed.), *Real Civil Societies*, London: Sage, pp. 1–19.

Alexander, J. C. and Smith, P. 1993, "The discourse of American civil society: a new proposal for cultural studies," in: *Theory and Society*, No. 22, pp. 151–207.

Allport, G. W., 1954, *The Nature of Prejudice*, Garden City, New York: Doubleday.

Almond, G. and Verba, S. 1965 (1963), *The Civic Culture: Political Attitudes and Democracy in Five Nations*, Boston: Little Brown.

Almond, G. and Verba, S. (eds.) 1980, *The Civic Culture Revisited*, Boston: Little Brown.

Arato, A. 1981, "Civil society against the state: Poland 1980–81," in: *Telos*, Vol. 47, pp. 23–47.

Archer, M. 1988, *Culture and Agency*, Cambridge, England: Cambridge University Press.

Baier, A. 1986, "Trust and antitrust," in: *Ethics*, No. 96, January, pp. 231–260.

Baier, A. 1995, *Moral Prejudices: Essays on Ethics*, Cambridge, Mass.: Harvard University Press.

Banfield, E. C. 1967 (1958), *The Moral Basis of a Backward Society*, New York: Free Press.

Barbalet, J. M. 1996, "Social emotions: confidence, trust and loyalty," in: *International Journal of Sociology and Social Policy*, Vol. 16, No. 9/10, pp. 75–96.

Barber, B. 1983, *The Logic and Limits of Trust*, New Brunswick, New Jersey: Rutgers University Press.

Barber, B. 1990, *Social Studies of Science*, New Brunswick, New Jersey: Transaction Publishers.

Bauman, Z. 1988, *Modernity and the Holocaust*, Cambridge, England: Polity Press.

Beck, U. 1992, *Risk Society*, London: Sage.

Beck, U., Giddens, A., and Lash, S., 1994, *Reflexive Modernization*, Cambridge, England: Polity Press.

Bellah, R. N., Madsen, R., Sullivan, W. M., Swindler, A., and Tipton, S. M. 1991, *The Good Society*, New York: Alfred Knopf.

Benn, S. I. and Peters, R. S. 1977, *Social Principles and the Democratic State*, London: Allen & Unwin.

Blumstein, P. and Kollock, P. 1988, "Personal relationships," in: *Annual Review of Sociology*, Vol. 14, pp. 467–490.

Bok, S. 1979, *Lying: Moral Choice in Public and Private Life*, New York: Vintage Books.

Bourdieu, P. 1977, *Outline of a Theory of Practice*, Cambridge, England: Cambridge University Press.

Bourdieu, P. 1996, *The State Nobility: Elite Schools in the Field of Power*, Cambridge, England: Polity Press.

Bourdieu, P. and Passeron, J.-C. 1979, *The Inheritors, French Students and their Relation to Culture*, Chicago: University of Chicago Press.

Brzeziński, Z. 1989, "Toward a common European home," in: *Problems of Communism*, November–December, pp. 1–10.

CBOS Bulletin = periodical of the Center for the Study of Social Opinions, Warsaw.

Central and Eastern Eurobarometer = periodical of the Commission of European Communities, Brussels.

Chong, D. 1992, "Reputation and cooperative behavior," in: *Social Science Information*, Vol. 31, No. 4, pp. 683–709.

Cladis, M. S. 1992, *A Communitarian Defense of Liberalism: Emile Durkheim and Contemporary Social Theory*, Stanford, Calif.: Stanford University Press.

Clarke, L. and Short, J. F., Jr. 1993, "Social organization and risk: some current controversies," in: *Annual Review of Sociology*, Vol. 19, pp. 375–399.

Cohen, J. L. and Arato, A. 1992, *Civil Society and Political Theory*, Cambridge, Mass.: MIT Press.

Coleman, J. C. 1990, *Foundations of Social Theory*, Cambridge, Mass.: Harvard University Press.

Cooley, C. H. 1909, *Social Organization*, New York: Scribner's.

Coser, L. A. 1974, *Greedy Institutions: Patterns of Undivided Commitment*, New York: Free Press.

Dahl, R. A. 1971, *Polyarchy*, New Haven, Conn.: Yale University Press.

Dahrendorf, R. 1980, "On representative activities," in: T. F. Gieryn (ed.), *Science and Social Structure*, New York: NY Academy of Sciences, pp. 15–27.

Dahrendorf, R. 1990, *Reflections on the Revolution in Europe*, New York: Times Books.

Dasgupta, P. 1988, "Trust as a commodity," in: D. Gambetta (ed.), *Trust: Making and Breaking Cooperative Relations*, Oxford: Basil Blackwell, pp. 49–71.

Davies, N. 1981, *God's Playground: A History of Poland*, Vols. I and II, Oxford: Clarendon Press.

Dawe, A. 1978, "Theories of social action," in: T. B. Bottomore and R. Nisbet (eds.) *A History of Sociological Analysis*, New York: Basic Books, pp. 362–417.

Dryzek, J. S. 1990, *Discoursive Democracy*, Cambridge, England: Cambridge University Press.

Dunn, J. 1988, "Trust and political agency," in: D. Gambetta (ed.), *Trust: Making and Breaking Cooperative Relations*, Oxford: Basil Blackwell, pp. 73–93.

Durkheim, E. 1951 (1897), *Suicide*, New York: Free Press.

Durkheim, E. 1964a (1895), *The Rules of Sociological Method*, New York: Free Press.

Durkheim, E. 1964b (1893), *The Division of Labor in Society*, New York: Free Press.

Durkheim, E. 1965 (1912), *The Elementary Forms of the Religious Life*, New York: Free Press.

Earle, T. and Cvetkovich, G. T. 1995, *Social Trust: Toward a Cosmopolitan Society*, New York: Praeger.

Eisenstadt, S. N. and Roniger, L., 1984, *Patrons, Clients and Friends*, Cambridge, England: Cambridge University Press.

Ekiert, G. 1996, *The State Against Society: Political Crises and their Aftermath in East-Central Europe*, Princeton, New Jersey: Princeton University Press.

Ekiert, G. and Kubik, J. 1997, "Collective protest and democratic consolidation in Poland, 1989–93," in: A. Seleny and E. Suleimann (eds.) *New Papers on Central Eastern European Reforms and Regionalism*, No. 3, Princeton, New Jersey: Center of International Studies, Princeton University.

Elias, N. 1978, *What is Sociology?*, London: Hutchinson.

Elster, J. 1989, *Solomonic Judgements*, Cambridge, England: Cambridge University Press.

Frieske, K. 1996, "Porządek społeczny i jego zagrożenia," (Threats to the social order), in: M. Marody and E. Gucwa-Leśny (eds.), *Podstawy Życia społecz-*

nego w Polsce (The foundations of social life in Poland), Warsaw: Instytut Studiów Społecznych, pp. 116–134.

Fukuyama, F. 1995, *Trust: The Social Virtues and the Creation of Prosperity*, New York: Free Press.

Gambetta, D. (ed.) 1988a, *Trust: Making and Breaking Cooperative Relations*, Oxford: Basil Blackwell.

Gambetta, D. 1988b, "Can we trust trust?," in: D. Gambetta (ed.), *Trust: Making and Breaking Cooperative Relations*, Oxford: Basil Blackwell, pp. 213–237.

Gambetta, D. 1988c, "Mafia: the price of distrust," in D. Gambetta (ed.), *Trust: Making and Breaking Cooperative Relations*, Oxford: Blackwell, pp. 154–175.

Gambetta, D. 1993, *The Sicilian Mafia*, Cambridge, Mass.: Harvard University Press.

Garton Ash, T. 1989, *The Uses of Adversity*, New York: Random House.

Garton Ash, T. 1990a, *We the People: The Revolution of 89*, Cambridge, England: Granta Books.

Garton Ash, T. 1990b, "Eastern Europe: the year of truth," in: *The New York Review of Books*, February 15, 1990, pp. 17–22.

Giddens, A. 1984, *The Constitution of Society*, Cambridge, England: Polity Press.

Giddens, A. 1990a, *The Consequences of Modernity*, Cambridge, England: Polity Press.

Giddens, A. 1990b, "Review of 'The Cement of Society' by J. Elster," in: *American Journal of Sociology*, Vol. 96, No. 1, pp. 223–225.

Giddens, A. 1991, *Modernity and Self-Identity*, Stanford, Calif.: Stanford University Press.

Giza-Poleszczuk, A. 1991, "Stosunki międzyludzkie i życie zbiorowe" (Interpersonal relations and collective life), in: M. Marody (ed.), *Co nam zostało z tych lat* (What has remained of those years), London: Aneks, pp. 69–105.

Goffman, E. 1959, *The Presentation of Self in Everyday Life*, Garden City, New York: Doubleday.

Goffman, E. 1967, *Interaction Ritual*, New York: Doubleday.

Good, D. 1988, "Individuals, interpersonal relations, and trust," in: D. Gambetta (ed.), *Trust: Making and Breaking Cooperative Relations*, Oxford: Basil Blackwell, pp. 31–48.

Gucwa-Leśny, E. 1996, "Zmiany poziomu życia i ich ocena," in: M. Marody and E. Gucwa-Leśny (eds.), *Podstawy życia społecznego w Polsce* (The foundations of social life in Poland), Warsaw: Instytut Studiów Społecznych, pp. 100–115.

Gurr, T. 1970, *Why Men Rebel?*, Princeton, New Jersey: Princeton University Press.

Habermas, J. 1984, *Theory of Communicative Action*, Vols. I and II, Boston: Beacon Press.

Habermas, J. 1987, *The Philosophical Discourse of Modernity*, Cambridge, Mass.: MIT Press.

Hannerz, U. 1993, "When culture is everywhere," in: *Ethnos*, Vol. 58, pp. 95–111.

Hannerz, U. 1996, *Transnational Connections; Culture, People, Places*, London: Routledge.

Hardin, R. 1991, "Trusting persons, trusting institutions," in: R. J. Zeckhauser (ed.), *Strategy and Choice*, Cambridge, Mass.: MIT Press, pp. 185–209.

Hardin, R. 1993, "The street-level epistemology of trust," in: *Politics and Society*, Vol. 21, No. 4, pp. 505–529.

Hardin, R. 1996, "Trustworthiness," in: *Ethics*, No. 107, pp. 26–42.

Hechter, M. and Kanazawa, S. 1993, "Group solidarity and social order in Japan," in: *Journal of Theoretical Politics*, Vol. 5, No. 4, pp. 455–493.

Himmelfarb, G. 1998, "Democratic remedies for democratic disorders," in: *The Public Interest*, Vol. 131, Spring, pp. 3–24.

Hirschman, A. O. 1970, *Exit, Voice, and Loyalty: Responses to Decline in Firms, Organizations, and States*, Cambridge, Mass.: Harvard University Press.

Holmes, J. G. and Rempel, J. K. 1989, "Trust in close relationships," in C. Hendrick (ed.), "Close relationships," special issue of *Personality and Social Psychology*, No. 10, Newbury Park, Calif.: Sage.

Holmes, S. 1993, "Tocqueville and democracy," in: D. Copp et al. (eds.), *The Idea of Democracy*, Cambridge, England: Cambridge University Press, pp. 23–63.

Inglehart, R. 1988, "The renaissance of political culture," in: *American Political Science Review*, No. 4, pp. 1203–1230.

Inglehart, R. 1990, *Culture Shift in Advanced Industrial Societies*, Princeton, New Jersey: Princeton University Press.

Janis, I. L. 1982, *Victims of Groupthink*, Boston: Houghton Mifflin.

Keane, J. 1988, *Democracy and Civil Society*, London: Verso.

Kolarska-Bobińska, L. 1994, "Social interests and their political representation: Poland in transition," CBOS conference paper (mimeo).

Kollock, P. 1994, "The emergence of exchange structures: an experimental study of uncertainty, commitment, and trust," in: *American Journal of Sociology*, Vol. 100, No. 2, pp. 313–345.

Koralewicz, J. and Ziółkowski, M. 1990, *Mentalność Polakow* (Mentality of the Poles), Poznan: Nakom.

Kozek, W. 1996, "Bezrobocie jako zjawisko społeczne" in: M. Marody and E. Gucwa-Leśny (eds.), *Podstawy życia społecznego w Polsce* (The foundations of social life in Poland), Warsaw: Instytut Studiów Społecznych, pp. 87–99.

Krygier, M. 1995, "The constitution of the heart," Sydney: University of New South Wales (mimeo).

Krzywicki, L. 1957, *Pierwociny więzi społecznej* (The rudiments of a social bond), Warsaw: KiW.

Kumar, K. 1993, "Civil society: an inquiry into the usefulness of an historical term," in: *British Journal of Sociology*, No. 3, pp. 375–401.

Lane, Ch. and Bachmann, R. 1994, "Risk, trust and power: The social constitution of supplier relations in Britain and Germany," University of Cambridge (mimeo).

Laub-Coser, R. 1975, "Complexity of roles as a seedbed of individual autonomy," in: L. A. Coser (ed.), *The Idea of Social Structure: Papers in Honor of Robert K. Merton*, New York: Harcourt Brace Jovanovich, pp. 237–263.

Lepenies, W. 1992, "Social surprises: Germany in Europe, three years after the revolution," Berlin: Fritz Thyssen Stiftung (mimeo).

Lewis, J. D. and Weigert, A. 1985, "Trust as a social reality," in: *Social Forces*, No. 63, pp. 967–985.

Lipset, S. M. and Schneider, W. 1987, *Confidence Gap: Business, Labor, and Government in the Public Mind*, Baltimore, Md.: The Johns Hopkins University Press.

Luhmann, N. 1979, *Trust and Power*, New York: John Wiley.

Luhmann, N. 1988, "Familiarity, confidence, trust: problems and alternatives," in: D. Gambetta (ed.), *Trust: Making and Breaking Cooperative Relations*, Oxford: Basil Blackwell, pp. 94–107.

Luhmann, N. 1994, *Risk: A Sociological Theory*, New York: Aldine de Gruyter.

Lutyński J. 1987 "Działania pozorne (take actions) in: *Kultura i Społeczenstwo* (Culture and Society), Vol. II, No. 2 (reprinted in Lutyński, 1990, pp. 105–120).

Lutyński, J. 1990, *Nauka i polskie problemy* (Science and the Polish challenge), Warsaw: PIW.

Malcolm N., 1988, "Wittgenstein's 'scepticism' in 'On Certainty'," in: *Inquiry*, No. 31, pp. 277–293.

Mansbridge, J. J. 1983, *Beyond Adversary Democracy*, Chicago: University of Chicago Press.

Marody, M. 1987, "Antynomie społecznej podświadomości" (Antinomies of social subconsciousness), in: *Odra*, No. 1, pp. 4–9 (also reprinted in *Studia Socjologiczne*, No. 2).

Marody, M. 1990, "Dylematy postaw politycznych i orientacji światopoglądowych" (The dilemmas of political attitudes and world views), in: J. J. Wiatr (ed.), *Polska 1980–1990*, Warsaw: Warsaw University Press, pp. 157–174.

Marody, M. (ed.) 1991, *Co nam zostalo z tych lat: społeczeństwo polskie u progu zmiany systemowej* (What has remained of those years: Polish society at the verge of systemic change), London: Aneks.

Marody, M. 1996 (ed.), *Oswajanie rzeczywistości* (Taming reality), Warsaw: Instytut Studiów Społecznych.

Marody, M. and Gucwa-Leśny, E. (eds.) (1996), *Podstawy życia społecznego w Polsce* (The foundations of social life in Poland), Warsaw: Instytut Studiów Społecznych.

Marx, K. 1975 (1844), *Economic and Philosophic Manuscripts of 1844* in: Vol. III of K. Marx and F. Engels, *Collected Works*, New York: International Publishers.

McAllister, D. 1995, "Affect and cognition based trust as foundations for interpersonal cooperation in organizations," in: *Academy of Management Journal*, Vol. 38, pp. 24–59.

Mead, G. H. 1964, *On Social Psychology*, Chicago: University of Chicago Press.

Merton, R. K. 1965, *On the Shoulders of Giants*, New York: Harcourt Brace.

Merton, R. K. 1968, *Social Theory and Social Structure*, 2nd edition, New York: Free Press.

Merton, R. K. 1973 (1963), "Multiple discoveries as strategic research site," in: R. K. Merton, *The Sociology of Science* (ed. by N. W. Storer), Chicago: University of Chicago Press, pp. 371–382.

Merton, R. K. 1976, *Sociological Ambivalence and Other Essays*, New York: Free Press.

Merton, R. K. 1982, "The self-fulfilling prophecy," in: A. Rosenblatt and T. F. Gieryn (eds.), *Social Research and the Practicing Professions*, Cambridge, Mass.: ABT Books, pp. 248–267.

Merton, R. K. 1996 (1938), *On Social Structure and Science* (edited and with an introduction by P. Sztompka), Chicago: University of Chicago Press.

Merton, R. K. and Kendall, P. L. 1944, "The boomerang response," in: *Channels*, No. 21/7, pp. 1–7.

Merton, V., Merton R. K., and Barber, E. 1983, "Client ambivalence in professional relationships: The problem of seeking help from strangers," in: B. M. DePaulo (ed.), *New Directions in Helping*, Vol. II, New York: Academic Press, pp. 13–44.

Mikołejko, A. 1991, *Poza autorytetem? Społeczeństwo polskie w sytuacji anomii* (Beyond authority? Polish society in conditions of anomie), Warsaw: KeyTex.

Miszalska, A. 1996, *Reakcje społeczne na przemiany ustrojowe* (Social reactions to regime change"), Łódź: Łódz University Press.

Misztal, B. A. 1996, *Trust in Modern Societies*, Cambridge, England: Polity Press.

Mokrzycki, E. 1995a, "Class interests, redistribution and corporatism," in: C. Bryant and E. Mokrzycki (eds.), *Democracy, Civil Society and Pluralism*, Warsaw: IFiS PAN, pp. 205–218.

Mokrzycki, E. 1995b, "A new middle class?," in: C. Bryant and E. Mokrzycki (eds), *Democracy, Civil Society and Pluralism*, Warsaw: IFiS PAN, pp. 219–238.

Nagorski, A. 1991, "The wall in our heads," in: *Newsweek*, April 29, p. 4.

Nowak, L. 1991, *U Podstaw Teorii Socjalizmu* (Foundations of the theory of socialism), Vols. I–II, Poznań: Nakom.

Nowak, S. 1979, "System wartości społeczeństwa polskiego" (The system of values of Polish society), in: *Studia Socjologiczne*, No. 4, pp. 7–29.

Nowak, S. 1987, "Społeczeństwo polskie drugiej połowy lat 80-tych" (Polish society in the second half of the eighties [The report for the Polish Socio-logical Association]), Warsaw: PTS (mimeo).

OBOP Bulletin = the periodical of the Institute for Public Opinion Research, affiliated with Polish public broadcasting.

Offe, C. 1996, "Trust and knowledge, rules and decisions," Washington: George-town University (mimeo).

Offe, C. and Preuss, UK 1991, "Democratic institutions and moral resources," in: D. Held (ed.), *Political Theory Today*, Stanford, Calif.: Stanford University Press, pp. 143–171.

Okólski, M. 1996, "Przemiany ludnościowe w Polsce w XX wieku" (Demographic change in twentieth-century Poland) in: M. Marody and E. Gucwa-Leśny (eds.), *Podstawy życia społecznego w Polsce* (The foundations of social life in Poland), Warsaw: Instytut Studiów Społecznych, pp. 17–38.

Ortega Y Gasset, J. 1957 (1930), *The Revolt of the Masses*, New York: Norton.

Ost, D. 1990, *Solidarity and the Politics of Anti-Politics*, Philadelphia: Temple University Press.

Parry, G. 1976, "Trust, distrust and consensus," in: *British Journal of Political Science*, Vol. 6, pp. 129–142.

Parsons, T. 1951, *The Social System*, New York: Free Press.

Parsons, T. 1968 (1937), *The Structure of Social Action*, New York: Free Press.

Poland: An International Economic Report 1993/1994, Warsaw: Warsaw School of Economics.

Popper, K. R. 1964 (1957), *The Poverty of Historicism*, New York: Harper & Row.

Przeworski, A., et al. 1995, *Sustainable Democracy*, Cambridge, England: Cambridge University Press.

Putnam, R. D. 1995a, *Making Democracy Work: Civic Traditions in Modern Italy*, Princeton, New Jersey: Princeton University Press.

Putnam, R. D. 1995b, "Tuning in, tuning out: the strange disappearance of social capital in America," in: *Political Science and Politics*, December, pp. 664–683.

Putnam, R. D. 1995c, "Bowling alone: America's declining social capital," in: *Journal of Democracy*, Vol. 6, No. 1, pp. 65–78.

Putnam, R. D. 1996, "The strange disappearance of civic America," in: *The American Prospect*, Winter, pp. 34–48.

Pye, L. and Verba, S. (eds.) 1965, *Political Culture and Political Development*, Princeton, New Jersey: Princeton University Press.

Rengger, N. 1997, "The ethics of trust in world politics," in: *International Affairs*, Vol. 73, No. 3, pp. 469–487.

Ridgeway, C. L. 1983, *The Dynamics of Small Groups*, New York: St. Martin's Press.

Riesman, D. 1950, *The Lonely Crowd*, New Haven, Conn.: Yale University Press.

Rocznik Statystyczny (Statistical yearbook), Warsaw: GUS (Central Statistical Office).

Rocznik Demograficzny (Demographic yearbook), Warsaw: GUS (Central Statistical Office).

Rose, R. 1994, "Postcommunism and the problem of trust," in: *Journal of Democracy*, July, pp. 18–30.

Seeman, M. 1959, "On the meaning of alienation," in: *American Sociological Review*, No. 24, pp. 783–789.

Seligman, A. 1992, *The Idea of Civil Society*, New York: Free Press.

Seligman, A. 1997, *The Problem of Trust*, Princeton, New Jersey: Princeton University Press.

Short, J. F. 1984, "The social fabric at risk: toward the social transformation of risk analysis" in: *American Sociological Review*, Vol. 49, December, pp. 711–725.

Short, J. F. Jr. 1990, "Hazards, risks, and enterprise: Approaches to science, law, and social policy," in: *Law and Society Review*, Vol. 24, No. 1, pp. 179–198.

Silver, A. 1985, " 'Trust' in social and political theory," in: G. D. Suttles and M. N. Zald (eds.), *The Challenge of Social Control*, Norwood, Mass.: Ablex Publishers.

Simmel, G. 1971, *Georg Simmel on Individuality and Social Forms* (ed. D. N. Levine), Chicago: University of Chicago Press.

Slany, K. 1997 (ed.), *Orientacje emigracyjne Polaków* (The emigrational orientation of Poles), Kraków: Jagiellonian University Press.

Stivers, R. 1994, *The Culture of Cynicism*, Oxford: Basil Blackwell.

Sufin, Z. 1981 "Praca i warunki życia" (Labor and life standards), in Z. Sufin (ed.) *Społeczeństwo Polskie W Drugiej Potowie Lat Siedemdziesiątych* (Polish society in the second half of the seventies), Warsaw: Institute of Marxism-Leninism, pp. 165–194.

Sztompka, P. 1986, *Robert K. Merton: An Intellectual Profile*, London: Macmillan Press.

Sztompka, P. 1991a, *Society in Action: The Theory of Social Becoming*, Cambridge, England: Polity Press (and University of Chicago Press).

Sztompka, P. 1991b, "The intangibles and imponderables of the transition to democracy," in: *Studies in Comparative Communism*, Vol. 24, No. 3, pp. 295–311.

Sztompka, P. 1992, "Dilemmas of the great transition," in: *Sisyphus*, Vol. 2, No. 8, pp. 9–28.

Sztompka, P. 1993a *The Sociology of Social Change*, Oxford: Blackwell.

Sztompka, P. 1993b, "Civilizational incompetence: the trap of post-communist societies," in: *Zeitschrift für Soziologie*, Vol. 2, pp. 85–95.

Sztompka, P. (ed.) 1994, *Agency and Structure: Reorienting Social Theory*, New York: Gordon & Breach.

Sztompka, P. 1995, "Vertrauen: Die fehlende Ressource in der postkommunistichen Gesellschaft" (Trust: A missing resource of postcommunist society, in: *Kolner Zeitschrift für Soziologie und Sozialpsychologie*, Special issue 35/1995

"Politische Institutionen in Wandel" (Political institutions in transition), (ed. by B. Nedelmann), September, pp. 254–276.

Sztompka, P. 1996a, *La fiducia nelle societa post-comuniste* (Trust in postcommunist societies), Messina: Rubbettino Editore.

Sztompka, P. 1996b, "Trust and emerging democracy: lessons from Poland," in: *International Sociology*, Vol. 11, No. 1, pp. 37–62.

Sztompka, P. 1996c, "Looking back: The year 1989 as a cultural and civilizational break," in: *Communist and Post-Communist Studies*, Vol. 29, No. 2, pp. 115–130.

Tarkowska, E. 1994, "A waiting society: The temporal dimension of transformation in Poland," in: A. Flis and P. Seel (eds.), *Social Time and Temporality*, Kraków: Goethe Institut, pp. 57–71.

Thomas, W. I. and Znaniecki, F. 1918–1920, *The Polish Peasant in Europe and America*, Vols. I–V, Boston: Badger.

Thompson, M., Ellis, R., and Wildavsky, A. 1990, *Cultural Theory*, Boulder, Colo.: Westview Press.

Tilly, C. 1993, *European Revolutions, 1492–1992*, Oxford: Basil Blackwell.

Tocqueville, A. de 1945, *Democracy in America*, Vols. I and II, New York: Knopf.

Tönnies, F. 1957 (1887), *Community and Society*, East Lansing: Michigan University Press.

Warnock, G. J. 1971, *The Object of Morality*, London: Methuen.

Weber, M. 1949, *The Methodology of the Social Sciences*, New York: Free Press.

Weber, M. 1968 (1922), *Economy and Society*, New York: Bedminster.

Wesołowski, W. 1995, "The nature of social ties and the future of postcommunist society: Poland after Solidarity," in: J. A. Hall (ed.), *Civil Society*, Cambridge, England: Polity Press, pp. 110–135.

Wilson, J. Q., 1993, *The Moral Sense*, New York: Free Press.

Wilson, J. Q. 1998, "Human remedies for social disorders," in: *The Public Interest*, Vol. 131, Spring, pp. 25–35.

Wirth, L. 1938, "Urbanism as a way of life," in: *American Journal of Sociology*, No. 44, pp. 1–24.

Wolfe, A. (ed.) 1991, *America at Century End*, Berkeley: University of California Press.

Zand, D. E. 1972, "Trust and managerial problem solving," in: *Administrative Science Quarterly*, Vol. 17, pp. 229–239.

Znaniecki, F. 1967 (1934), *Social Actions*, New York: Russell.

Index

Name index